JULIO'S DAY

GILBERT HERNANDEZ

JULIO

by GILBERT HERNANDEZ

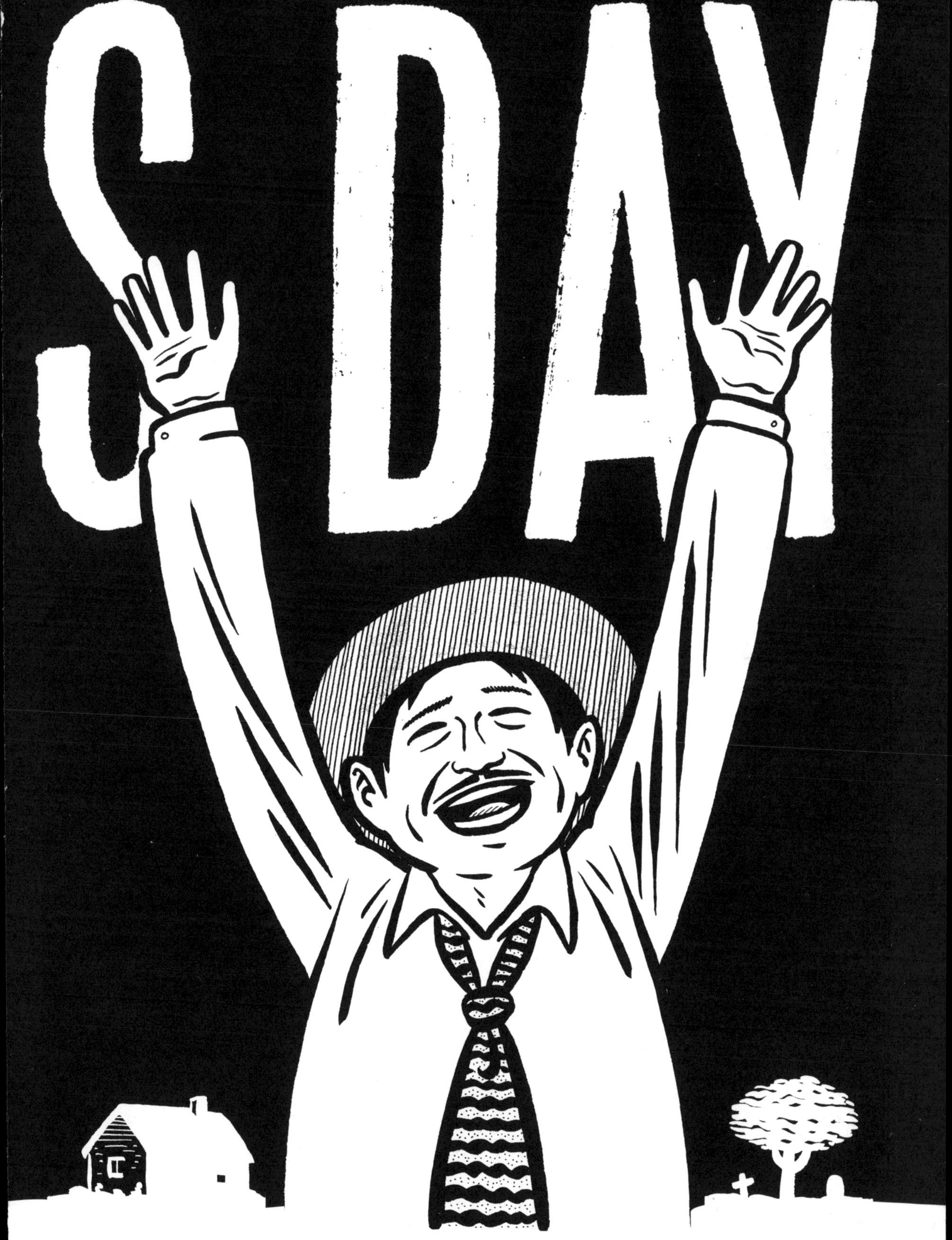
S DAY

Fantagraphics Books
7563 Lake City Way NE
Seattle, WA 98115

Edited by Jason T. Miles
Design by Emory Liu
Associate Publisher, Eric Reynolds
Published by Gary Groth and Kim Thompson

First edition: February 2013
ISBN: 978-1-60699-606-5
Printed in Singapore

INTRODUCTION

by Brian Evenson

"...one day we were born, one day we shall die, the same day, the same second, is that not enough for you?"

—Samuel Beckett, *Waiting for Godot*

Gilbert Hernandez's *Julio's Day* might be read as an illustration of the above quotation from Beckett's play, and of the words that follow it: "They give birth astride a grave, the light gleams an instant, then it's night once more." The graphic novel begins with a panel of darkness, nothingness, but by the second panel we've pulled back far enough to see that the darkness is the inside of a baby's mouth. The baby is Julio, and we'll stay with him and his family for exactly one hundred pages as he grows from zero to the ripe old age of one hundred and then dies. We'll leave him in the same way as we first met him, but in reverse order: the second to the last panel offers an old man's ravaged mouth, followed by a final panel of darkness, nothingness.

But where Beckett sees the shortness of a man's life as cause for despair and dismay, Hernandez is interested in celebrating a life fully, in all its shortcomings and joys, all its ups and downs, all its risks and limitations. Despite the death, illness, abuse, and war that fill these pages, despite many serious familial and personal struggles, there is little bitterness here. Hernandez's characters have a remarkable ability to persist, to keep on. Even those that struggle to find their place in one generation (including those who never shake free from denial about who they are), help pave the way for the freedoms claimed by those that follow them.

Julio's Day is a story of one man's life, but it's a great deal more than that as well. It's the story of the life of a century, also told as if a day. Beginning with Julio's birth in 1900 and ending with his death in 2000, the graphic novel touches on most of the major events that shaped the 20th century. We see wars, ruinous weather, changing fashion, changing attitudes, but Hernandez very wisely doesn't give us these things in historical terms. In fact, outside of the images and the characters' speech (there are no panel captions), he does nothing to let us know where we are in the century on a given page, and often we don't know quite what year we're in. The characters don't feed us information: Hernandez's guiding principle is to let them only say what's natural, and only say it when it's natural. Hernandez operates quite deftly, by inference and suggestion. We don't know, for instance, why Julio's father takes the trip that nearly kills him (and which ends up sealing Julio's brother's fate years later as well) until he arrives at his destination, and then we're only given it with several well-placed images and two speech bubbles.

That's one of the great strengths of *Julio's Day* and one of the great qualities of Hernandez's style in general. He touches a great many serious topics, but does so with remarkable lightness. He gives whatever is at hand an attention that at once seems fleeting and full, and he can switch quickly from one scene to another without losing our interest or attention. Characters can flit by, be present and amazingly rendered for a few panels, and then suddenly disappear for good. But they can just as easily reappear after an eighty-year absence. Even the more central characters can age dramatically from one page to the next as the years pass and yet still be recognizable.

The amazing speed with which things change from page to page and even from panel to panel is one of the real charms of *Julio's Day*. Hernandez doesn't overdirect us: he lets us figure things out for ourselves, just as we do in life. He doesn't insist on the echoes that occur across generations or between characters, but leaves the threads there for us to pick up. He lets us make our own tenuous connections, which makes them all the more powerful, and all the more valuable. This is a stunning graphic novel, by someone who is one of the major voices in the field, and is sure to hold surprises even for those aficionados of Hernandez's other work.

• •

Brian Evenson is the author of *Windeye, Last Days, Fugue State, The Open Curtain, Immobility,* and *Altmann's Tongue,* among others. He is the recipient of numerous awards including an NEA fellowship, three O. Henry Prizes, and the American Library Association's award for Best Horror Novel. He lives and works in Providence, Rhode Island, where he directs Brown University's Literary Arts Program, translates literature from French into English, and of course, writes.

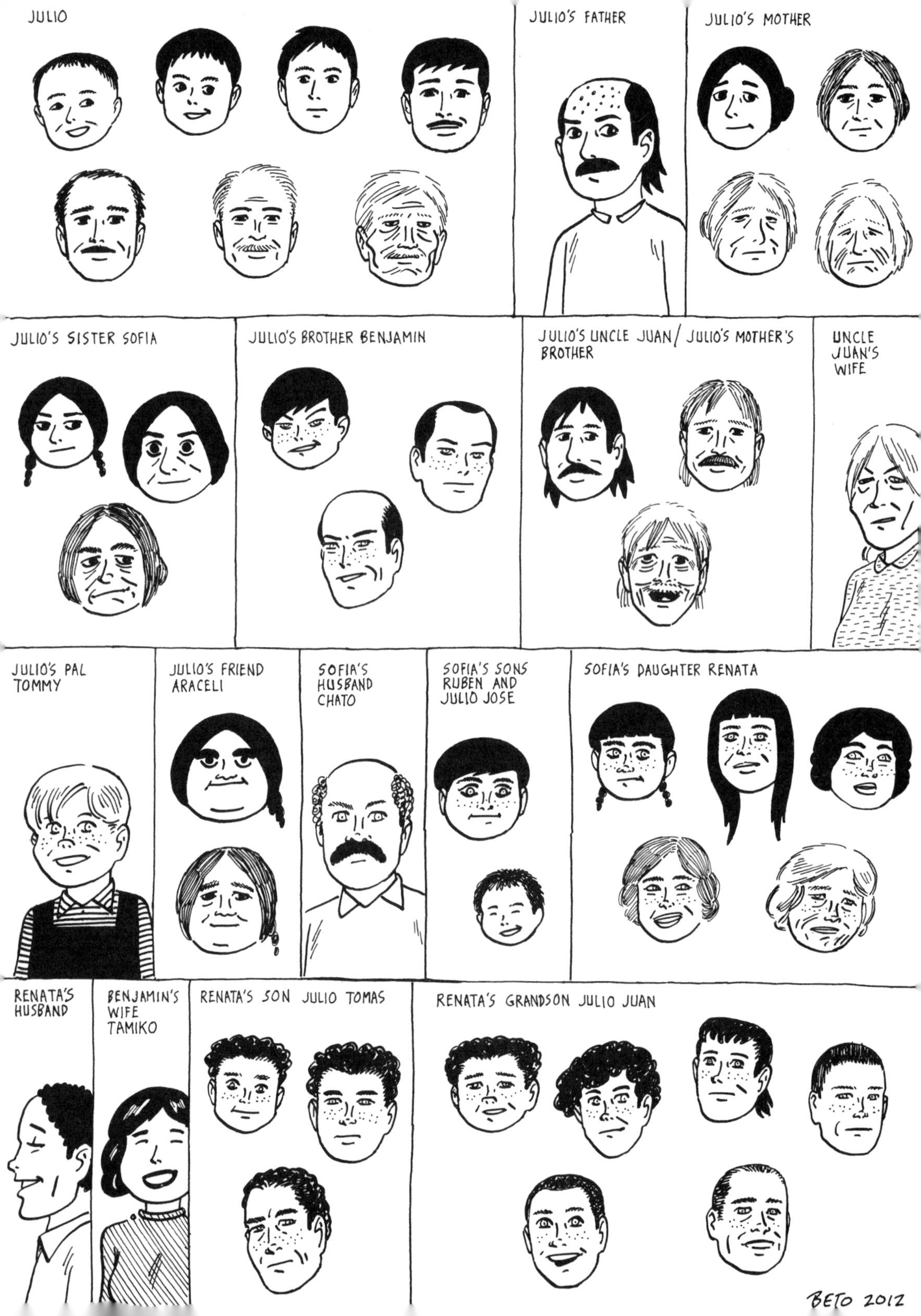
JULIO
JULIO'S FATHER
JULIO'S MOTHER
JULIO'S SISTER SOFIA
JULIO'S BROTHER BENJAMIN
JULIO'S UNCLE JUAN / JULIO'S MOTHER'S BROTHER
UNCLE JUAN'S WIFE
JULIO'S PAL TOMMY
JULIO'S FRIEND ARACELI
SOFIA'S HUSBAND CHATO
SOFIA'S SONS RUBEN AND JULIO JOSE
SOFIA'S DAUGHTER RENATA
RENATA'S HUSBAND
BENJAMIN'S WIFE TAMIKO
RENATA'S SON JULIO TOMAS
RENATA'S GRANDSON JULIO JUAN
BETO 2012

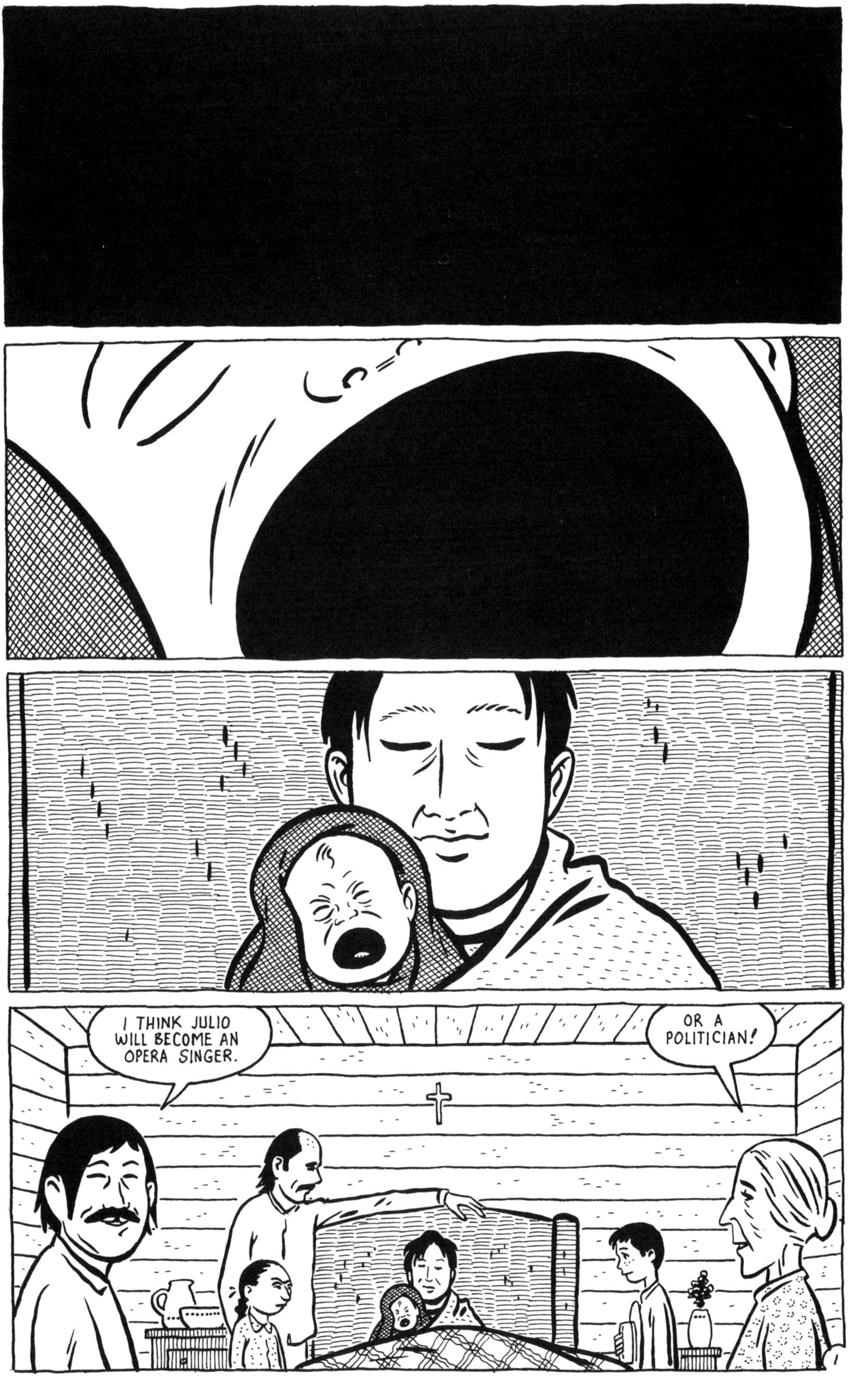
I THINK JULIO WILL BECOME AN OPERA SINGER.
OR A POLITICIAN!

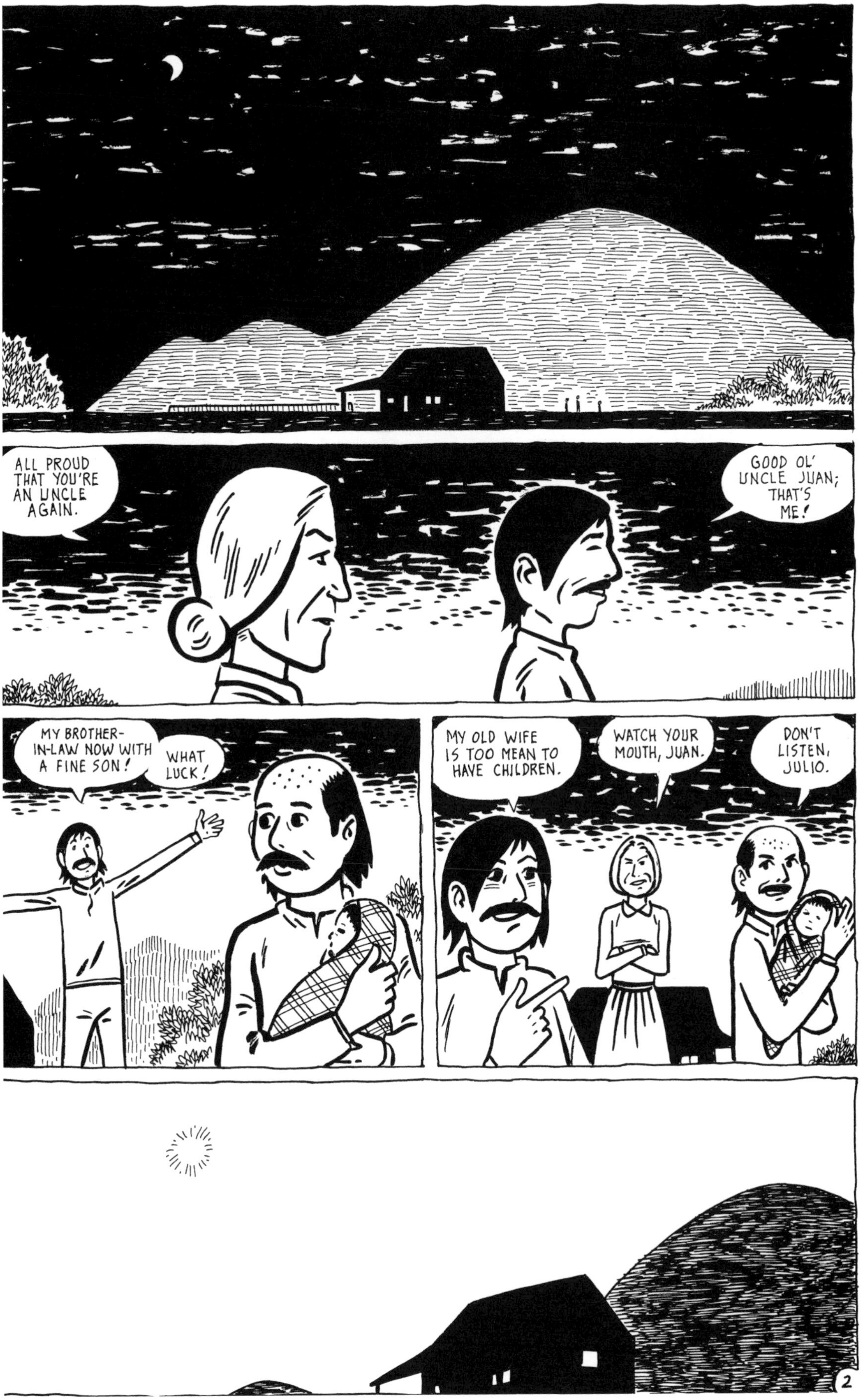

ALL PROUD THAT YOU'RE AN UNCLE AGAIN.
GOOD OL' UNCLE JUAN; THAT'S ME!
MY BROTHER-IN-LAW NOW WITH A FINE SON!
WHAT LUCK!
MY OLD WIFE IS TOO MEAN TO HAVE CHILDREN.
WATCH YOUR MOUTH, JUAN.
DON'T LISTEN, JULIO.

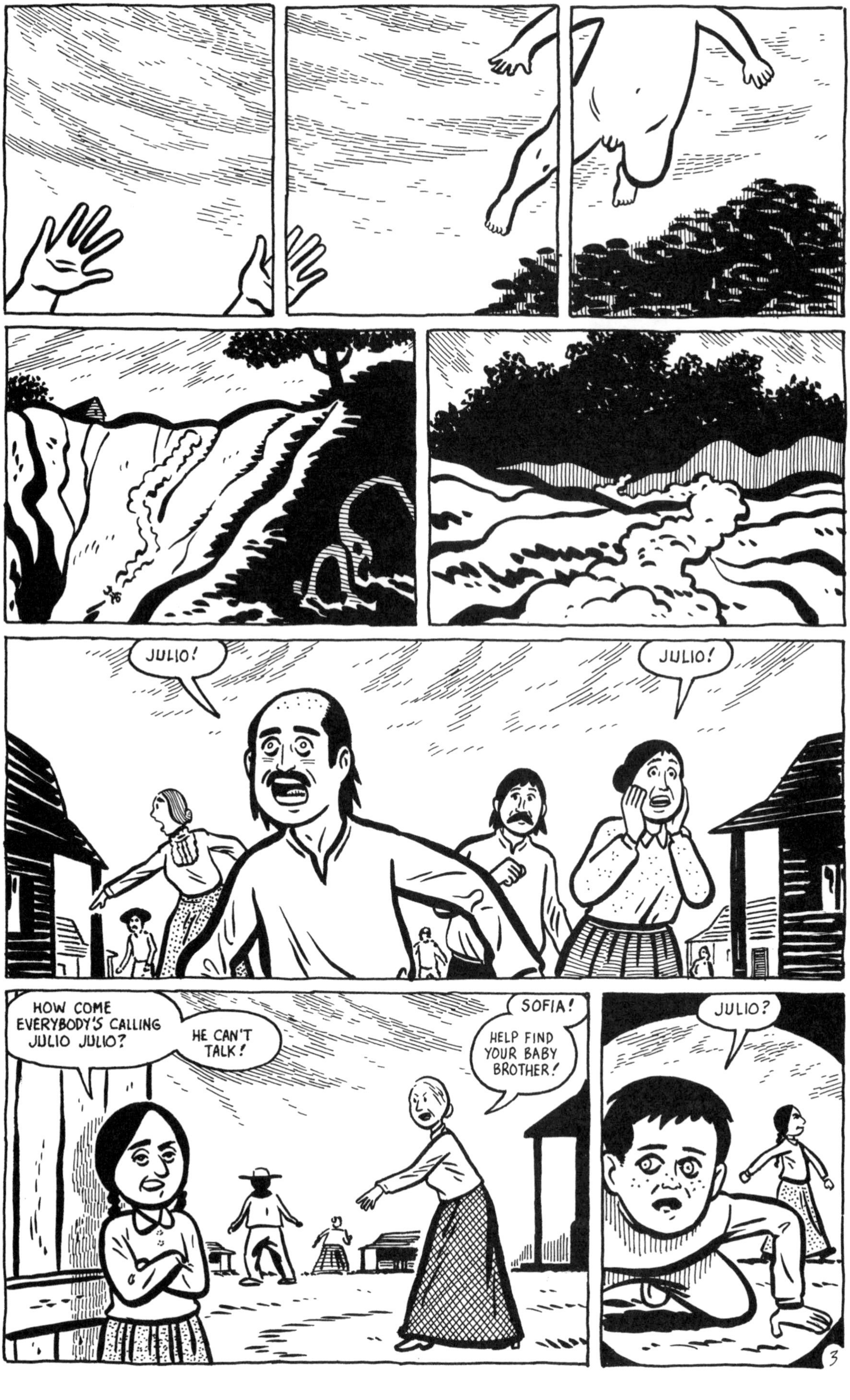

JULIO!
JULIO!
HOW COME EVERYBODY'S CALLING JULIO JULIO?
HE CAN'T TALK!
SOFIA!
HELP FIND YOUR BABY BROTHER!
JULIO?

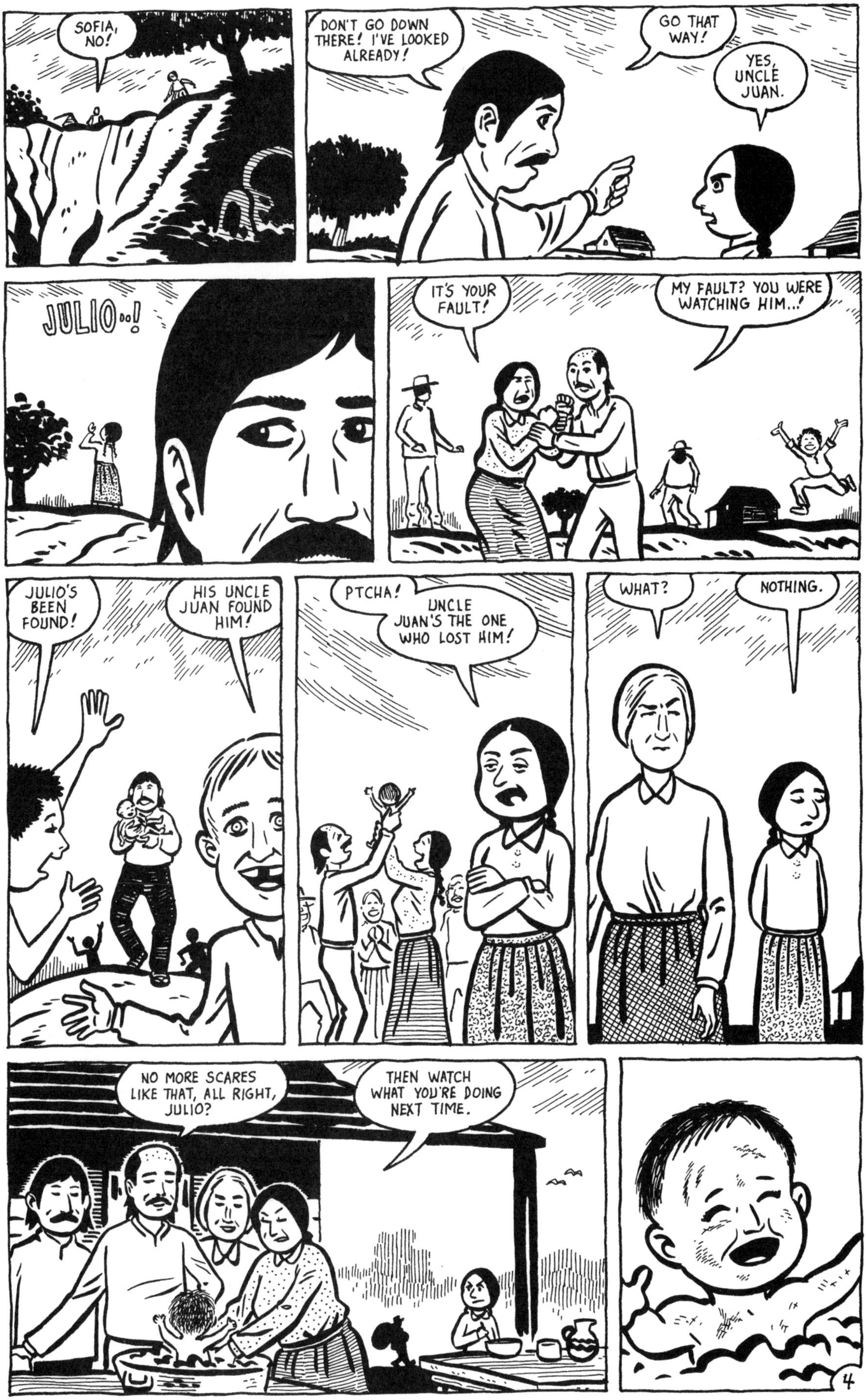
SOFIA, NO!
DON'T GO DOWN THERE! I'VE LOOKED ALREADY!
GO THAT WAY!
YES, UNCLE JUAN.
JULIO..!
IT'S YOUR FAULT!
MY FAULT? YOU WERE WATCHING HIM...!
JULIO'S BEEN FOUND!
HIS UNCLE JUAN FOUND HIM!
PTCHA!
UNCLE JUAN'S THE ONE WHO LOST HIM!
WHAT?
NOTHING.
NO MORE SCARES LIKE THAT, ALL RIGHT, JULIO?
THEN WATCH WHAT YOU'RE DOING NEXT TIME.
4

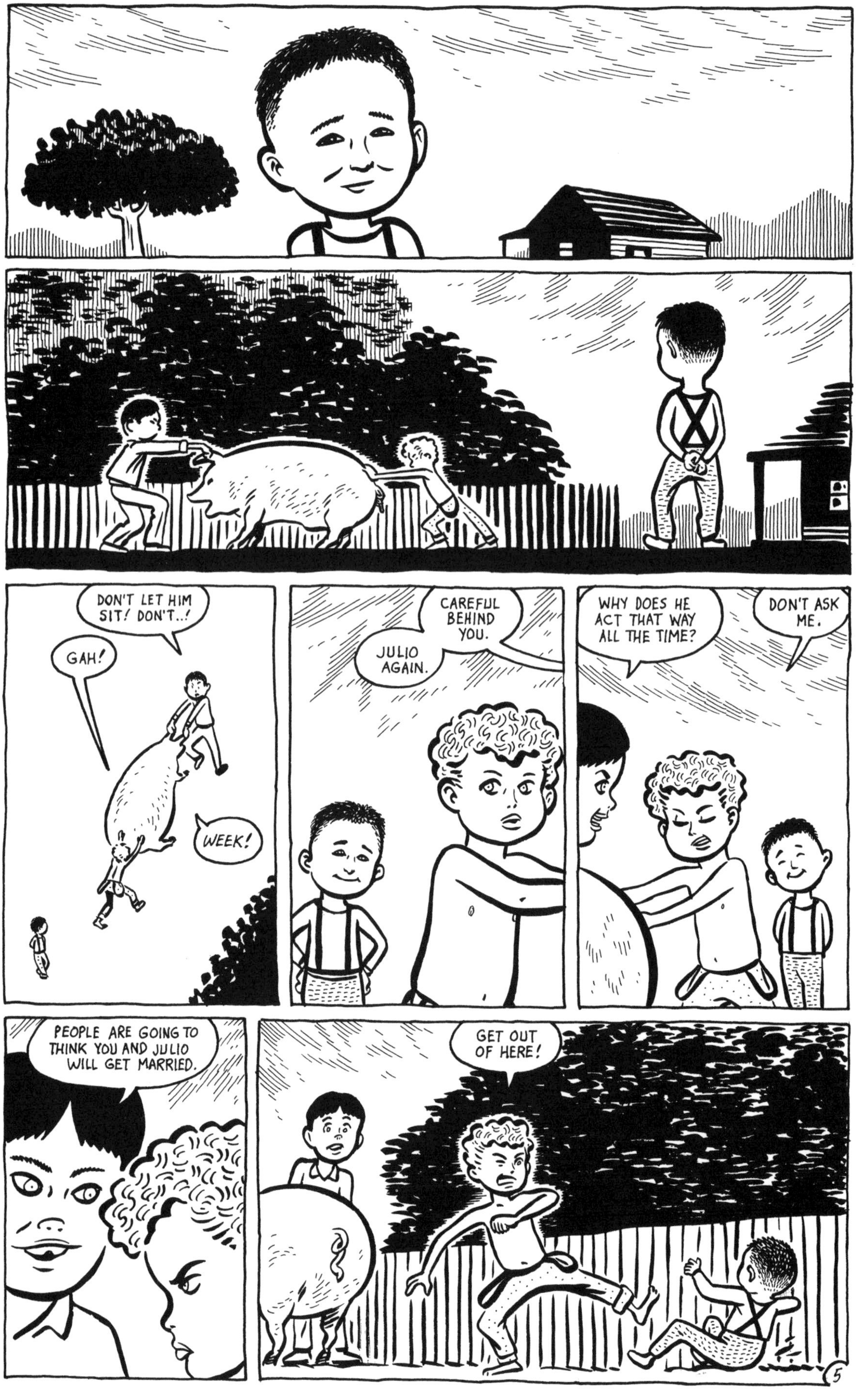

DON'T LET HIM SIT! DON'T..!
GAH!
WEEK!
CAREFUL BEHIND YOU.
JULIO AGAIN.
WHY DOES HE ACT THAT WAY ALL THE TIME?
DON'T ASK ME.
PEOPLE ARE GOING TO THINK YOU AND JULIO WILL GET MARRIED.
GET OUT OF HERE!

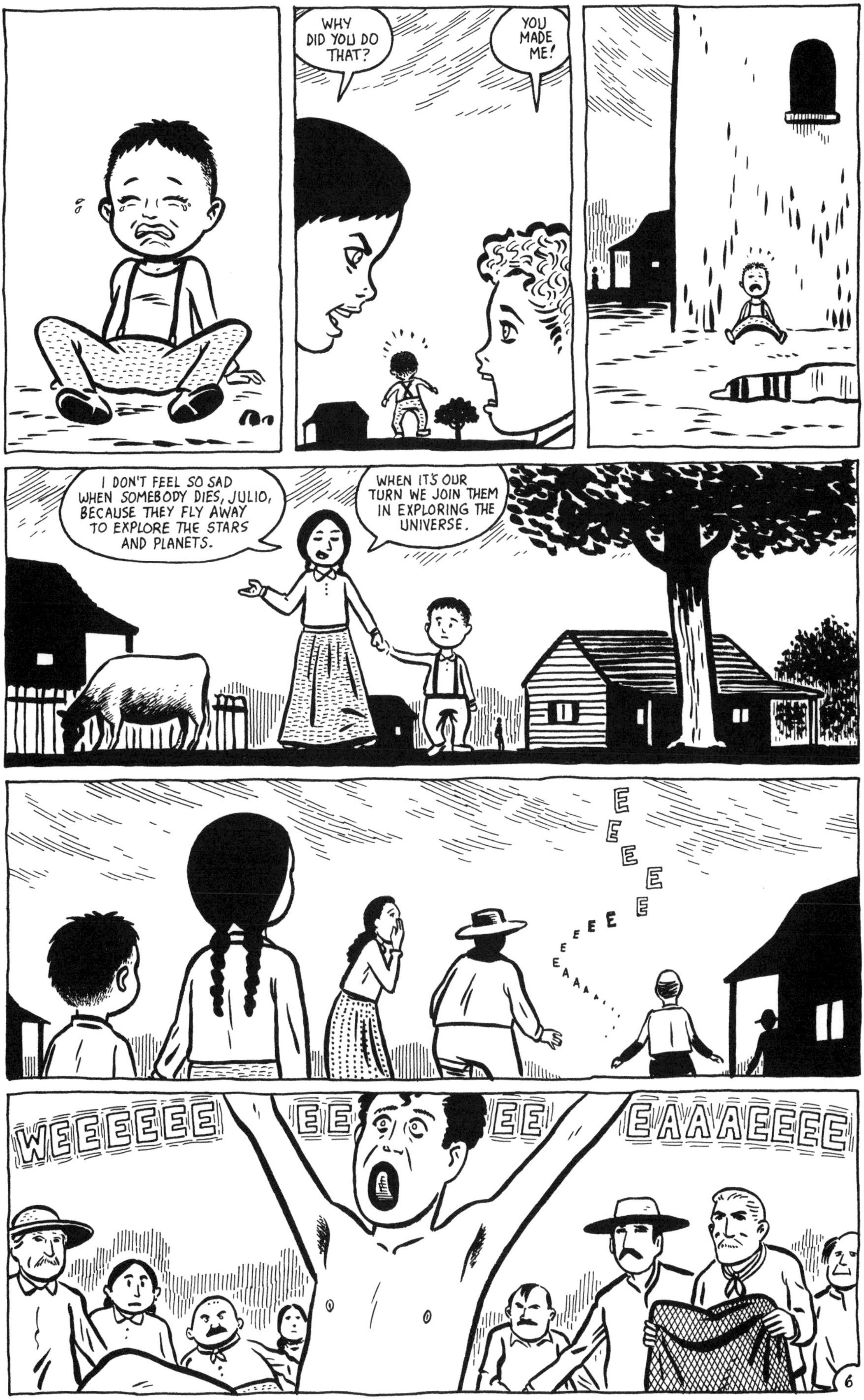
WHY DID YOU DO THAT?
YOU MADE ME!
I DON'T FEEL SO SAD WHEN SOMEBODY DIES, JULIO, BECAUSE THEY FLY AWAY TO EXPLORE THE STARS AND PLANETS.
WHEN IT'S OUR TURN WE JOIN THEM IN EXPLORING THE UNIVERSE.
EEEEEEEEEEEAAAA....
WEEEEEEE EE EE EAAAEEEE

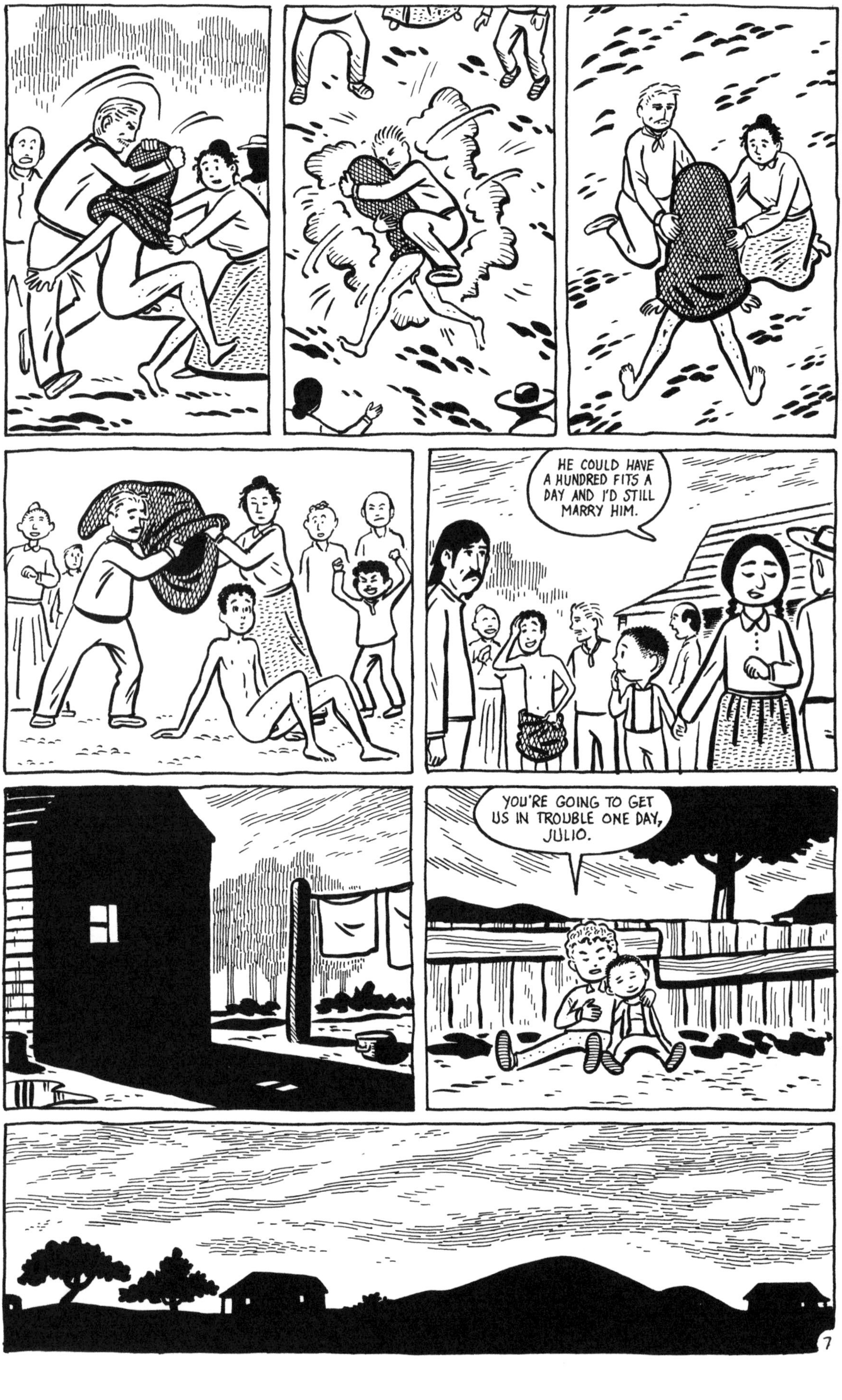
HE COULD HAVE A HUNDRED FITS A DAY AND I'D STILL MARRY HIM.
YOU'RE GOING TO GET US IN TROUBLE ONE DAY, JULIO.

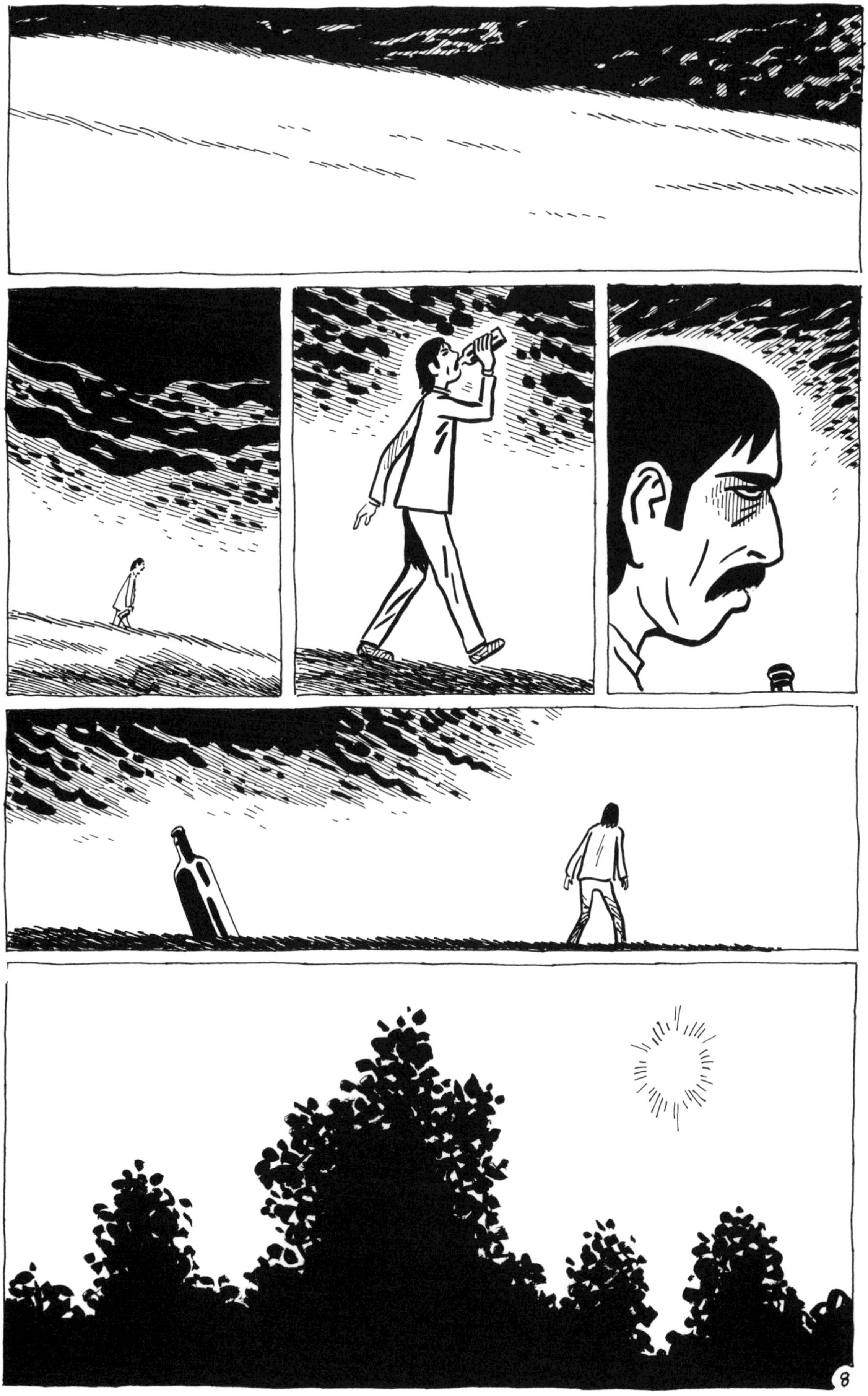

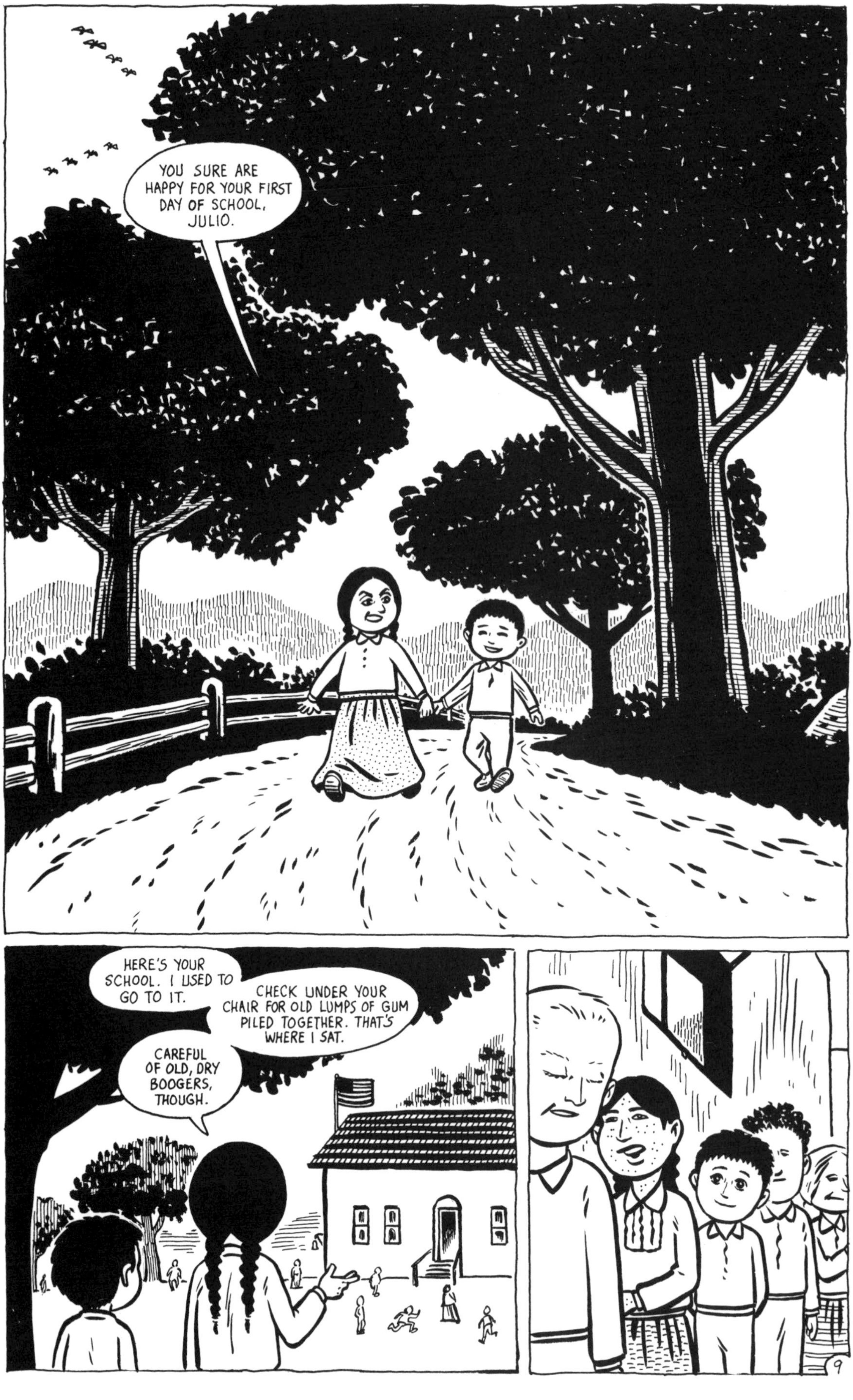
YOU SURE ARE HAPPY FOR YOUR FIRST DAY OF SCHOOL, JULIO.
HERE'S YOUR SCHOOL. I USED TO GO TO IT.
CHECK UNDER YOUR CHAIR FOR OLD LUMPS OF GUM PILED TOGETHER. THAT'S WHERE I SAT.
CAREFUL OF OLD, DRY BOOGERS, THOUGH.

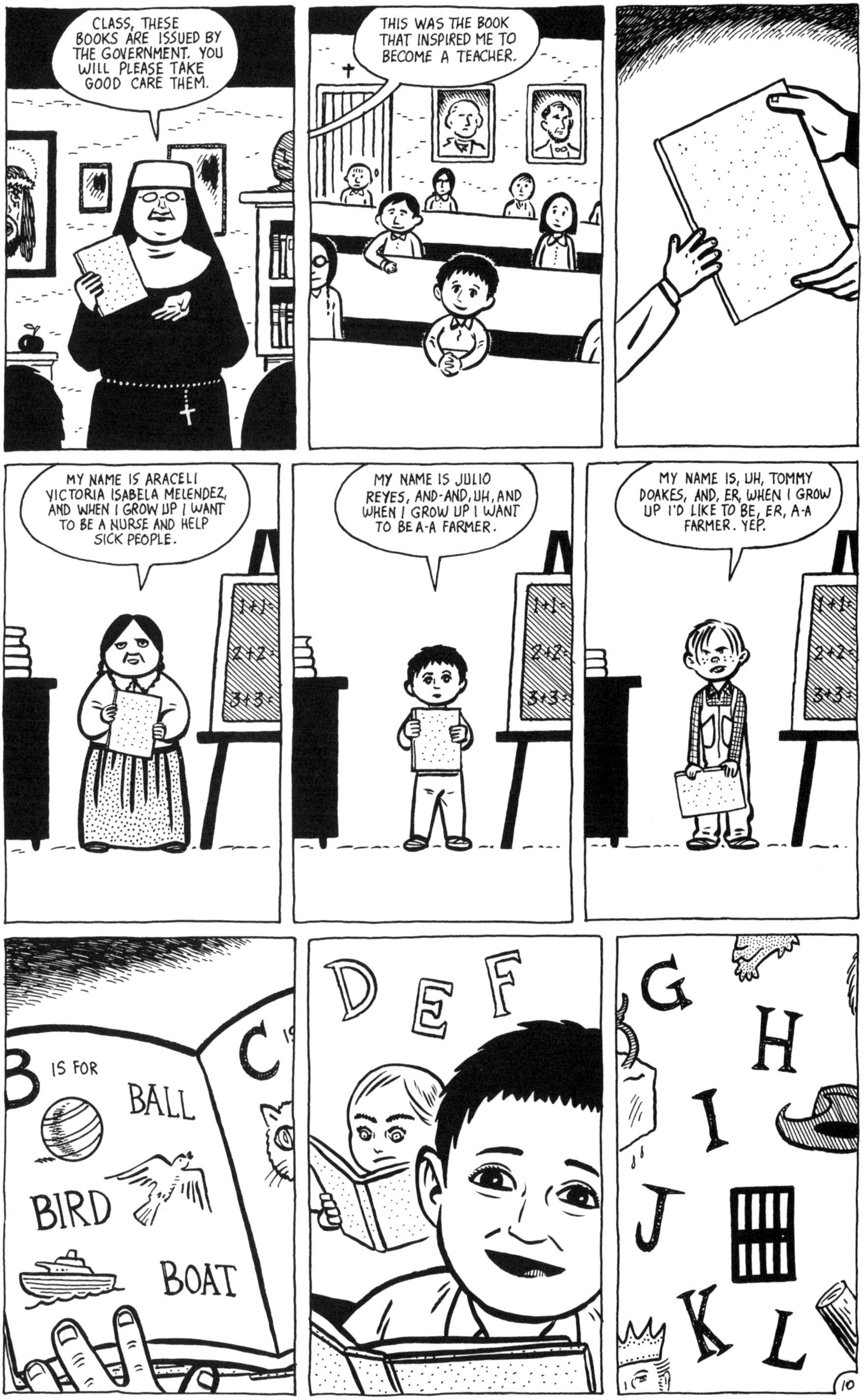

CLASS, THESE BOOKS ARE ISSUED BY THE GOVERNMENT. YOU WILL PLEASE TAKE GOOD CARE THEM.
THIS WAS THE BOOK THAT INSPIRED ME TO BECOME A TEACHER.
MY NAME IS ARACELI VICTORIA ISABELA MELENDEZ, AND WHEN I GROW UP I WANT TO BE A NURSE AND HELP SICK PEOPLE.
1+1=
2+2=
3+3=
MY NAME IS JULIO REYES, AND-AND, UH, AND WHEN I GROW UP I WANT TO BE A-A FARMER.
MY NAME IS, UH, TOMMY DOAKES, AND, ER, WHEN I GROW UP I'D LIKE TO BE, ER, A-A FARMER. YEP.
B IS FOR
BALL
BIRD
BOAT
C
D E F
G
H
I
J
K
L

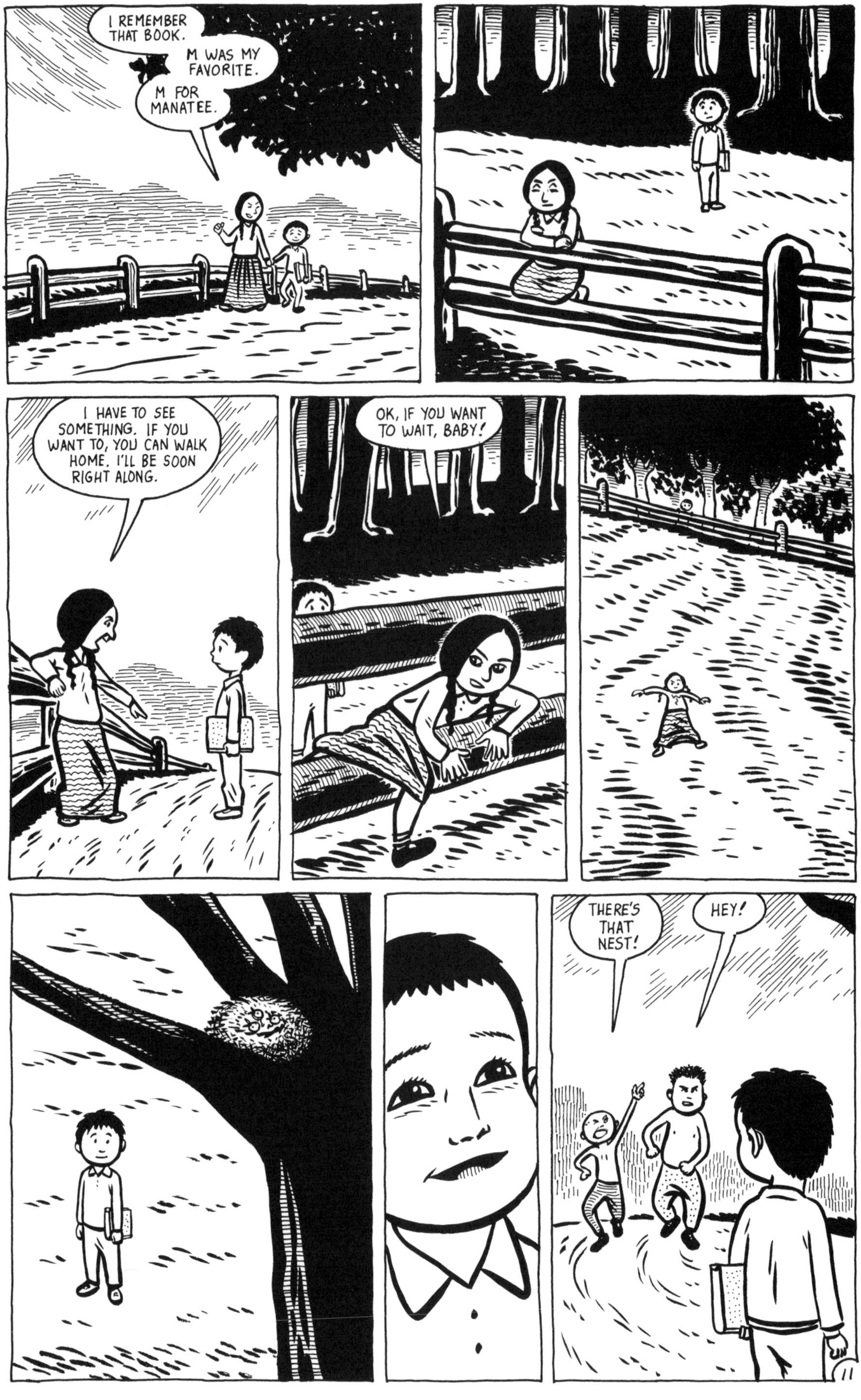
I REMEMBER THAT BOOK.
M WAS MY FAVORITE.
M FOR MANATEE.
I HAVE TO SEE SOMETHING. IF YOU WANT TO, YOU CAN WALK HOME. I'LL BE SOON RIGHT ALONG.
OK, IF YOU WANT TO WAIT, BABY!
THERE'S THAT NEST!
HEY!

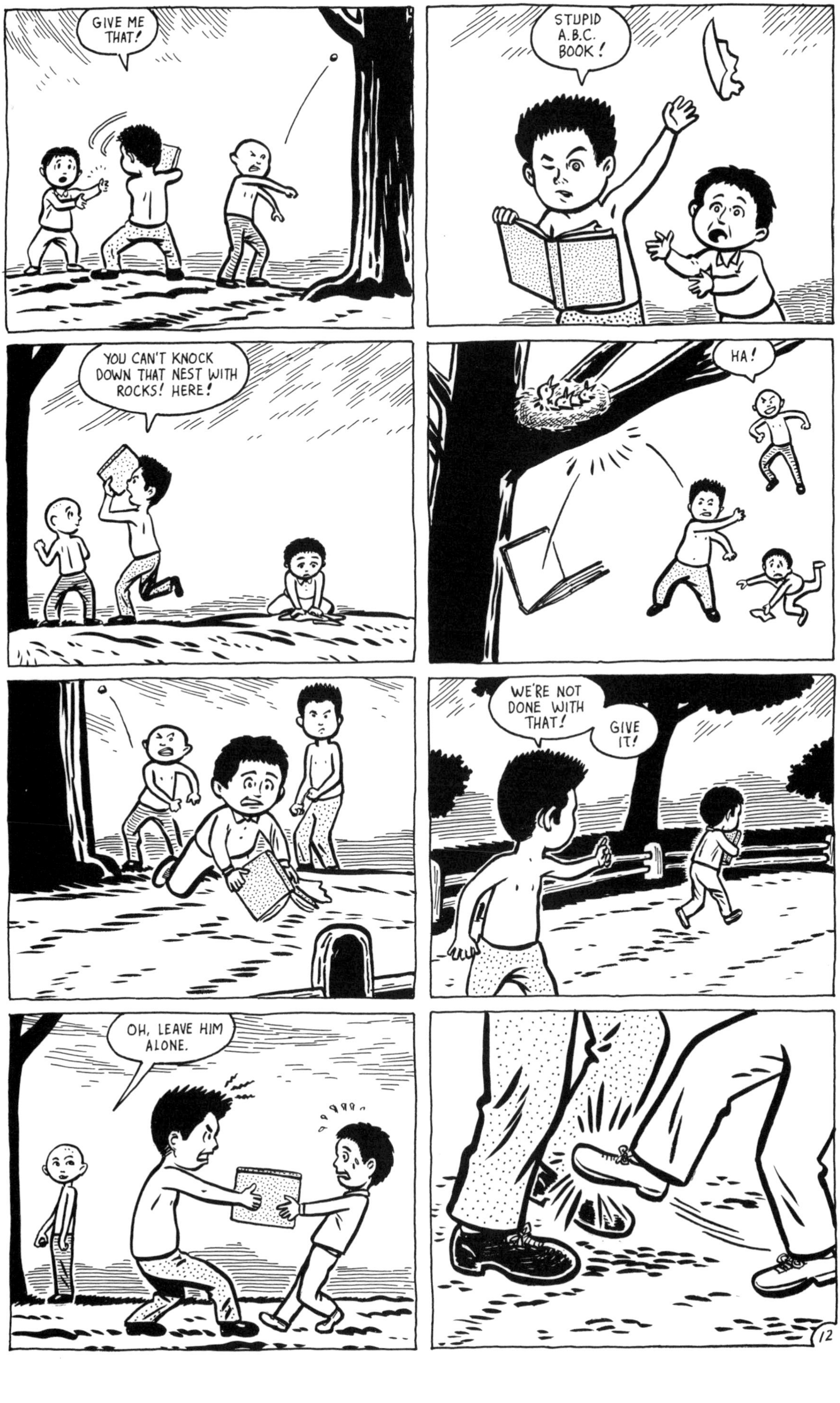
GIVE ME THAT!
STUPID A.B.C. BOOK!
YOU CAN'T KNOCK DOWN THAT NEST WITH ROCKS! HERE!
HA!
WE'RE NOT DONE WITH THAT!
GIVE IT!
OH, LEAVE HIM ALONE.

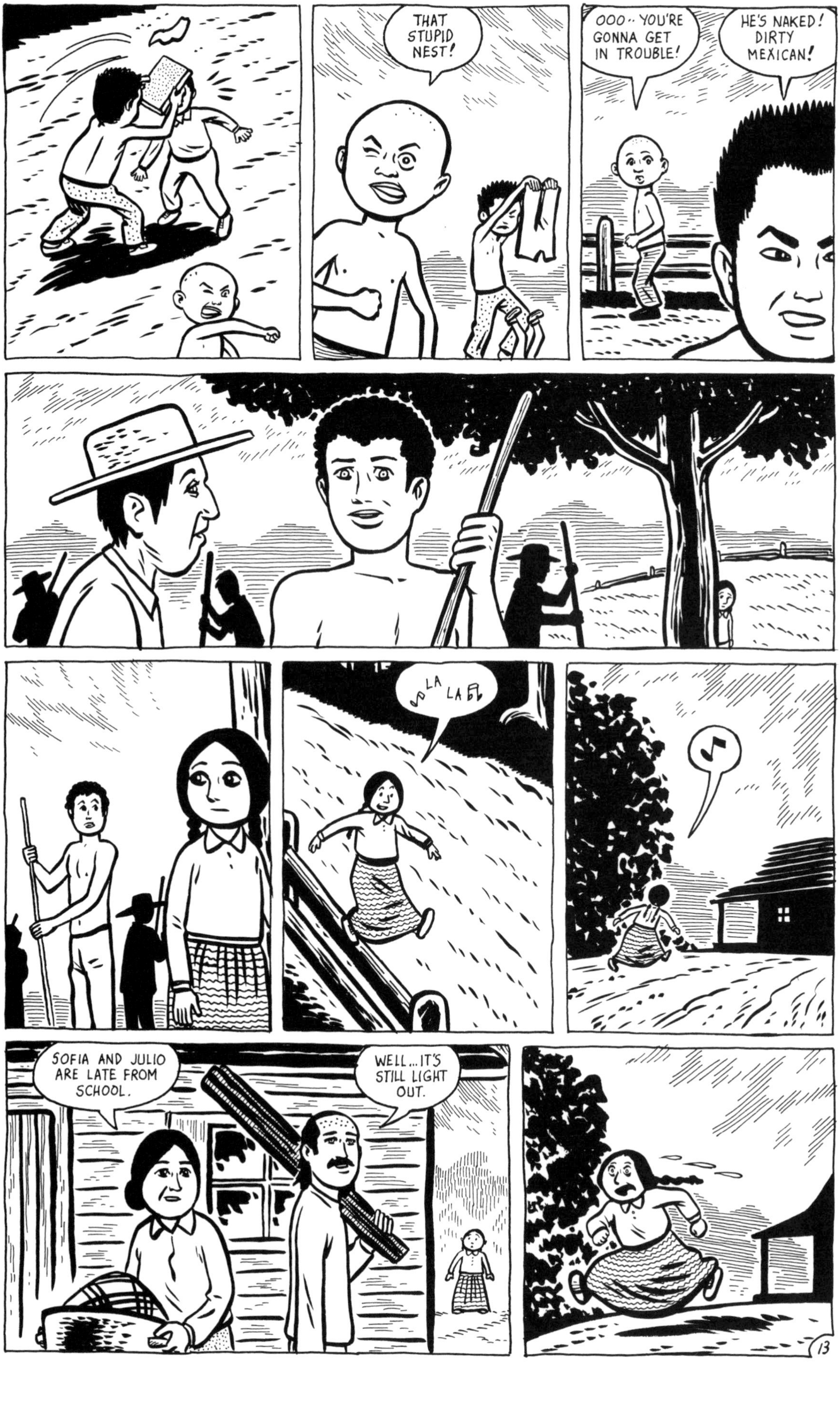
THAT STUPID NEST!
OOO.. YOU'RE GONNA GET IN TROUBLE!
HE'S NAKED! DIRTY MEXICAN!
LA LA
SOFIA AND JULIO ARE LATE FROM SCHOOL.
WELL... IT'S STILL LIGHT OUT.

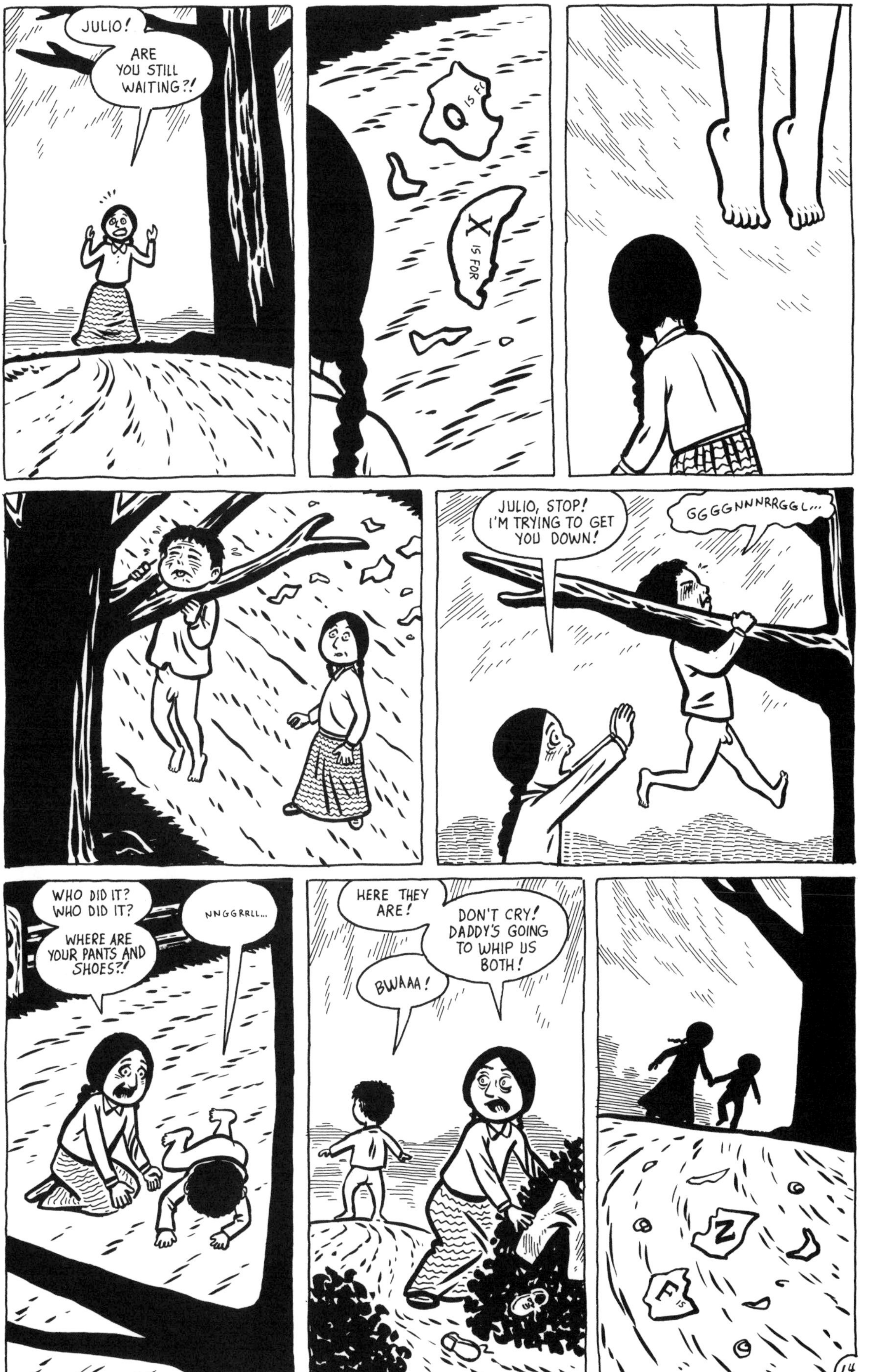
JULIO!
ARE YOU STILL WAITING?!
Q IS F
X IS FOR
JULIO, STOP! I'M TRYING TO GET YOU DOWN!
GGGGNNNRRGGL...
WHO DID IT? WHO DID IT?
WHERE ARE YOUR PANTS AND SHOES?!
NNGGRRLL...
HERE THEY ARE!
DON'T CRY! DADDY'S GOING TO WHIP US BOTH!
BWAAA!
Z
F IS

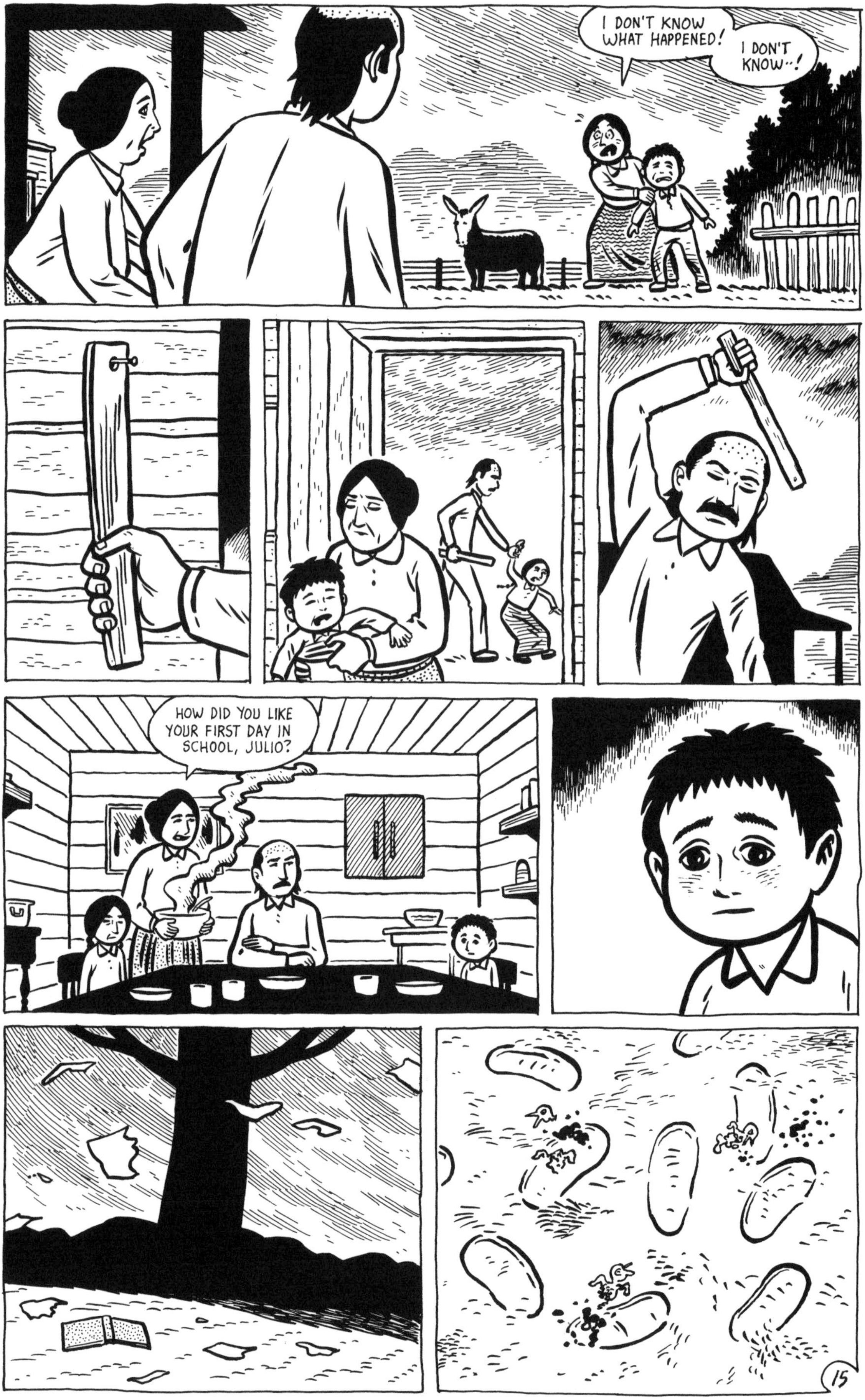
I DON'T KNOW WHAT HAPPENED!
I DON'T KNOW..!
HOW DID YOU LIKE YOUR FIRST DAY IN SCHOOL, JULIO?

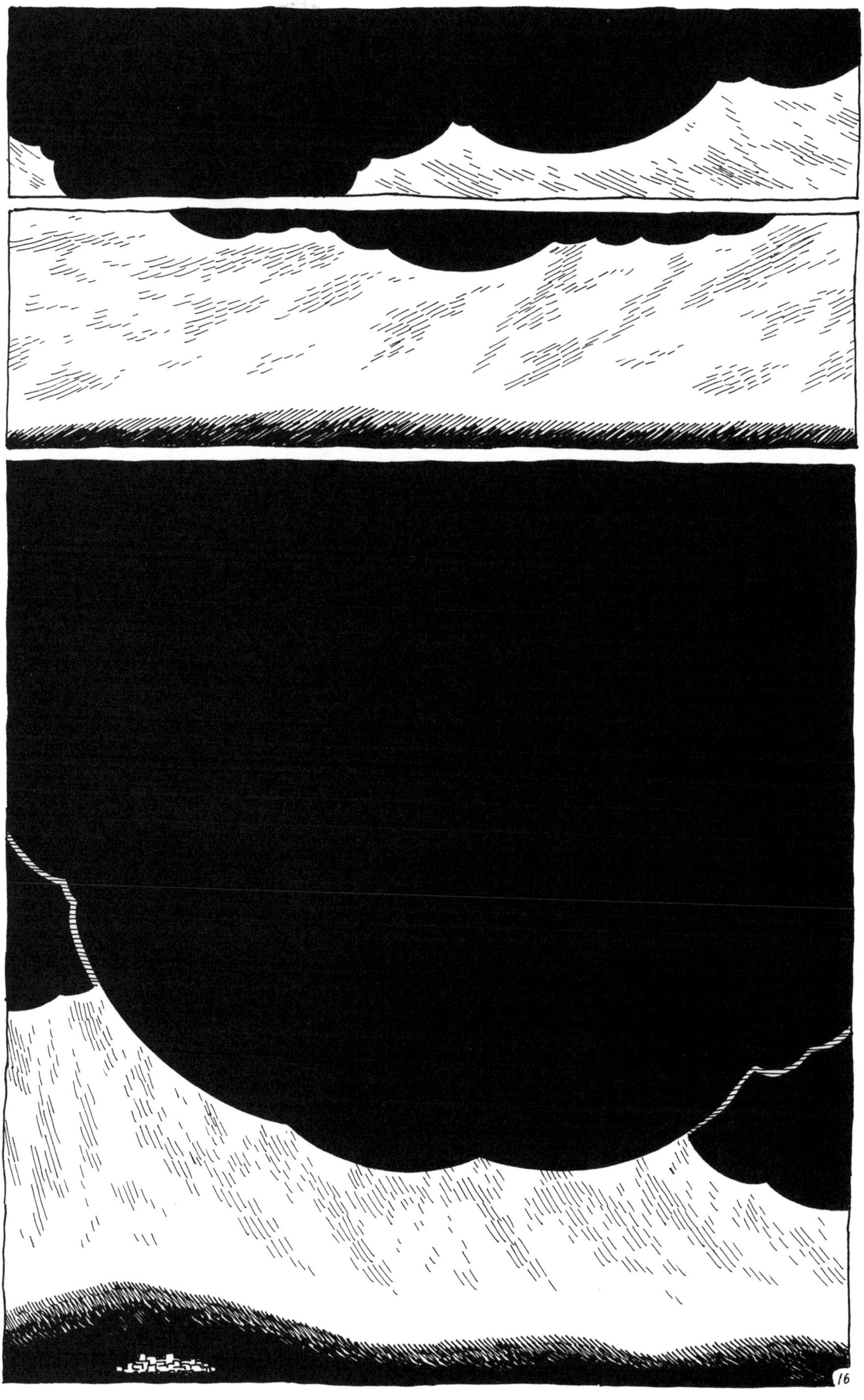

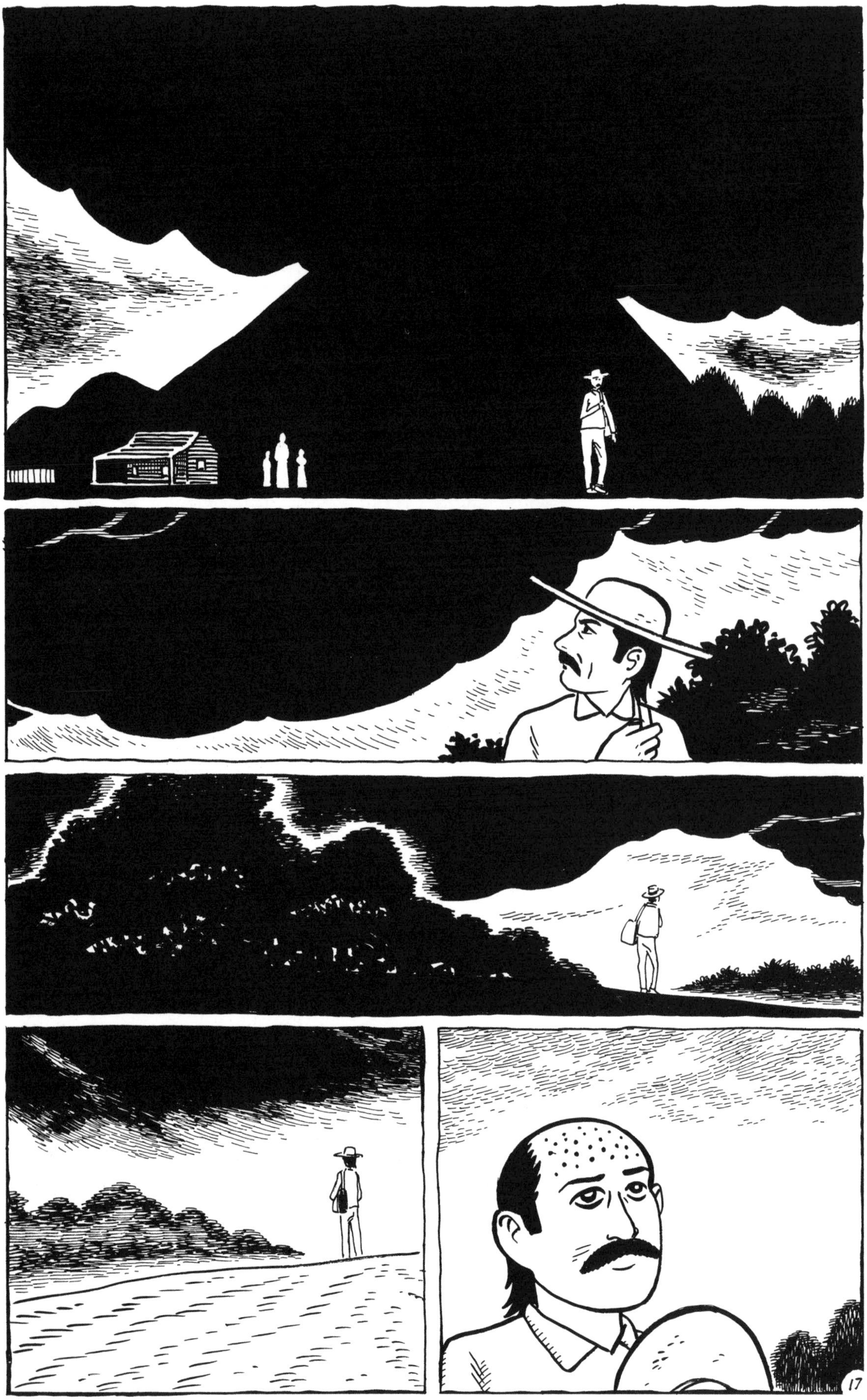

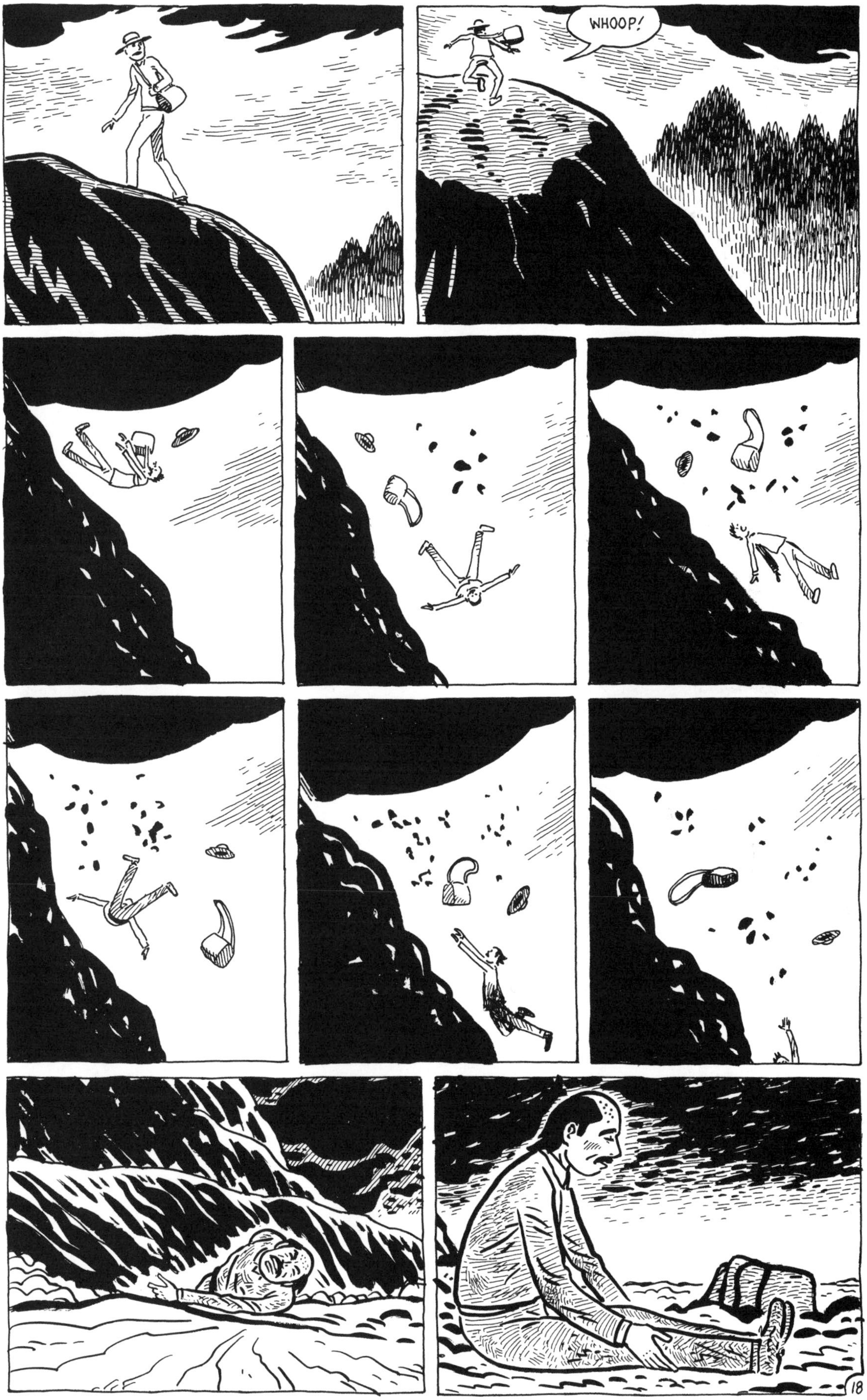
WHOOP!

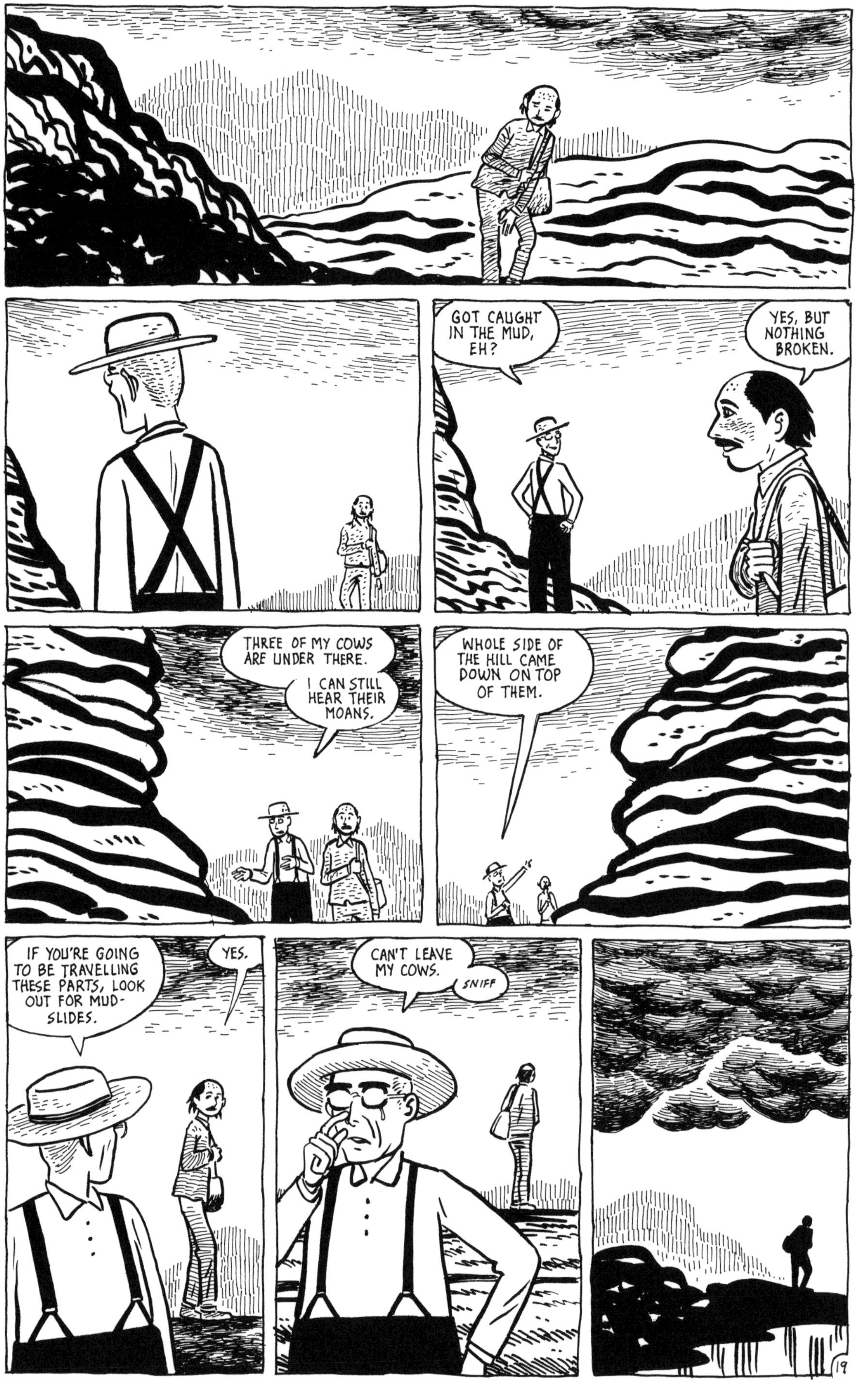
GOT CAUGHT IN THE MUD, EH?
YES, BUT NOTHING BROKEN.
THREE OF MY COWS ARE UNDER THERE.
I CAN STILL HEAR THEIR MOANS.
WHOLE SIDE OF THE HILL CAME DOWN ON TOP OF THEM.
IF YOU'RE GOING TO BE TRAVELLING THESE PARTS, LOOK OUT FOR MUD-SLIDES.
YES.
CAN'T LEAVE MY COWS.
SNIFF

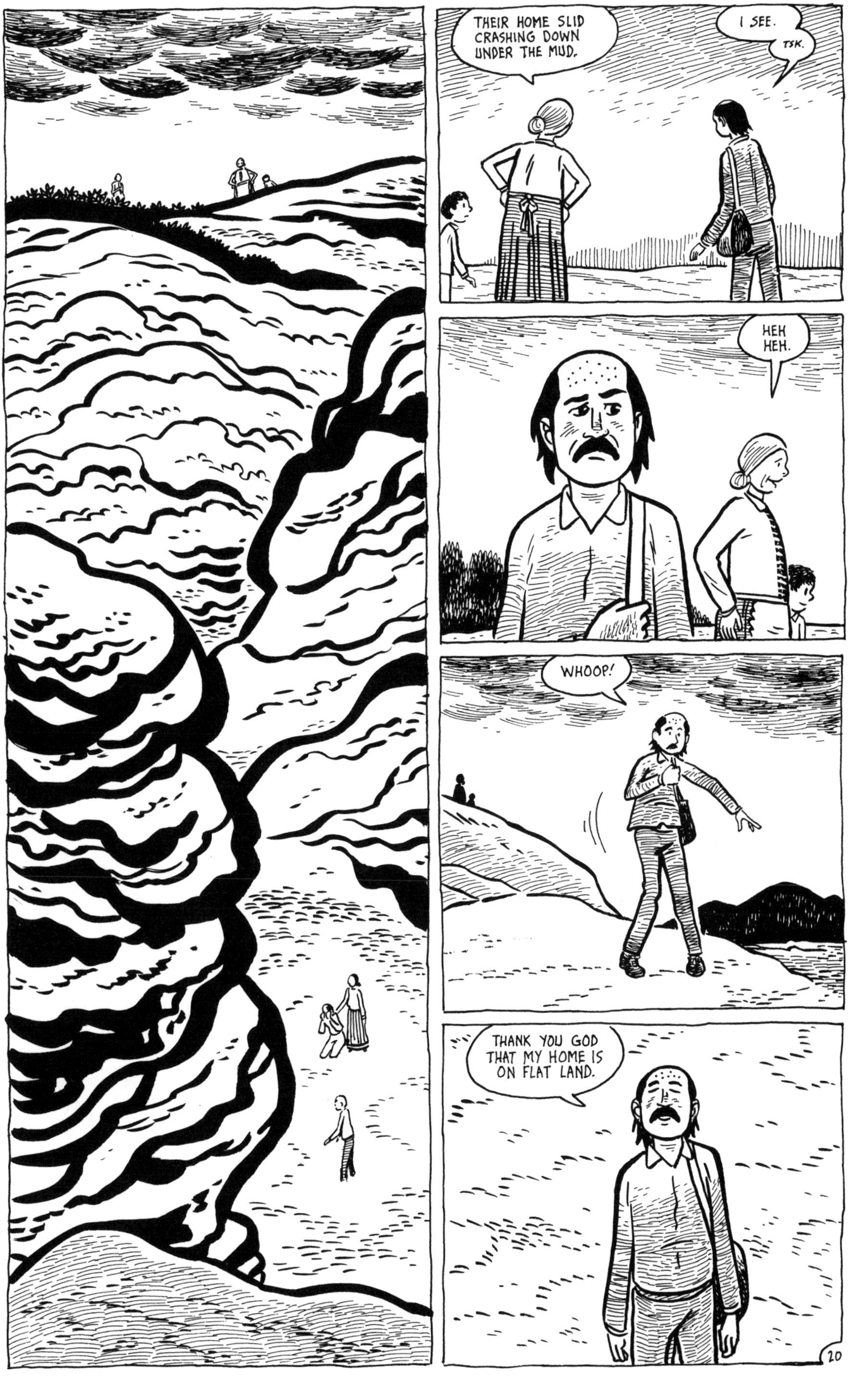
THEIR HOME SLID CRASHING DOWN UNDER THE MUD.
I SEE.
TSK.
HEH HEH.
WHOOP!
THANK YOU GOD THAT MY HOME IS ON FLAT LAND.

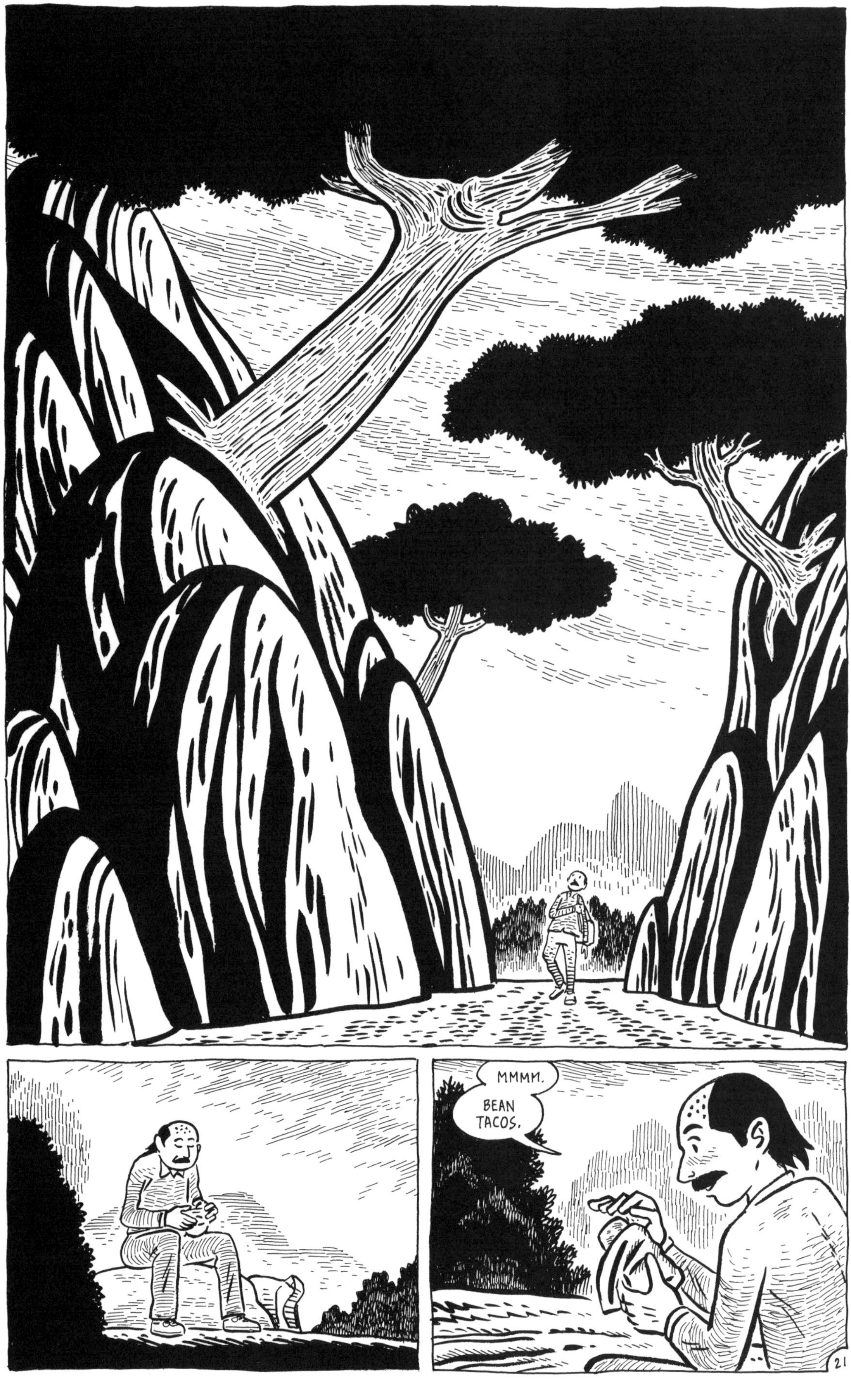
MMMM.
BEAN TACOS.

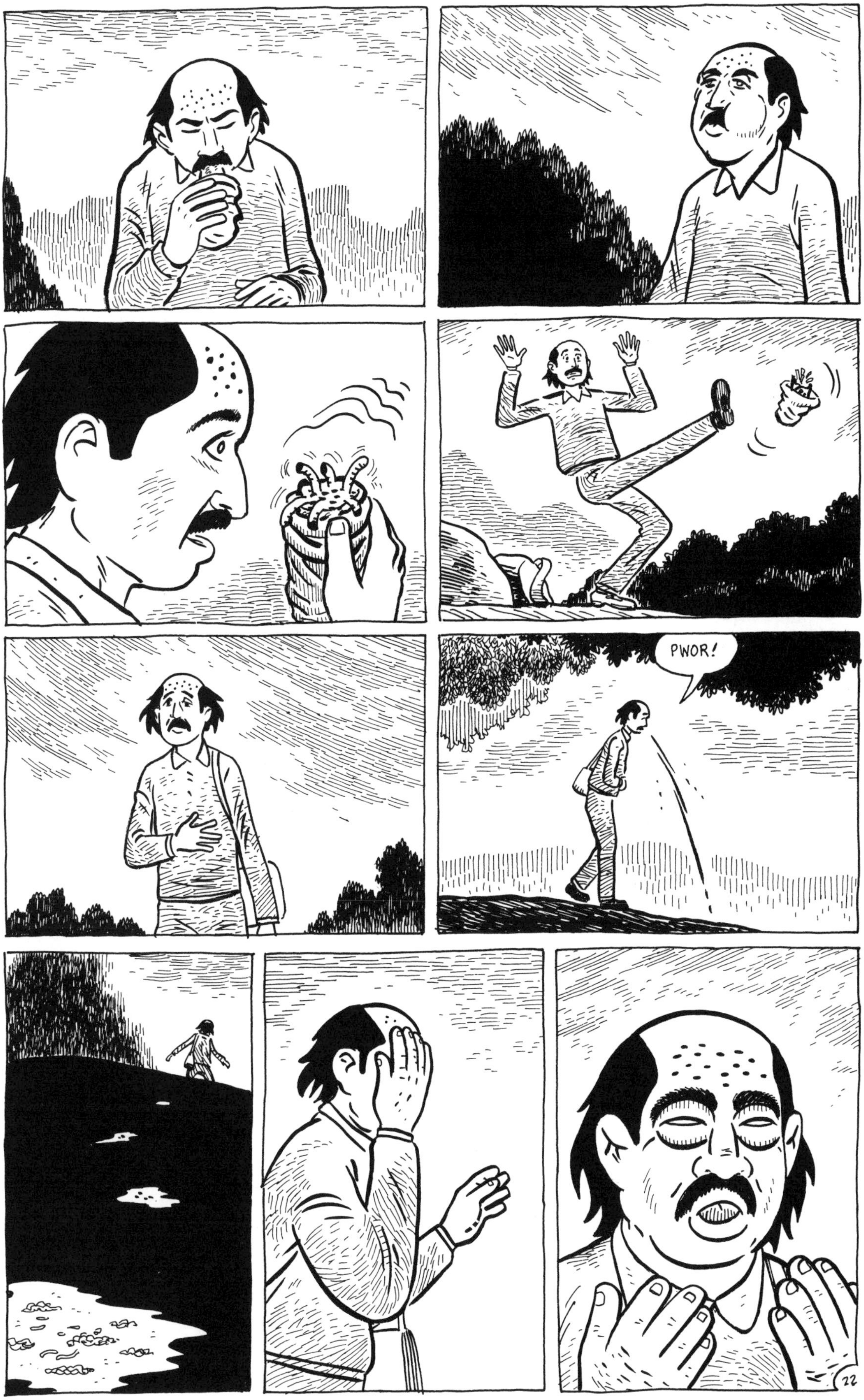
PWOR!

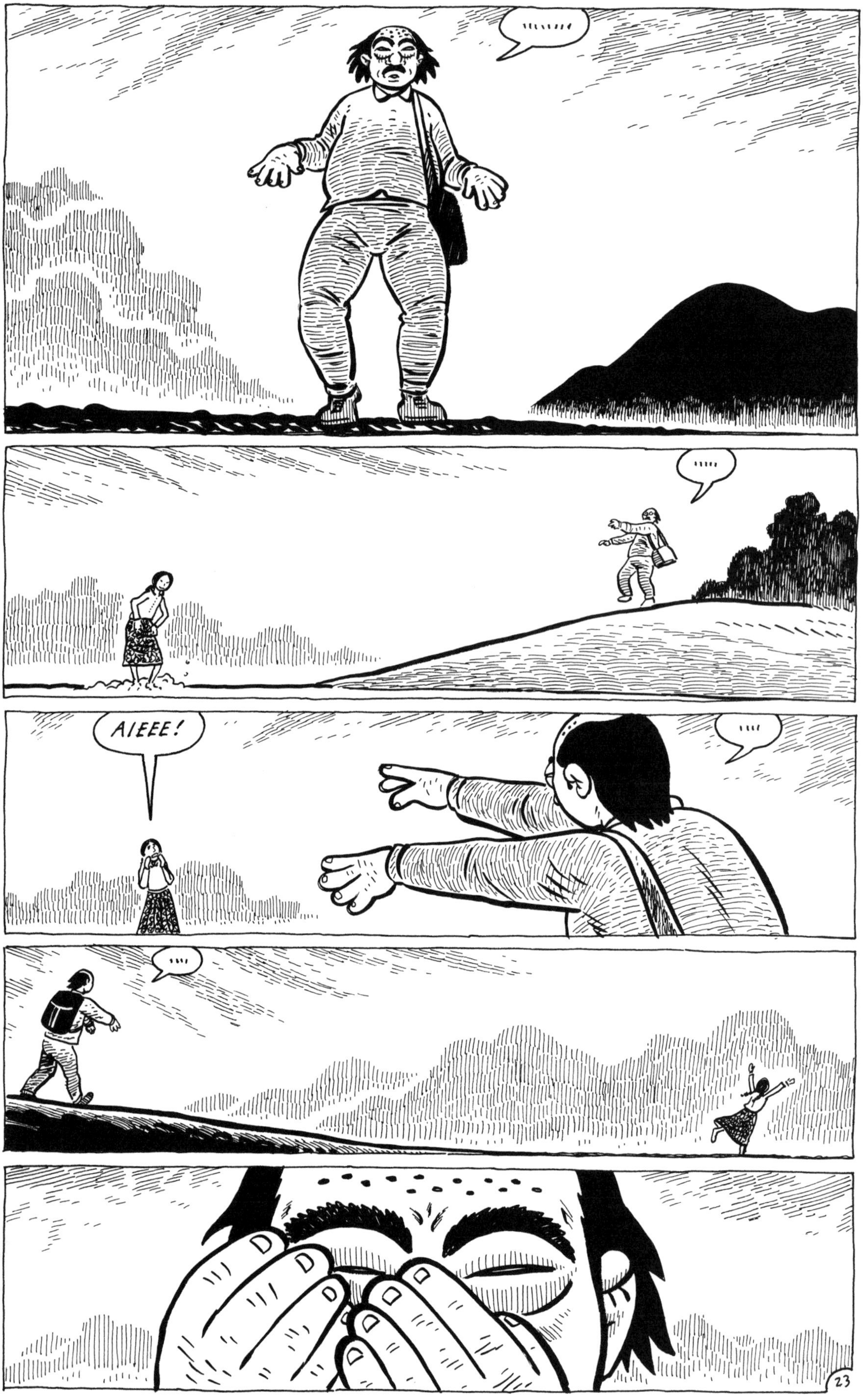
AIEEE!

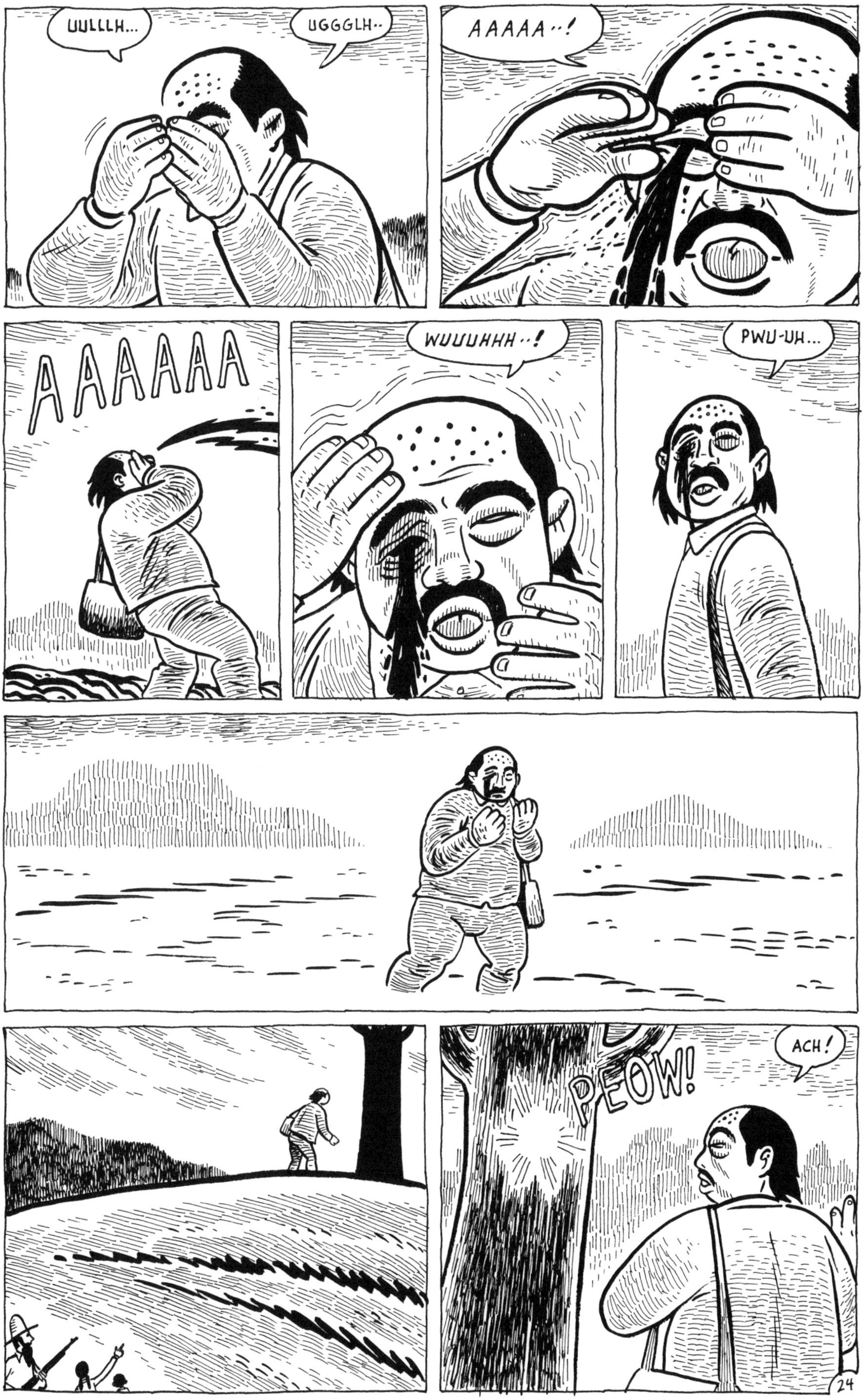
UULLLH...
UGGGLH..
AAAAA..!
AAAAAA
WUUUHHH..!
PWU-UH...
PEOW!
ACH!

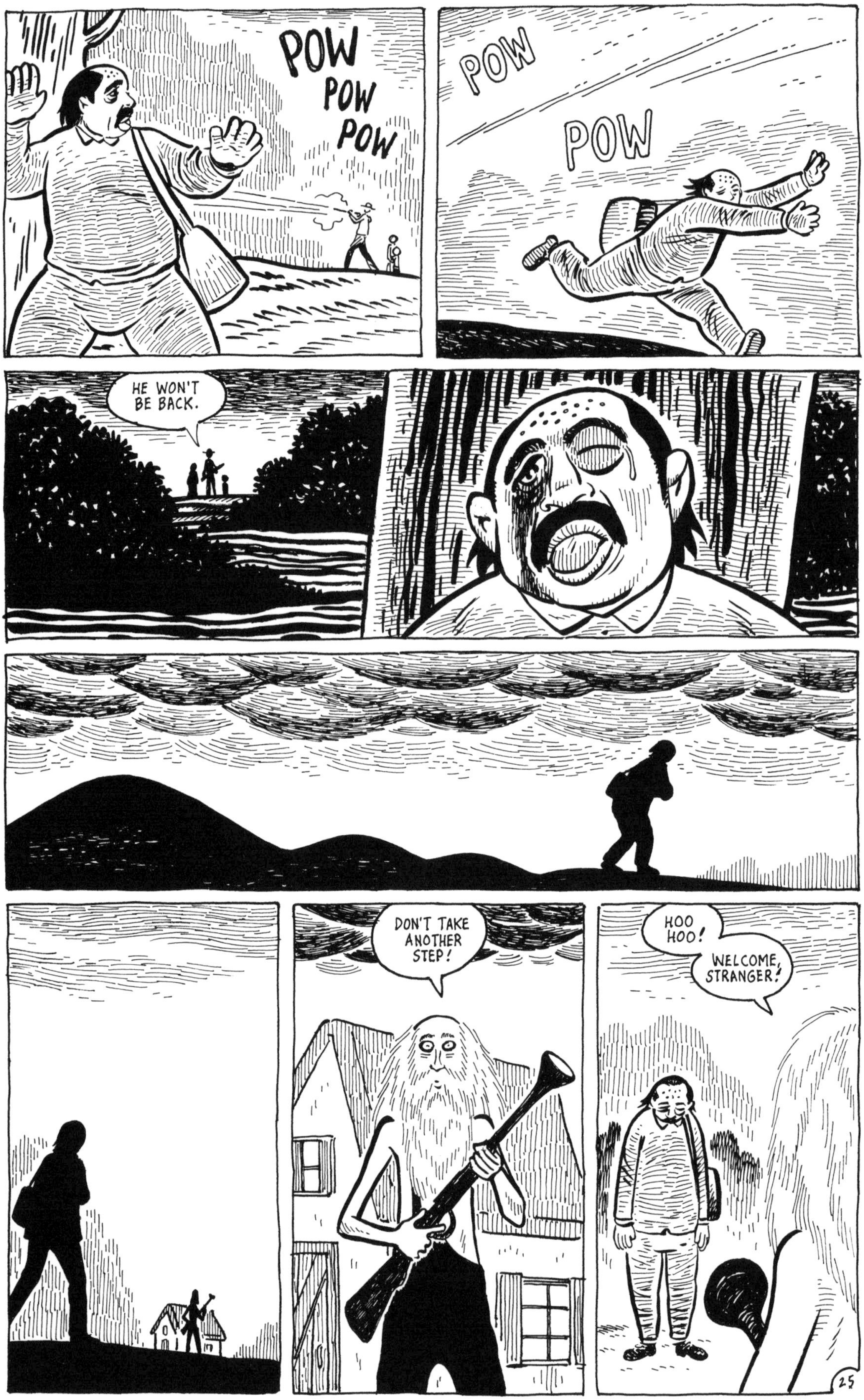
POW
POW
POW
POW
POW
HE WON'T BE BACK.
DON'T TAKE ANOTHER STEP!
HOO HOO!
WELCOME, STRANGER!

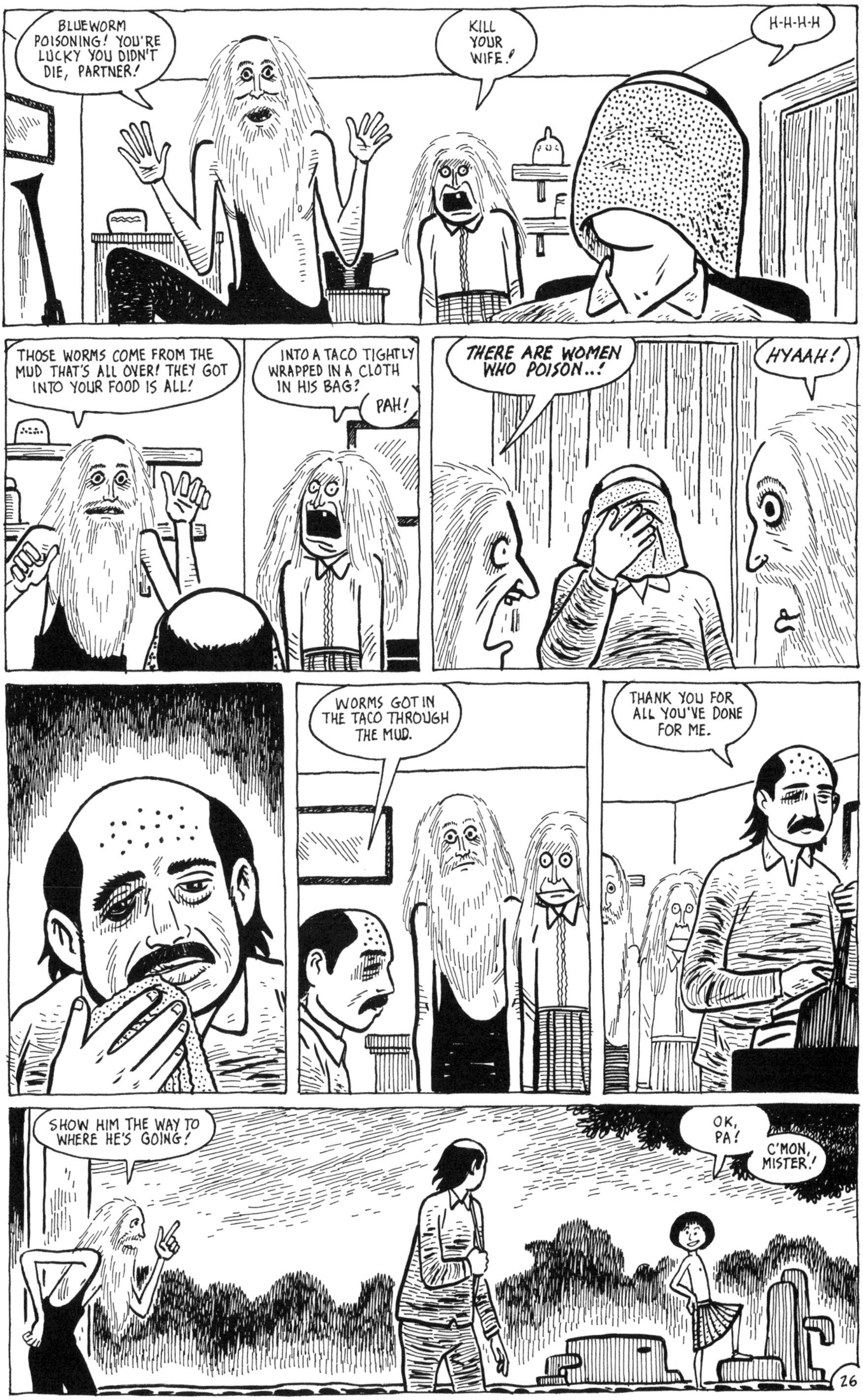
BLUEWORM POISONING! YOU'RE LUCKY YOU DIDN'T DIE, PARTNER!
KILL YOUR WIFE!
H-H-H-H
THOSE WORMS COME FROM THE MUD THAT'S ALL OVER! THEY GOT INTO YOUR FOOD IS ALL!
INTO A TACO TIGHTLY WRAPPED IN A CLOTH IN HIS BAG?
PAH!
THERE ARE WOMEN WHO POISON..!
HYAAH!
WORMS GOT IN THE TACO THROUGH THE MUD.
THANK YOU FOR ALL YOU'VE DONE FOR ME.
SHOW HIM THE WAY TO WHERE HE'S GOING!
OK, PA!
C'MON, MISTER!

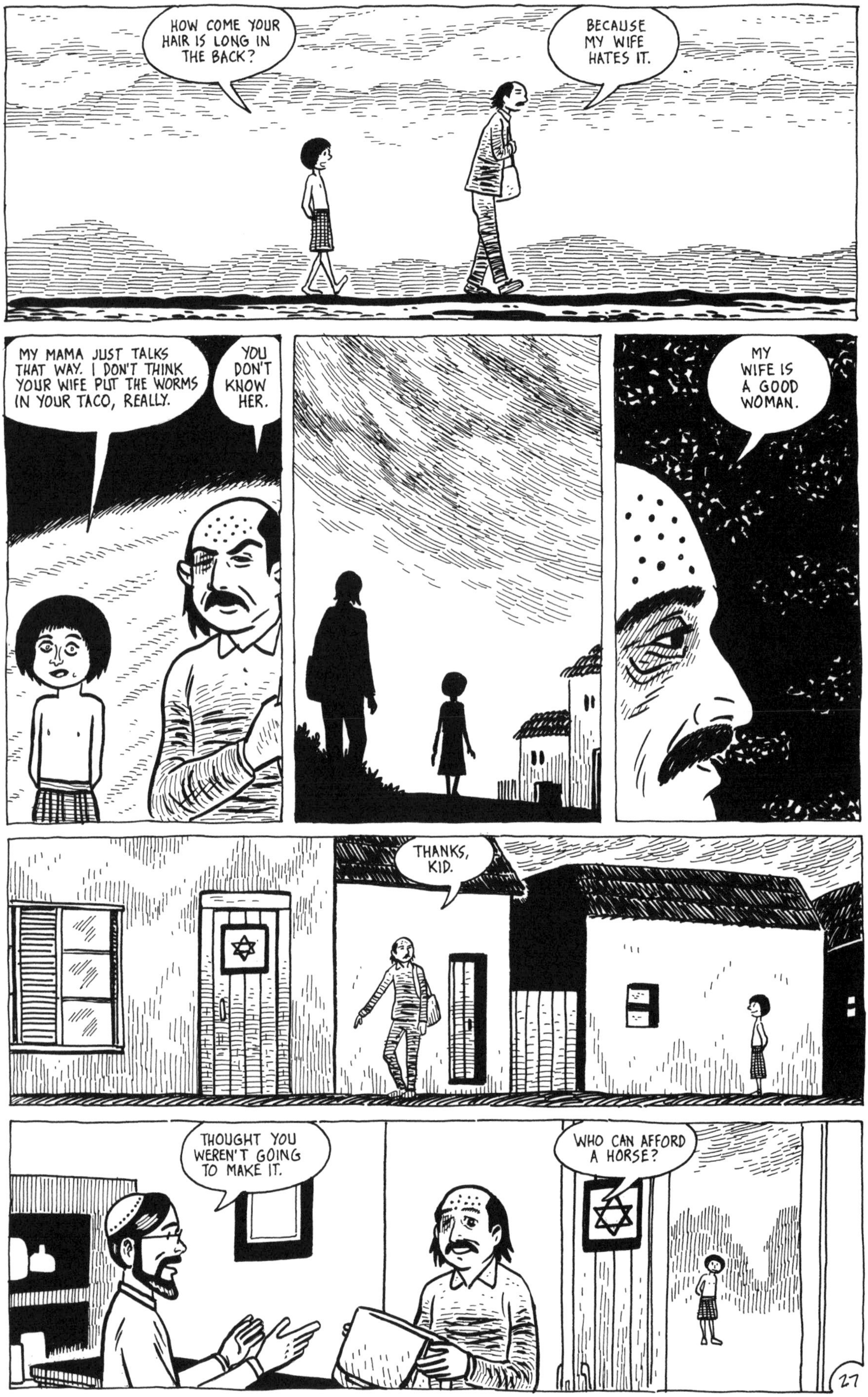
HOW COME YOUR HAIR IS LONG IN THE BACK?
BECAUSE MY WIFE HATES IT.
MY MAMA JUST TALKS THAT WAY. I DON'T THINK YOUR WIFE PUT THE WORMS IN YOUR TACO, REALLY.
YOU DON'T KNOW HER.
MY WIFE IS A GOOD WOMAN.
THANKS, KID.
THOUGHT YOU WEREN'T GOING TO MAKE IT.
WHO CAN AFFORD A HORSE?

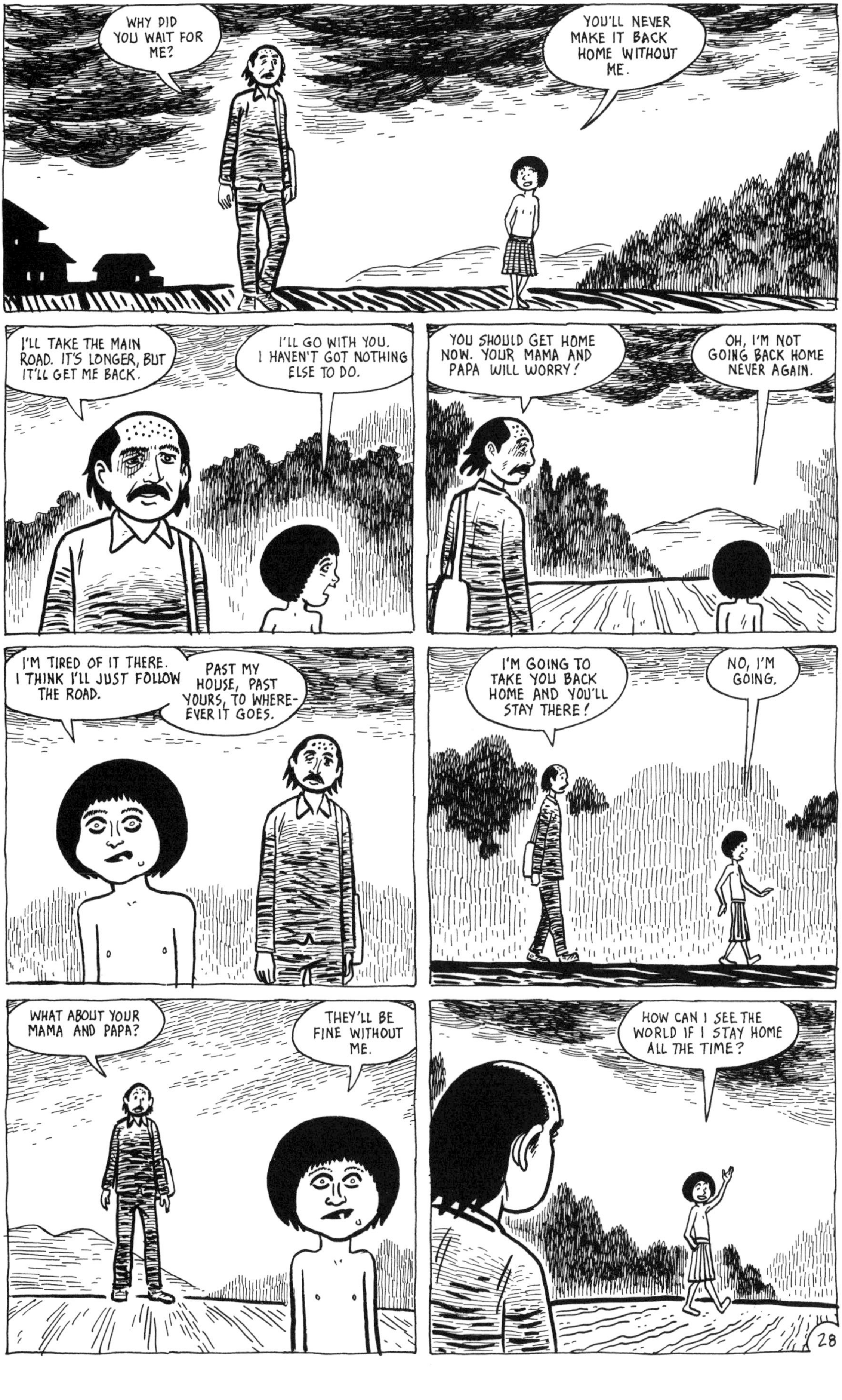
WHY DID YOU WAIT FOR ME?
YOU'LL NEVER MAKE IT BACK HOME WITHOUT ME.
I'LL TAKE THE MAIN ROAD. IT'S LONGER, BUT IT'LL GET ME BACK.
I'LL GO WITH YOU. I HAVEN'T GOT NOTHING ELSE TO DO.
YOU SHOULD GET HOME NOW. YOUR MAMA AND PAPA WILL WORRY!
OH, I'M NOT GOING BACK HOME NEVER AGAIN.
I'M TIRED OF IT THERE. I THINK I'LL JUST FOLLOW THE ROAD.
PAST MY HOUSE, PAST YOURS, TO WHERE-EVER IT GOES.
I'M GOING TO TAKE YOU BACK HOME AND YOU'LL STAY THERE!
NO, I'M GOING.
WHAT ABOUT YOUR MAMA AND PAPA?
THEY'LL BE FINE WITHOUT ME.
HOW CAN I SEE THE WORLD IF I STAY HOME ALL THE TIME?

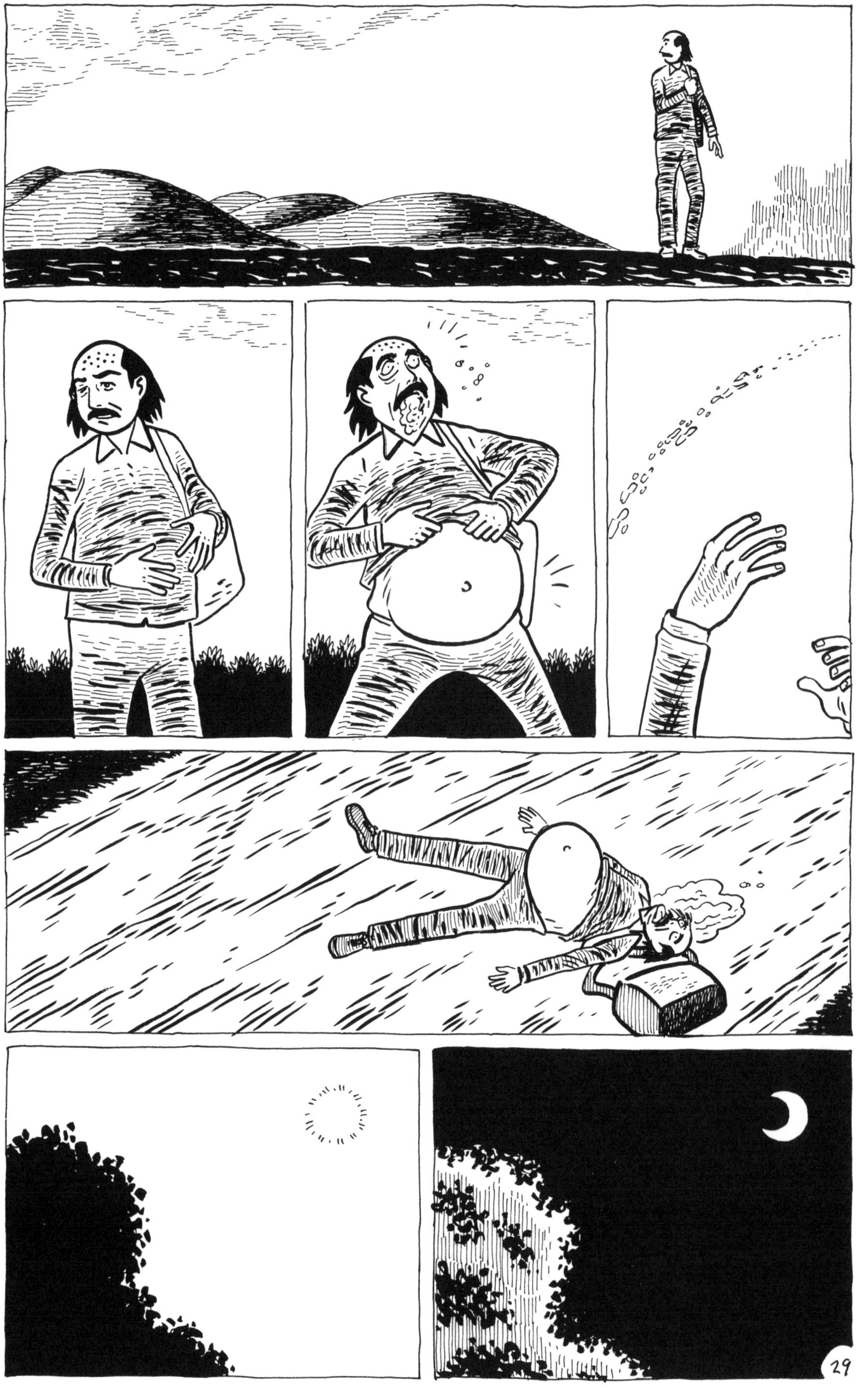

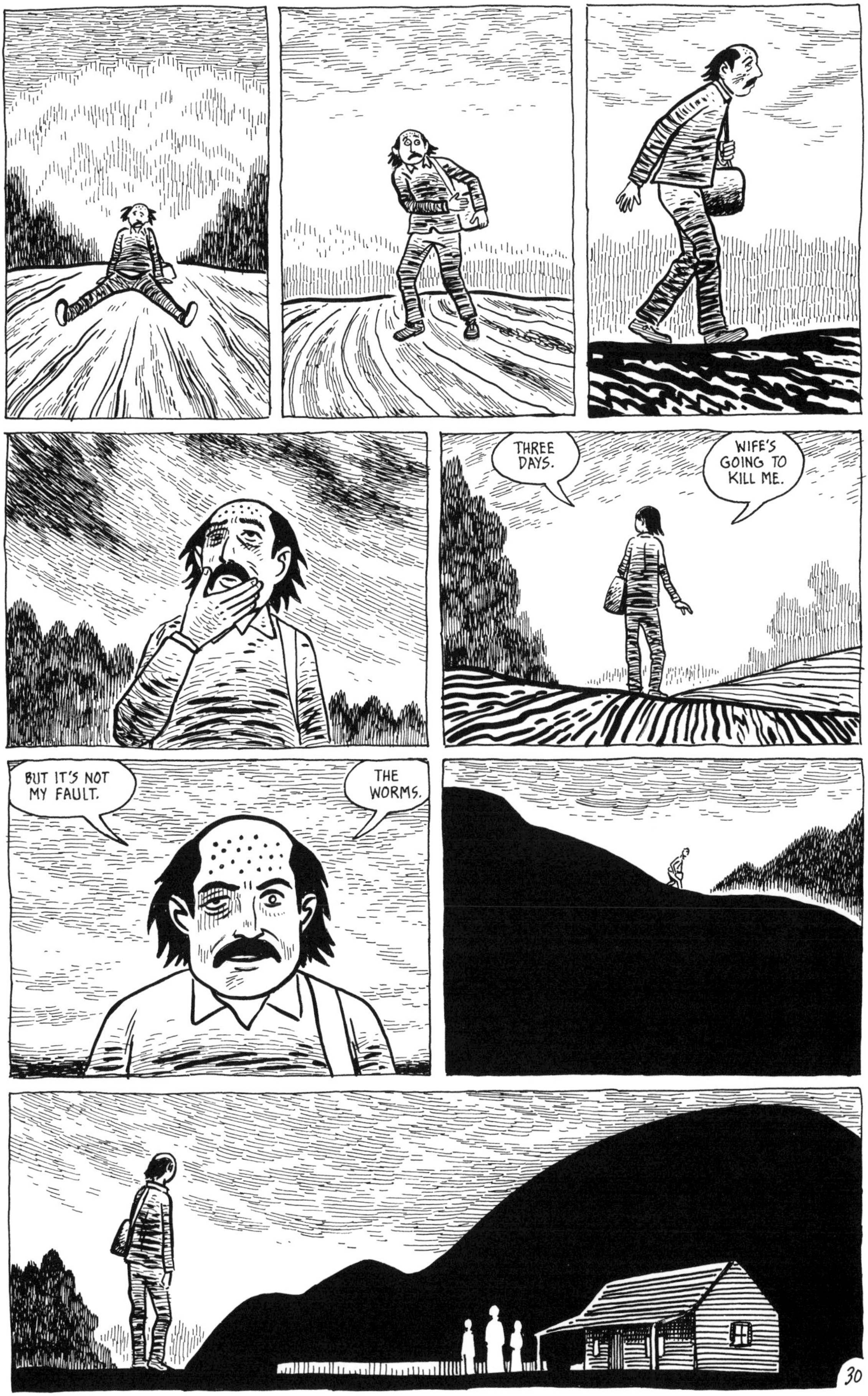
THREE DAYS.
WIFE'S GOING TO KILL ME.
BUT IT'S NOT MY FAULT.
THE WORMS.

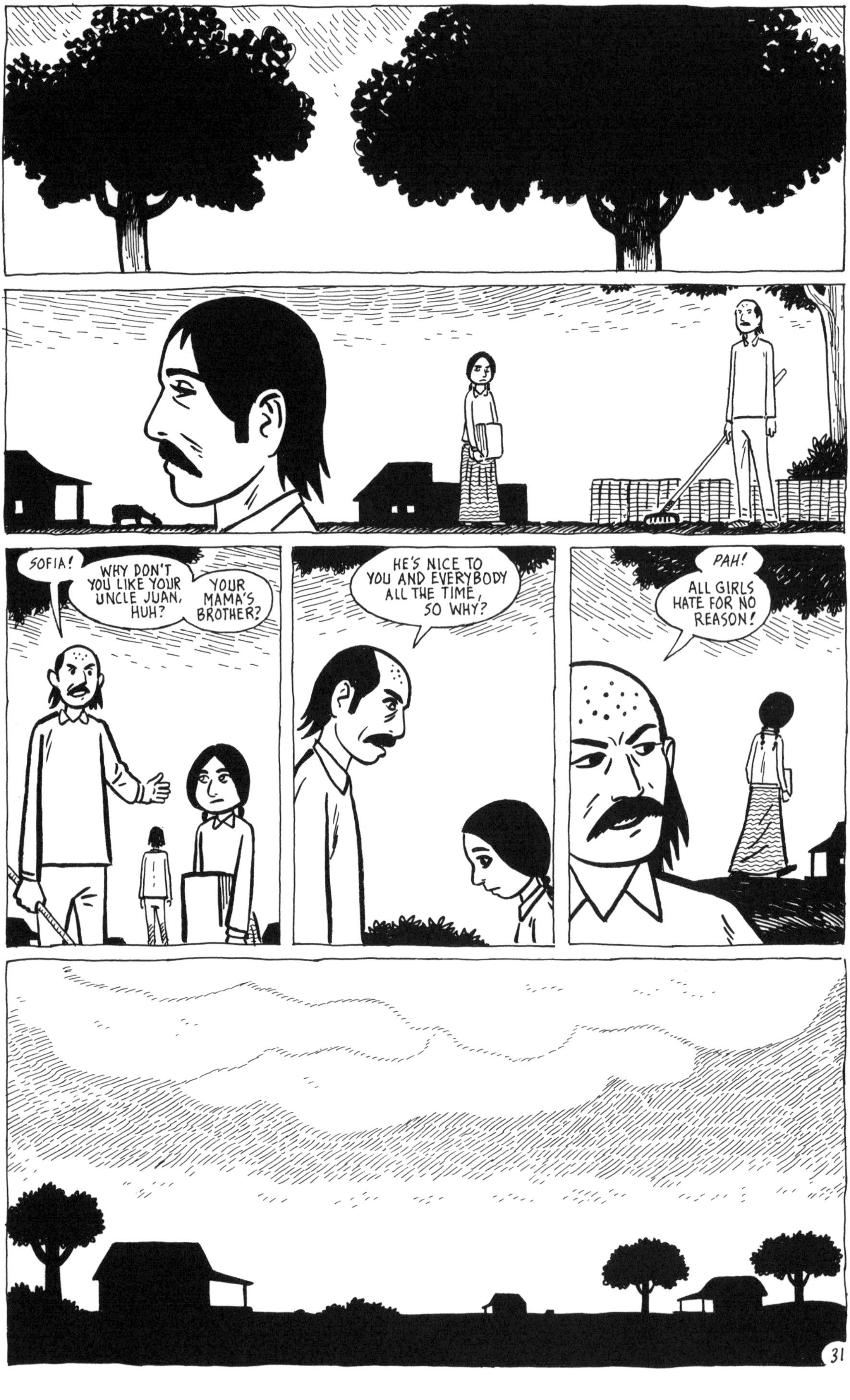
SOFIA!
WHY DON'T YOU LIKE YOUR UNCLE JUAN, HUH?
YOUR MAMA'S BROTHER?
HE'S NICE TO YOU AND EVERYBODY ALL THE TIME, SO WHY?
PAH!
ALL GIRLS HATE FOR NO REASON!

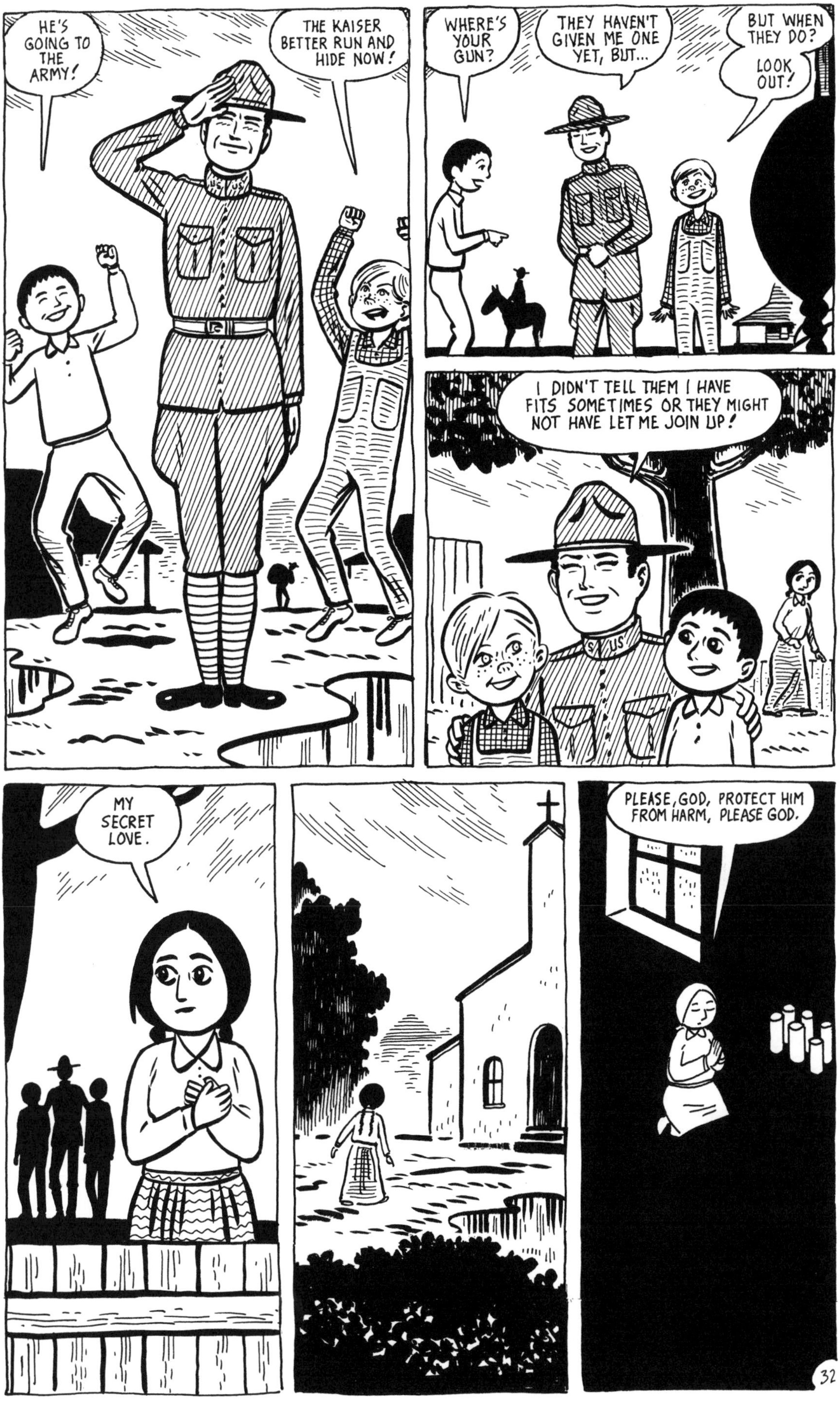
HE'S GOING TO THE ARMY!
THE KAISER BETTER RUN AND HIDE NOW!
WHERE'S YOUR GUN?
THEY HAVEN'T GIVEN ME ONE YET, BUT...
BUT WHEN THEY DO?
LOOK OUT!
I DIDN'T TELL THEM I HAVE FITS SOMETIMES OR THEY MIGHT NOT HAVE LET ME JOIN UP!
MY SECRET LOVE.
PLEASE, GOD, PROTECT HIM FROM HARM, PLEASE GOD.

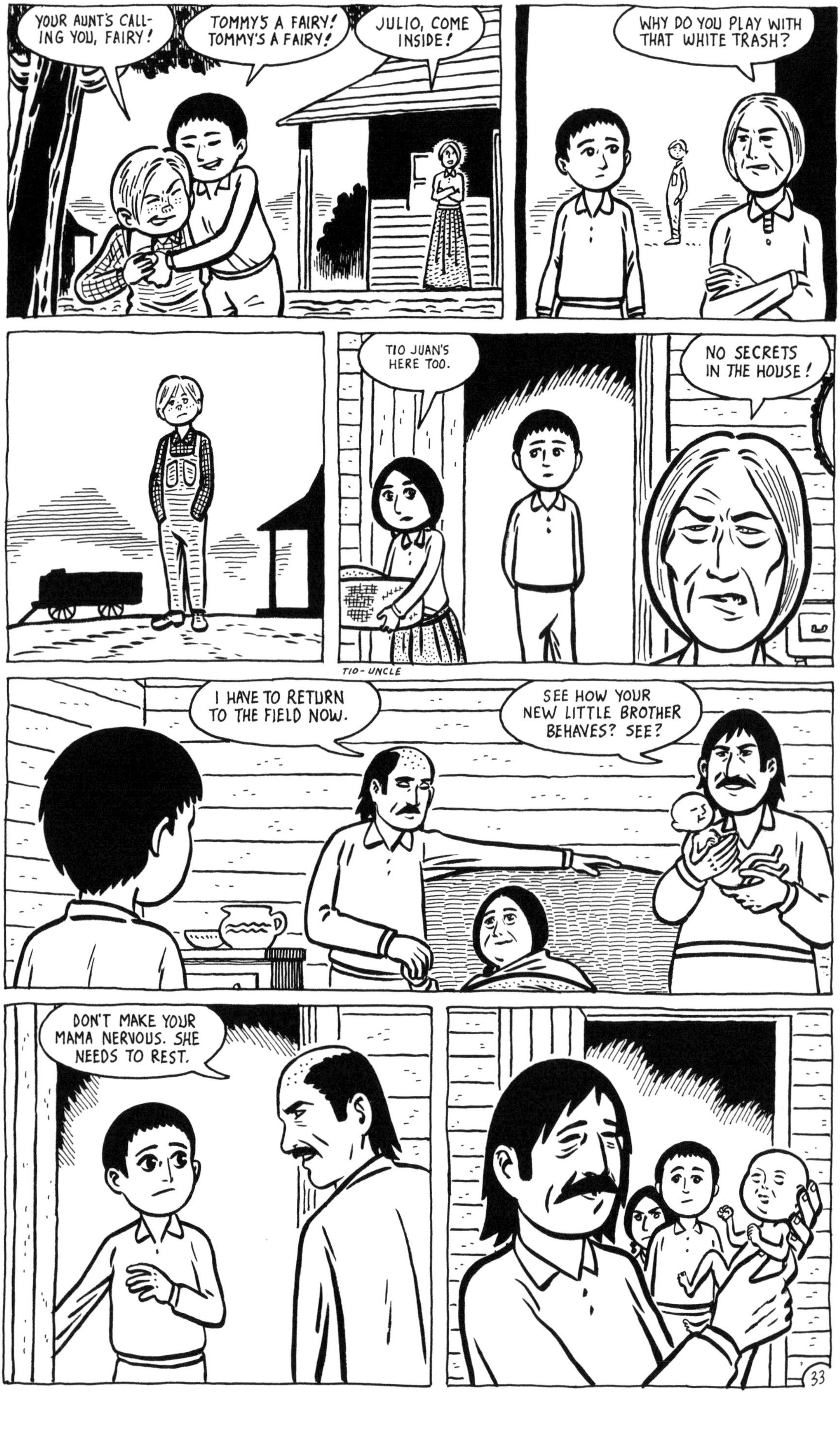
YOUR AUNT'S CALL-ING YOU, FAIRY!
TOMMY'S A FAIRY! TOMMY'S A FAIRY!
JULIO, COME INSIDE!
WHY DO YOU PLAY WITH THAT WHITE TRASH?
TIO JUAN'S HERE TOO.
NO SECRETS IN THE HOUSE!
TIO- UNCLE
I HAVE TO RETURN TO THE FIELD NOW.
SEE HOW YOUR NEW LITTLE BROTHER BEHAVES? SEE?
DON'T MAKE YOUR MAMA NERVOUS. SHE NEEDS TO REST.

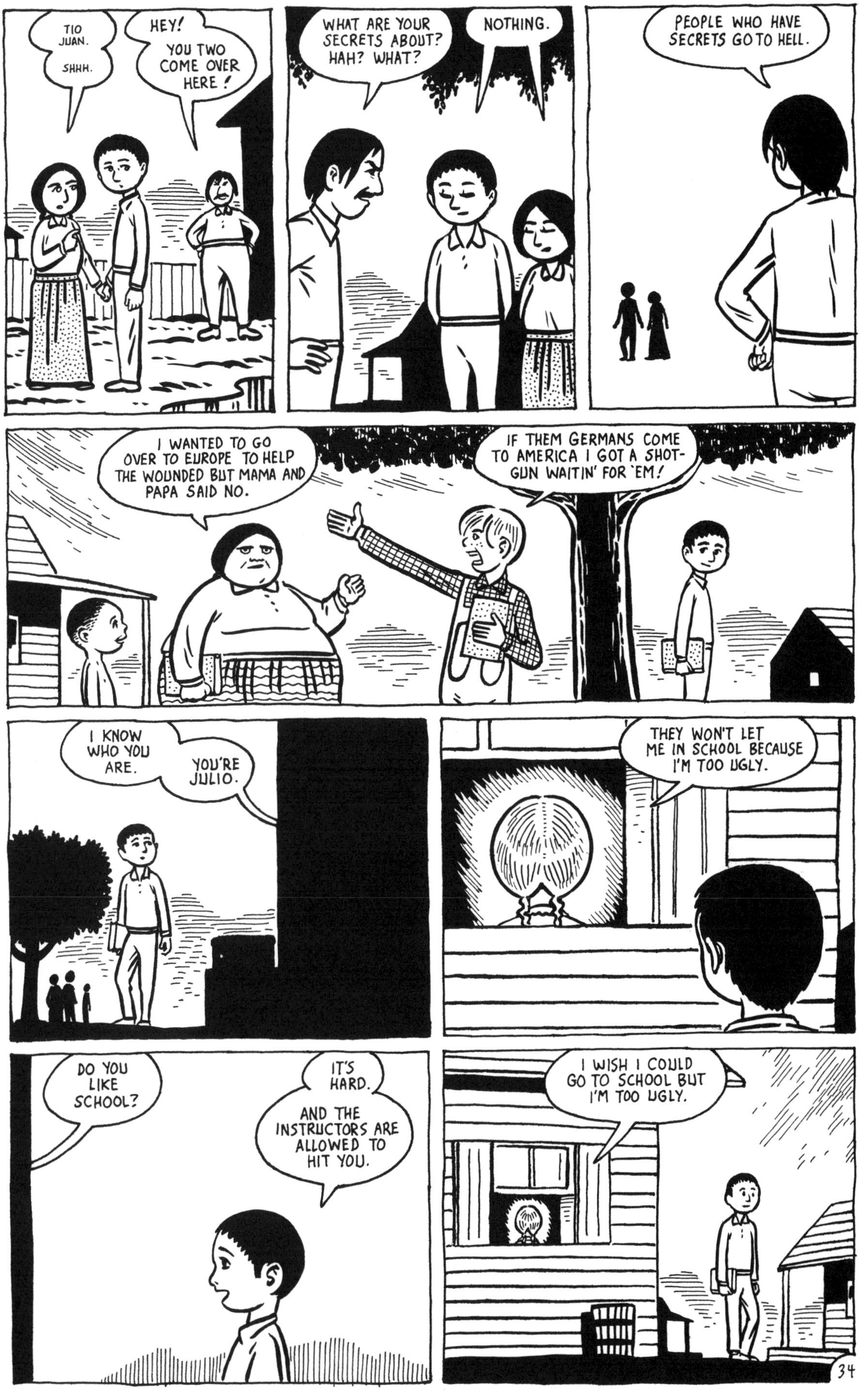
TIO JUAN.
SHHH.
HEY!
YOU TWO COME OVER HERE!
WHAT ARE YOUR SECRETS ABOUT? HAH? WHAT?
NOTHING.
PEOPLE WHO HAVE SECRETS GO TO HELL.
I WANTED TO GO OVER TO EUROPE TO HELP THE WOUNDED BUT MAMA AND PAPA SAID NO.
IF THEM GERMANS COME TO AMERICA I GOT A SHOT-GUN WAITIN' FOR 'EM!
I KNOW WHO YOU ARE.
YOU'RE JULIO.
THEY WON'T LET ME IN SCHOOL BECAUSE I'M TOO UGLY.
DO YOU LIKE SCHOOL?
IT'S HARD.
AND THE INSTRUCTORS ARE ALLOWED TO HIT YOU.
I WISH I COULD GO TO SCHOOL BUT I'M TOO UGLY.

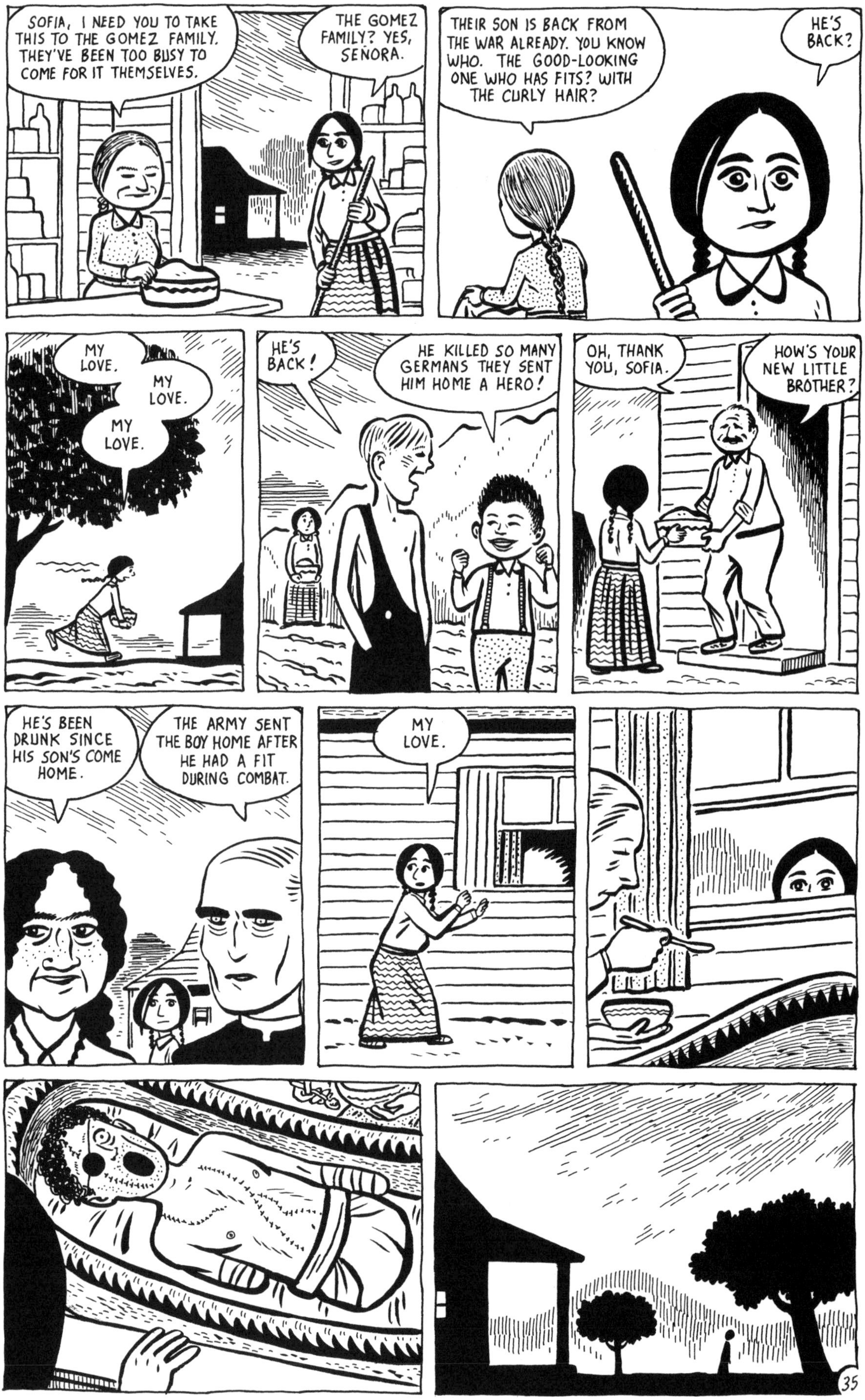
SOFIA, I NEED YOU TO TAKE THIS TO THE GOMEZ FAMILY. THEY'VE BEEN TOO BUSY TO COME FOR IT THEMSELVES.
THE GOMEZ FAMILY? YES, SEÑORA.
THEIR SON IS BACK FROM THE WAR ALREADY. YOU KNOW WHO. THE GOOD-LOOKING ONE WHO HAS FITS? WITH THE CURLY HAIR?
HE'S BACK?
MY LOVE.
MY LOVE.
MY LOVE.
HE'S BACK!
HE KILLED SO MANY GERMANS THEY SENT HIM HOME A HERO!
OH, THANK YOU, SOFIA.
HOW'S YOUR NEW LITTLE BROTHER?
HE'S BEEN DRUNK SINCE HIS SON'S COME HOME.
THE ARMY SENT THE BOY HOME AFTER HE HAD A FIT DURING COMBAT.
MY LOVE.

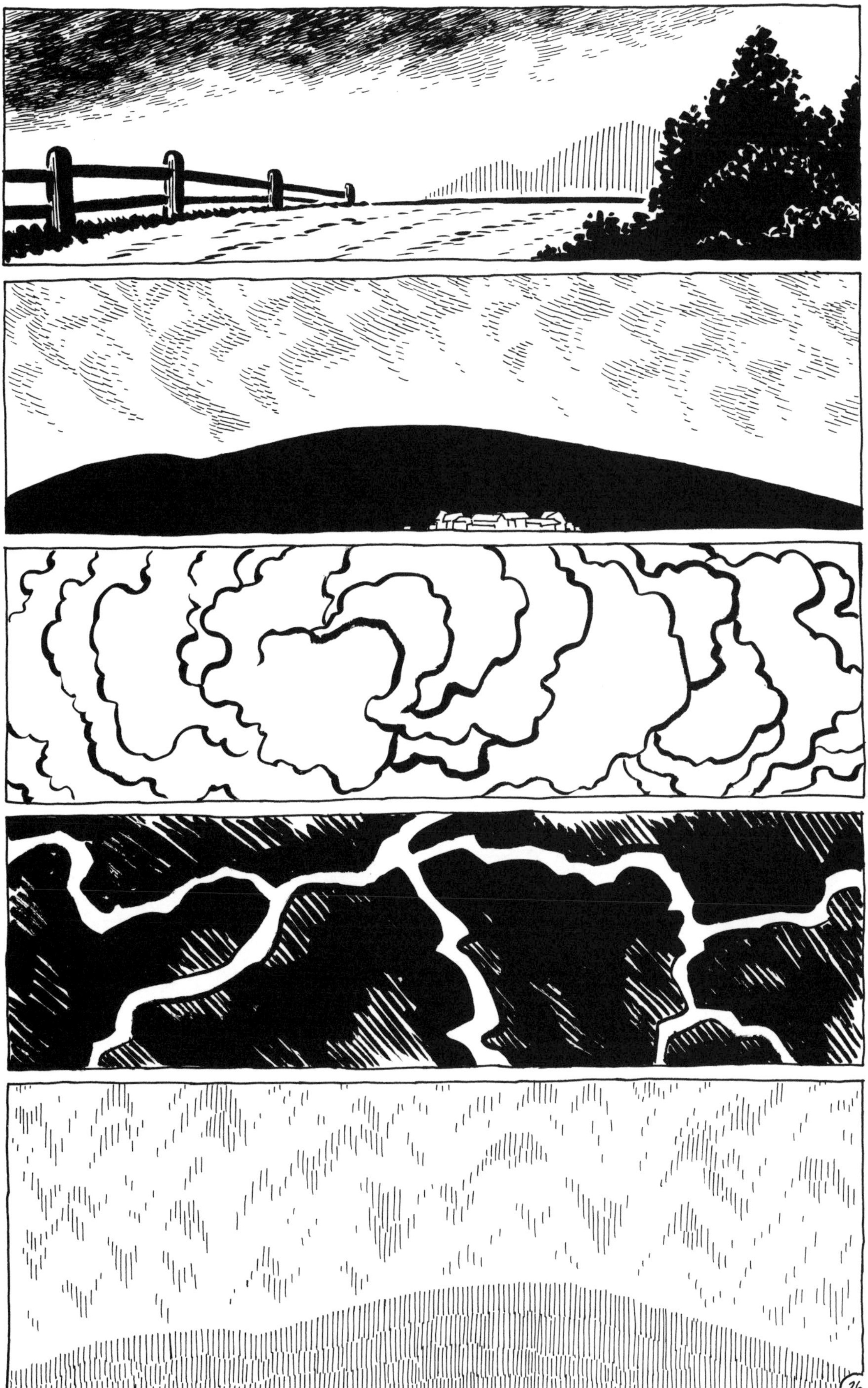

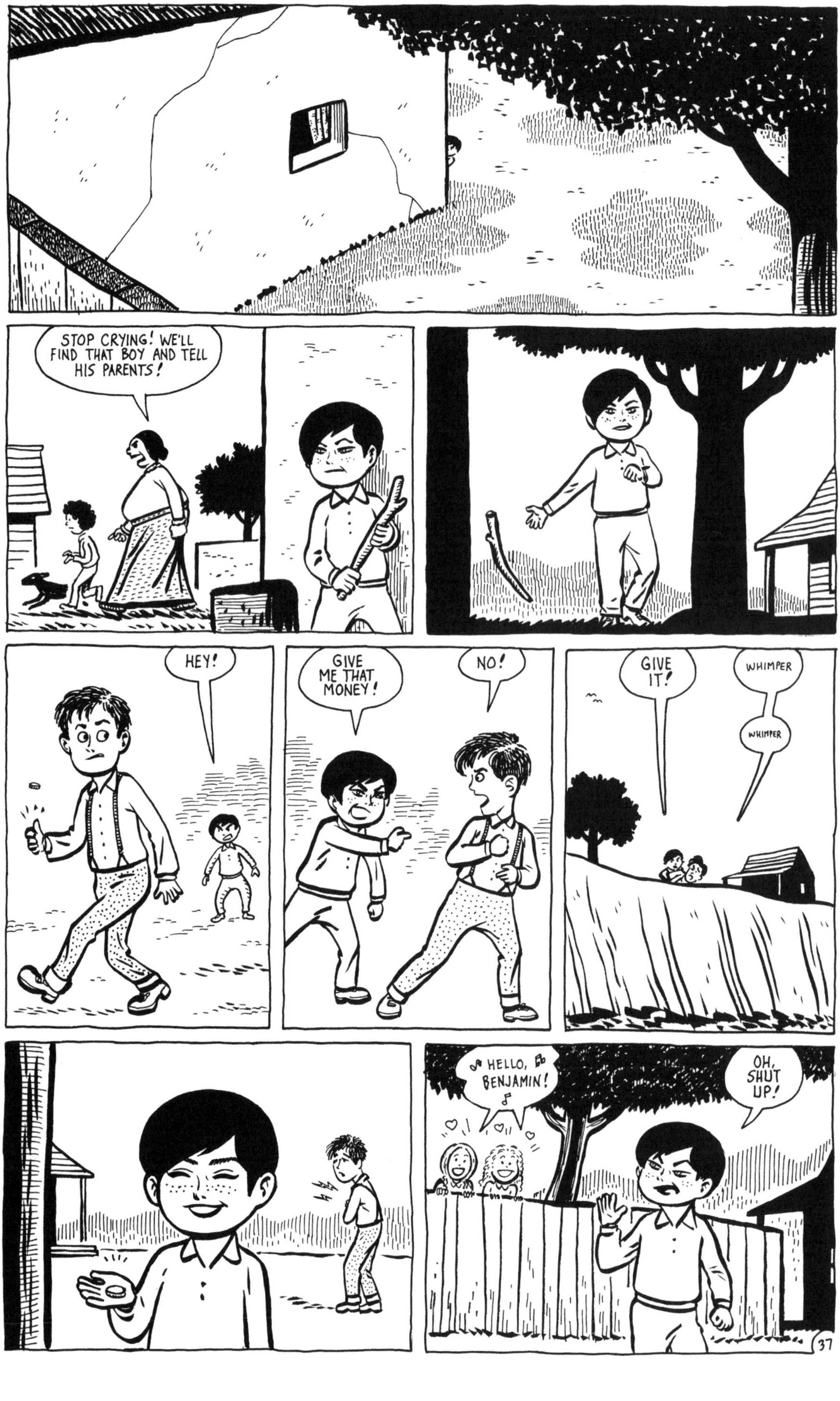
STOP CRYING! WE'LL FIND THAT BOY AND TELL HIS PARENTS!
HEY!
GIVE ME THAT MONEY!
NO!
GIVE IT!
WHIMPER
WHIMPER
HELLO, BENJAMIN!
OH, SHUT UP!

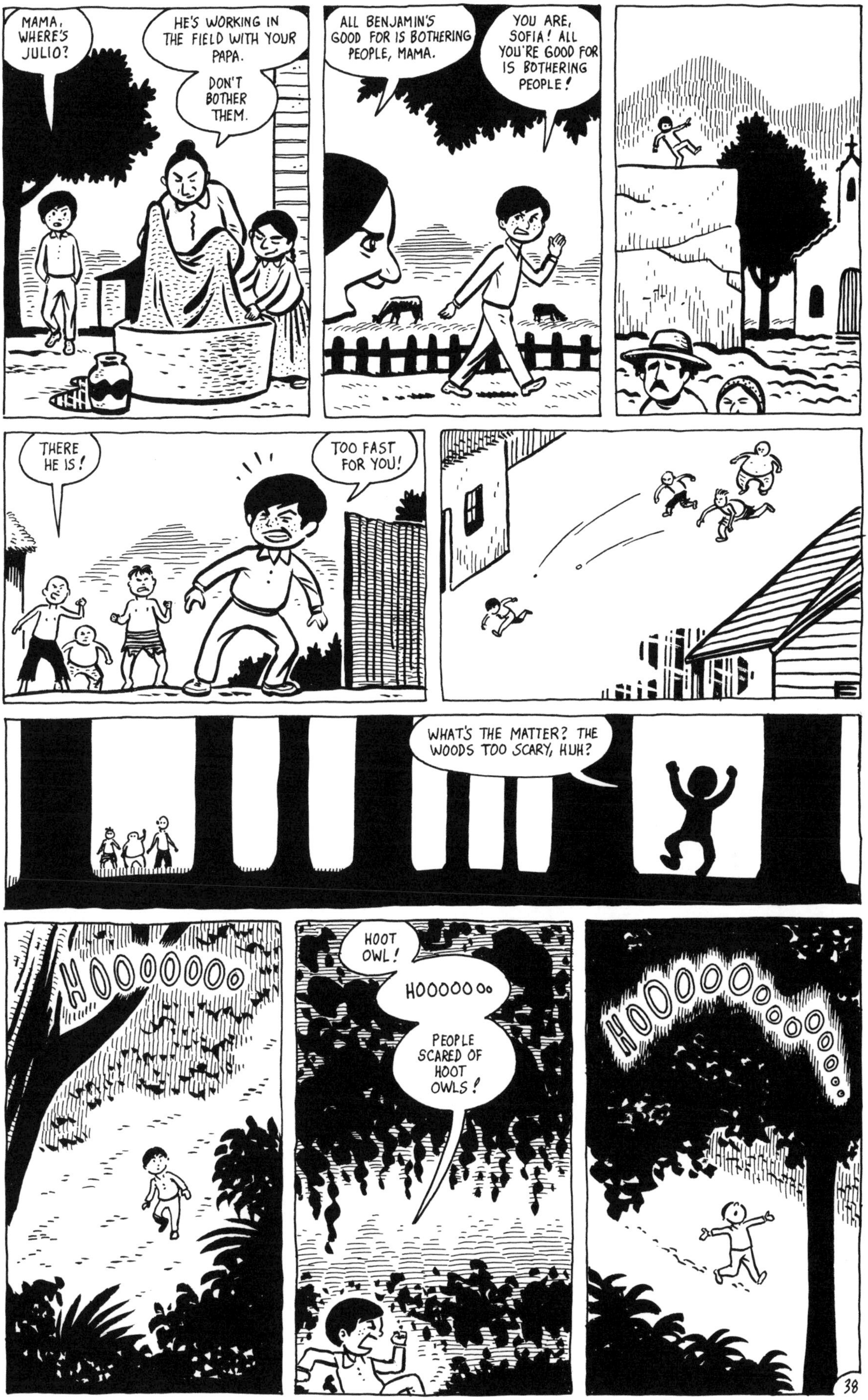

MAMA, WHERE'S JULIO?
HE'S WORKING IN THE FIELD WITH YOUR PAPA.
DON'T BOTHER THEM.
ALL BENJAMIN'S GOOD FOR IS BOTHERING PEOPLE, MAMA.
YOU ARE, SOFIA! ALL YOU'RE GOOD FOR IS BOTHERING PEOPLE!
THERE HE IS!
TOO FAST FOR YOU!
WHAT'S THE MATTER? THE WOODS TOO SCARY, HUH?
HOOOOOOo
HOOT OWL!
HOOOOOoo
PEOPLE SCARED OF HOOT OWLS!
HOOOOOOooooooo
38

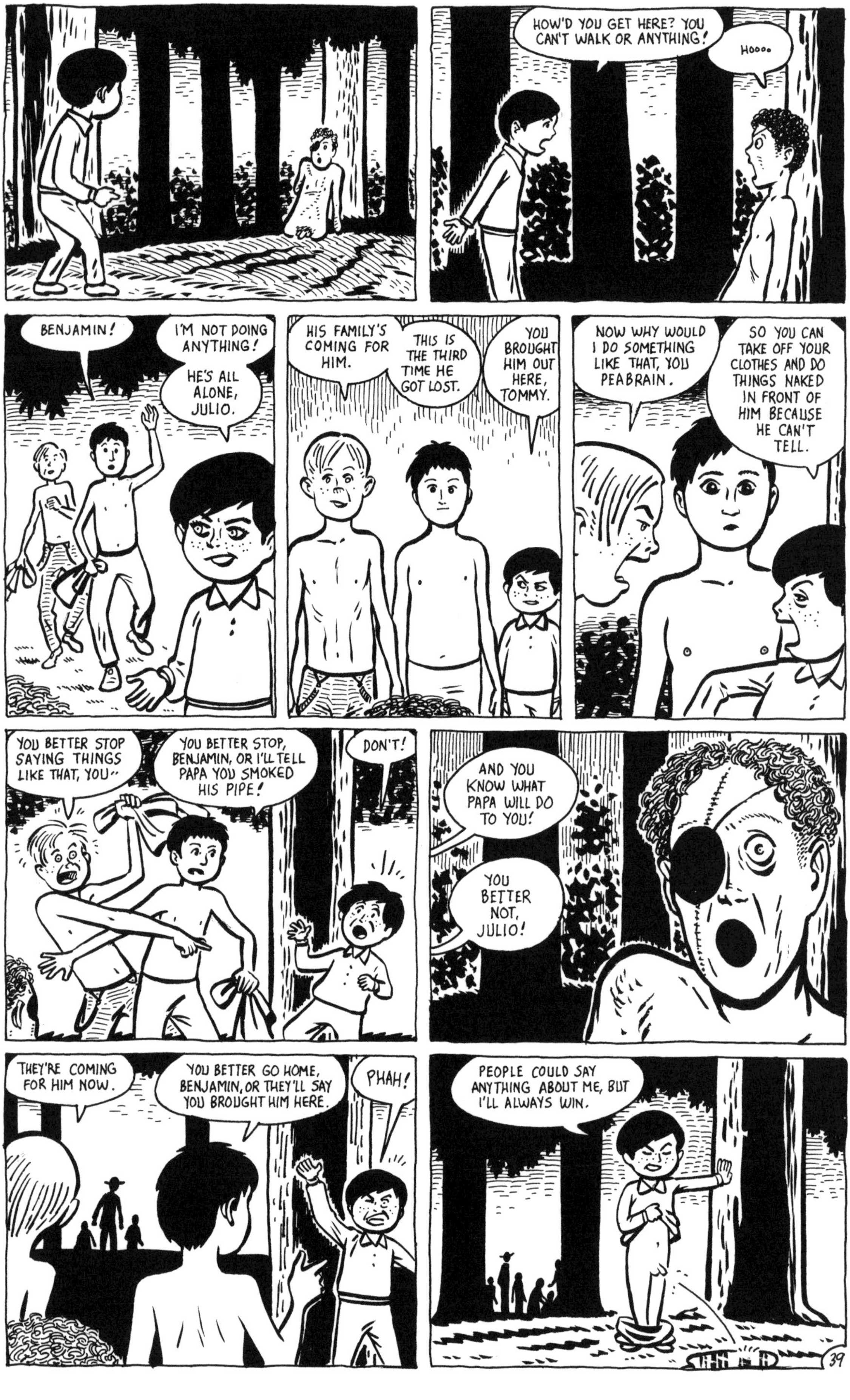
HOW'D YOU GET HERE? YOU CAN'T WALK OR ANYTHING!
Hoooo
BENJAMIN!
I'M NOT DOING ANYTHING!
HE'S ALL ALONE, JULIO.
HIS FAMILY'S COMING FOR HIM.
THIS IS THE THIRD TIME HE GOT LOST.
YOU BROUGHT HIM OUT HERE, TOMMY.
NOW WHY WOULD I DO SOMETHING LIKE THAT, YOU PEABRAIN.
SO YOU CAN TAKE OFF YOUR CLOTHES AND DO THINGS NAKED IN FRONT OF HIM BECAUSE HE CAN'T TELL.
YOU BETTER STOP SAYING THINGS LIKE THAT, YOU--
YOU BETTER STOP, BENJAMIN, OR I'LL TELL PAPA YOU SMOKED HIS PIPE!
DON'T!
AND YOU KNOW WHAT PAPA WILL DO TO YOU!
YOU BETTER NOT, JULIO!
THEY'RE COMING FOR HIM NOW.
YOU BETTER GO HOME, BENJAMIN, OR THEY'LL SAY YOU BROUGHT HIM HERE.
PHAH!
PEOPLE COULD SAY ANYTHING ABOUT ME, BUT I'LL ALWAYS WIN.

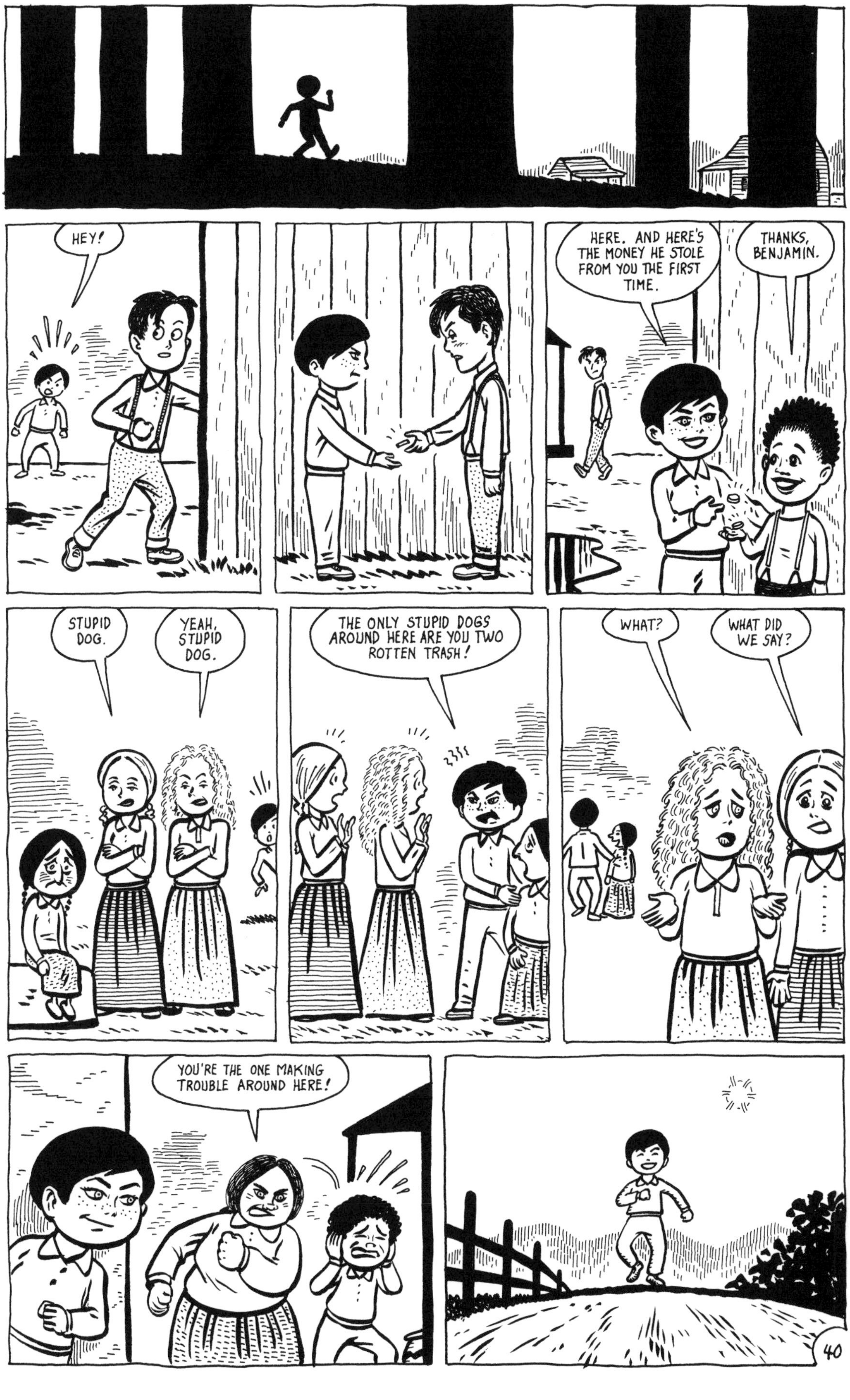
HEY!
HERE. AND HERE'S THE MONEY HE STOLE FROM YOU THE FIRST TIME.
THANKS, BENJAMIN.
STUPID DOG.
YEAH, STUPID DOG.
THE ONLY STUPID DOGS AROUND HERE ARE YOU TWO ROTTEN TRASH!
WHAT?
WHAT DID WE SAY?
YOU'RE THE ONE MAKING TROUBLE AROUND HERE!

HERE COMES THE RAIN!

IT'S GOING TO LAST A LONG TIME.

CAN FEEL IT IN MY HEAD HOLES.

WATCH OUT FOR THE WORMS!

THE BLUE ONES!

THE RAIN WILL FORCE THEM RIGHT UP OUT OF THE GROUND!

BLUE WORMS!

HEY, SOMEBODY SEE IF THAT KID'S OK!

MIGHT GET LOST WANDERING AROUND THE WORLD LIKE THAT!

AND WATCH OUT FOR THE WORMS!

. . . .

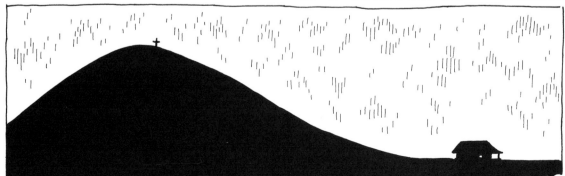

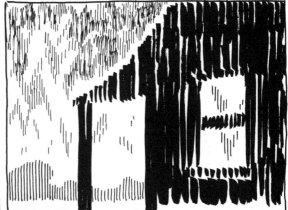

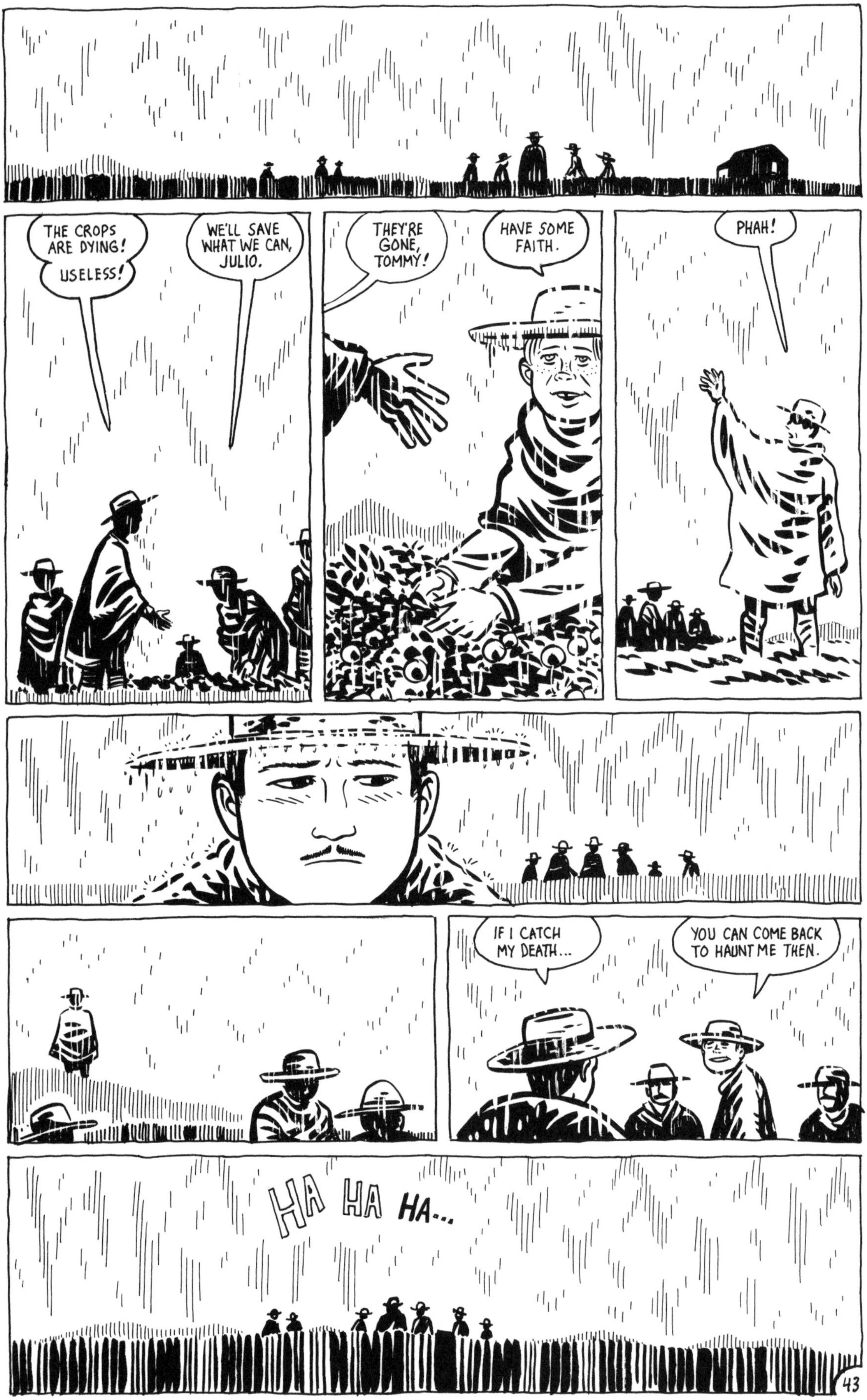
THE CROPS ARE DYING!
USELESS!
WE'LL SAVE WHAT WE CAN, JULIO.
THEY'RE GONE, TOMMY!
HAVE SOME FAITH.
PHAH!
IF I CATCH MY DEATH...
YOU CAN COME BACK TO HAUNT ME THEN.
HA HA HA...

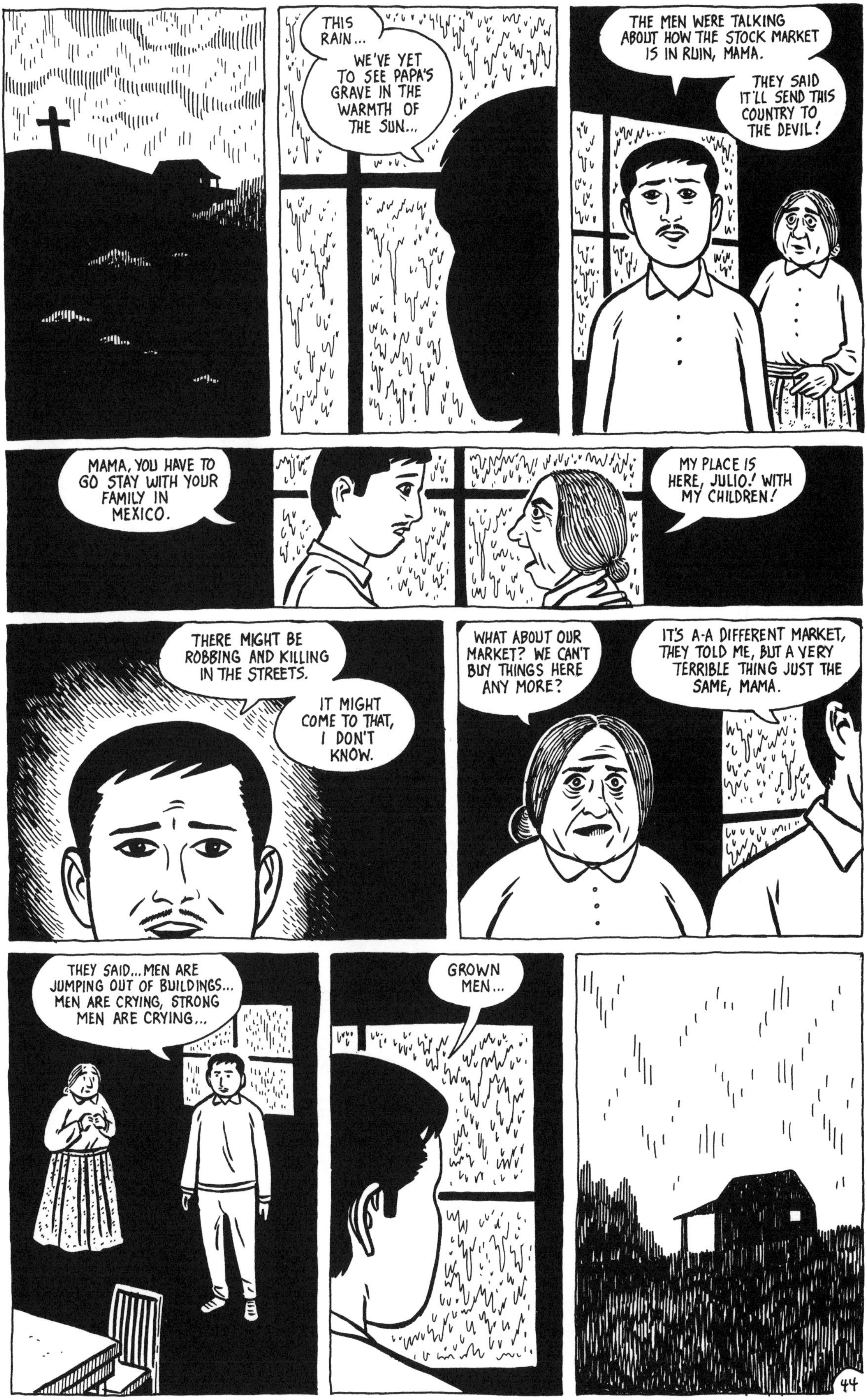

THIS RAIN...
WE'VE YET TO SEE PAPA'S GRAVE IN THE WARMTH OF THE SUN...
THE MEN WERE TALKING ABOUT HOW THE STOCK MARKET IS IN RUIN, MAMA.
THEY SAID IT'LL SEND THIS COUNTRY TO THE DEVIL!
MAMA, YOU HAVE TO GO STAY WITH YOUR FAMILY IN MEXICO.
MY PLACE IS HERE, JULIO! WITH MY CHILDREN!
THERE MIGHT BE ROBBING AND KILLING IN THE STREETS.
IT MIGHT COME TO THAT, I DON'T KNOW.
WHAT ABOUT OUR MARKET? WE CAN'T BUY THINGS HERE ANY MORE?
IT'S A-A DIFFERENT MARKET, THEY TOLD ME, BUT A VERY TERRIBLE THING JUST THE SAME, MAMA.
THEY SAID... MEN ARE JUMPING OUT OF BUILDINGS... MEN ARE CRYING, STRONG MEN ARE CRYING...
GROWN MEN...

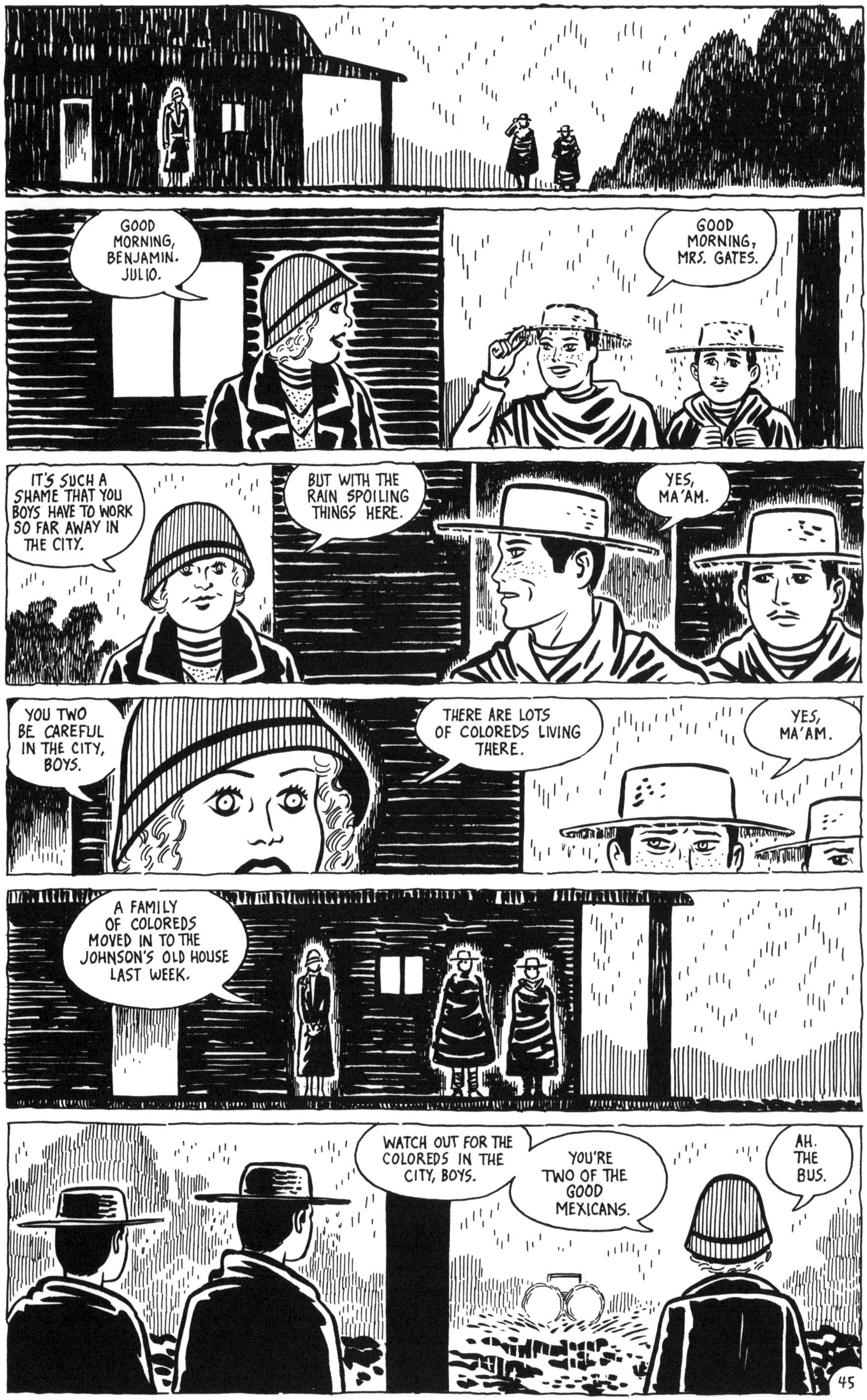
GOOD MORNING, BENJAMIN. JULIO.
GOOD MORNING, MRS. GATES.
IT'S SUCH A SHAME THAT YOU BOYS HAVE TO WORK SO FAR AWAY IN THE CITY.
BUT WITH THE RAIN SPOILING THINGS HERE.
YES, MA'AM.
YOU TWO BE CAREFUL IN THE CITY, BOYS.
THERE ARE LOTS OF COLOREDS LIVING THERE.
YES, MA'AM.
A FAMILY OF COLOREDS MOVED IN TO THE JOHNSON'S OLD HOUSE LAST WEEK.
WATCH OUT FOR THE COLOREDS IN THE CITY, BOYS.
YOU'RE TWO OF THE GOOD MEXICANS.
AH. THE BUS.

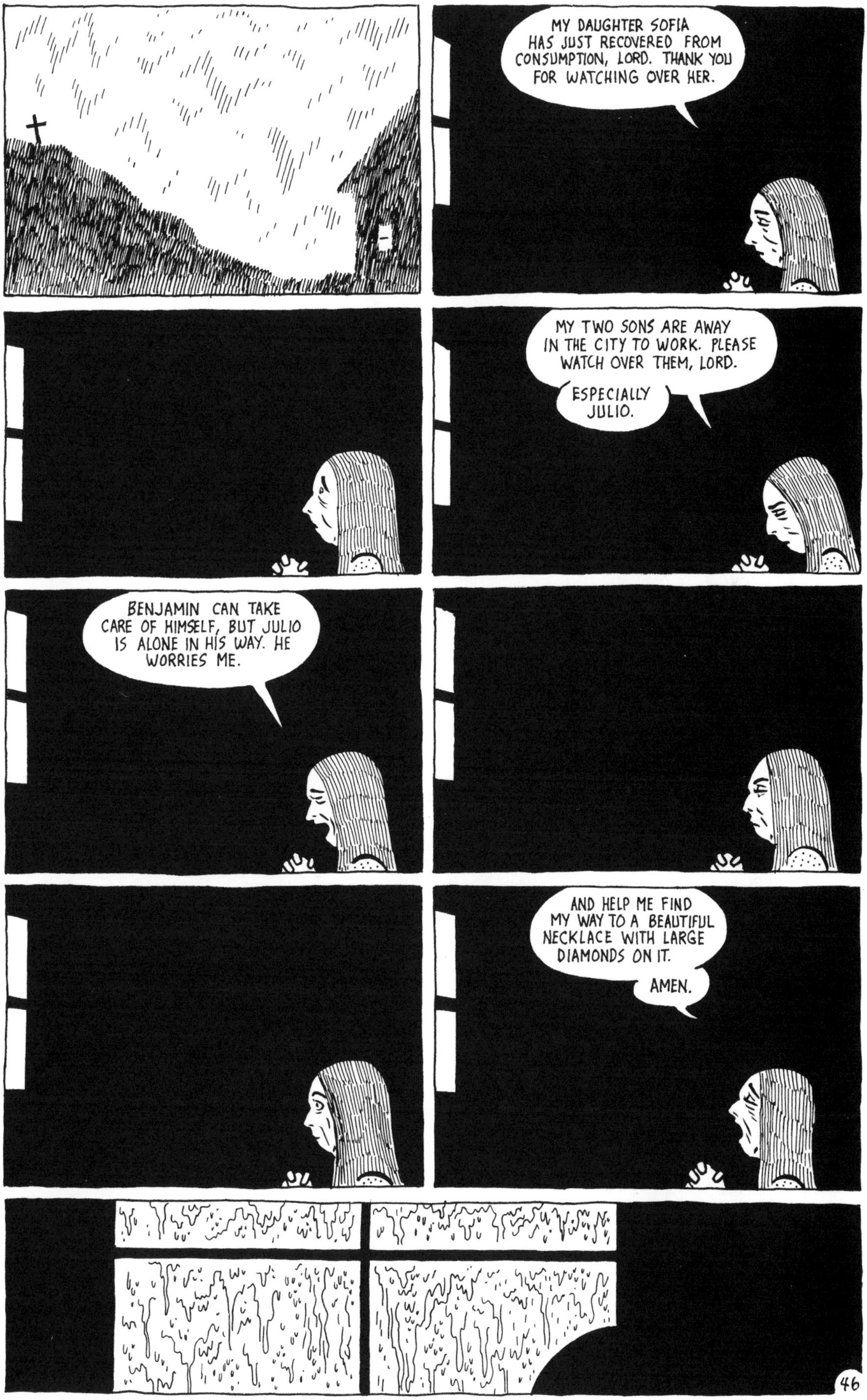
MY DAUGHTER SOFIA HAS JUST RECOVERED FROM CONSUMPTION, LORD. THANK YOU FOR WATCHING OVER HER.
MY TWO SONS ARE AWAY IN THE CITY TO WORK. PLEASE WATCH OVER THEM, LORD.
ESPECIALLY JULIO.
BENJAMIN CAN TAKE CARE OF HIMSELF, BUT JULIO IS ALONE IN HIS WAY. HE WORRIES ME.
AND HELP ME FIND MY WAY TO A BEAUTIFUL NECKLACE WITH LARGE DIAMONDS ON IT.
AMEN.

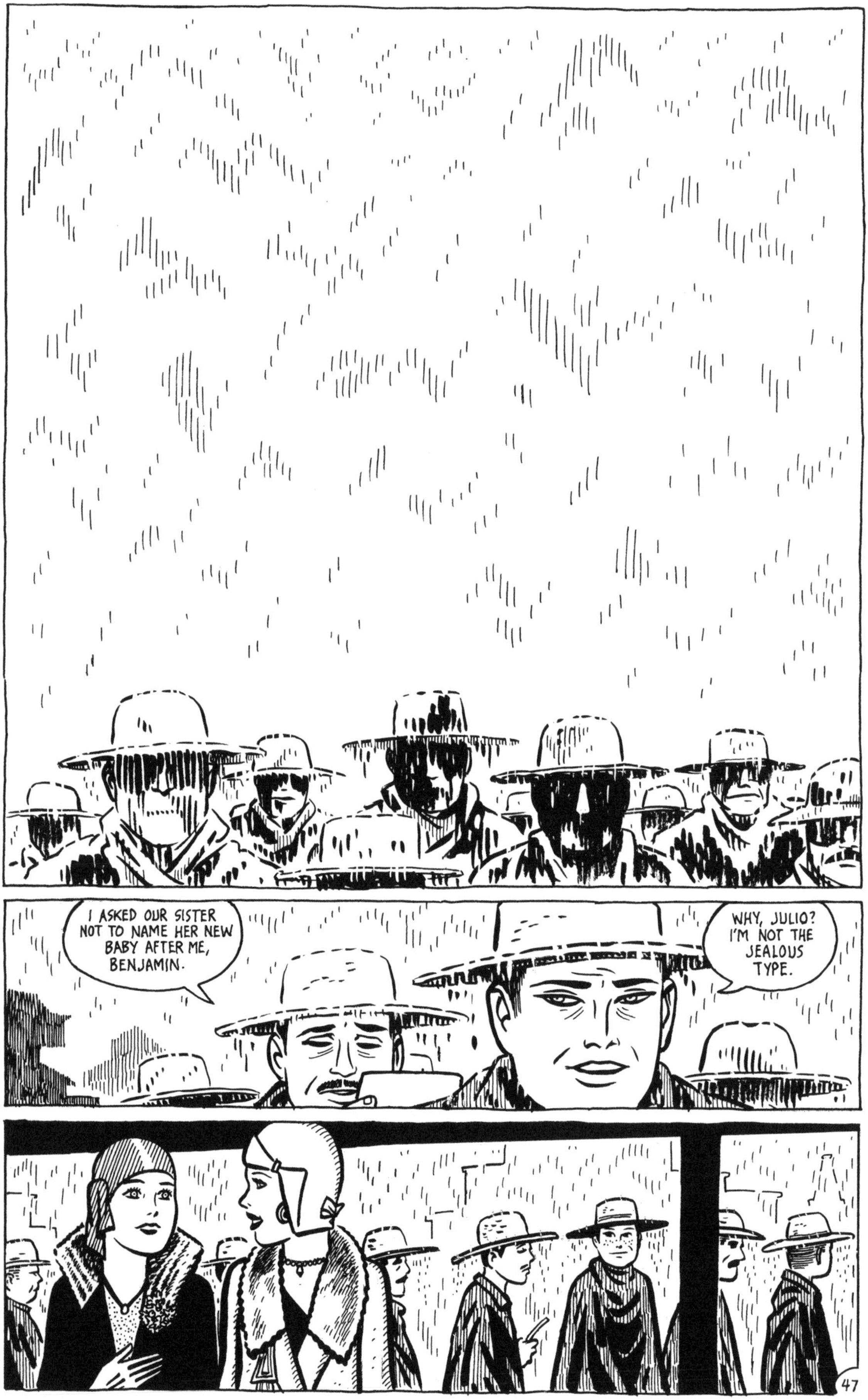
I ASKED OUR SISTER NOT TO NAME HER NEW BABY AFTER ME, BENJAMIN.
WHY, JULIO? I'M NOT THE JEALOUS TYPE.

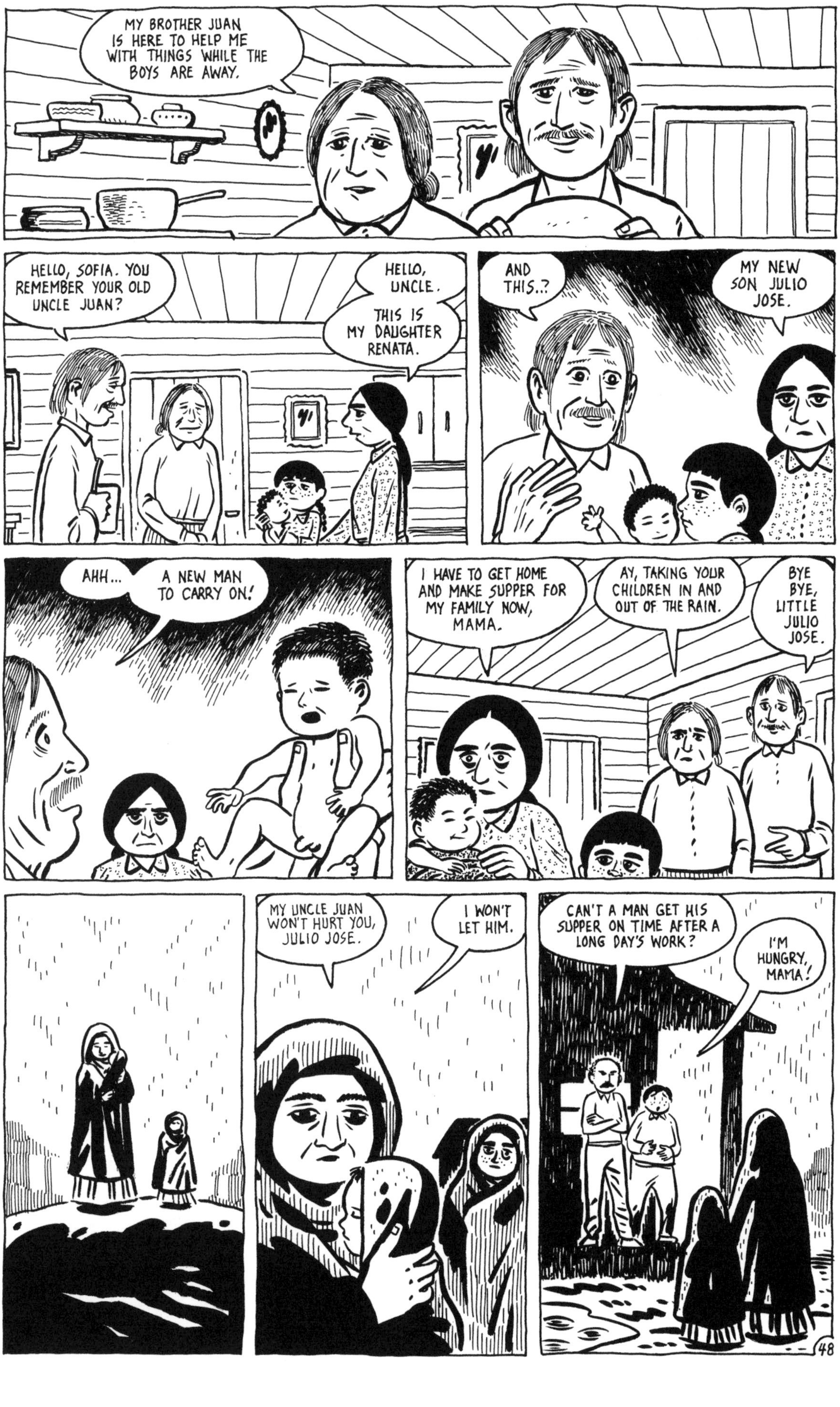

MY BROTHER JUAN IS HERE TO HELP ME WITH THINGS WHILE THE BOYS ARE AWAY.
HELLO, SOFIA. YOU REMEMBER YOUR OLD UNCLE JUAN?
HELLO, UNCLE.
THIS IS MY DAUGHTER RENATA.
AND THIS..?
MY NEW SON JULIO JOSE.
AHH...
A NEW MAN TO CARRY ON!
I HAVE TO GET HOME AND MAKE SUPPER FOR MY FAMILY NOW, MAMA.
AY, TAKING YOUR CHILDREN IN AND OUT OF THE RAIN.
BYE BYE, LITTLE JULIO JOSE.
MY UNCLE JUAN WON'T HURT YOU, JULIO JOSE.
I WON'T LET HIM.
CAN'T A MAN GET HIS SUPPER ON TIME AFTER A LONG DAY'S WORK?
I'M HUNGRY, MAMA!

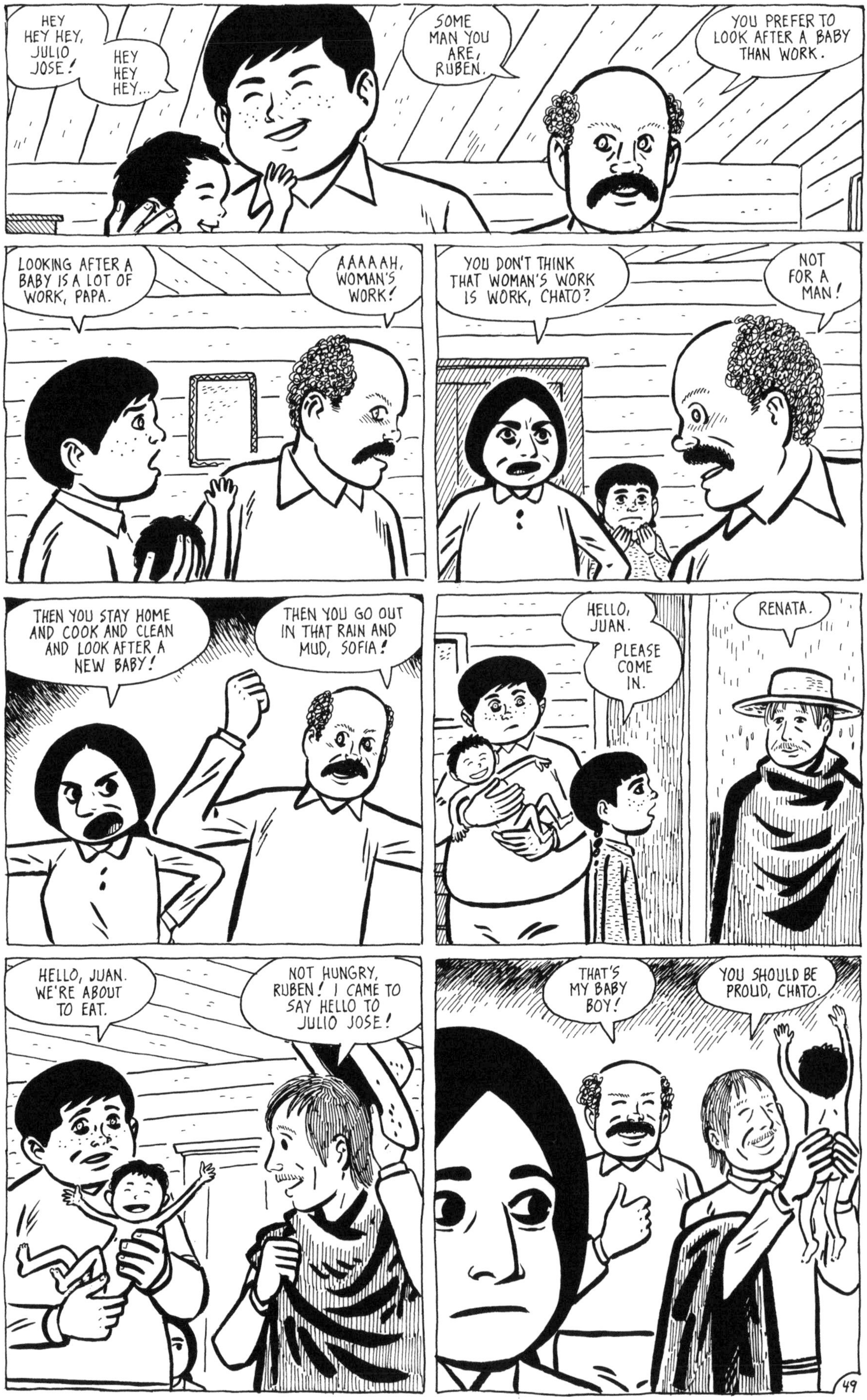
HEY HEY HEY, JULIO JOSE!
HEY HEY HEY...
SOME MAN YOU ARE, RUBEN.
YOU PREFER TO LOOK AFTER A BABY THAN WORK.
LOOKING AFTER A BABY IS A LOT OF WORK, PAPA.
AAAAAH, WOMAN'S WORK!
YOU DON'T THINK THAT WOMAN'S WORK IS WORK, CHATO?
NOT FOR A MAN!
THEN YOU STAY HOME AND COOK AND CLEAN AND LOOK AFTER A NEW BABY!
THEN YOU GO OUT IN THAT RAIN AND MUD, SOFIA!
HELLO, JUAN.
PLEASE COME IN.
RENATA.
HELLO, JUAN. WE'RE ABOUT TO EAT.
NOT HUNGRY, RUBEN! I CAME TO SAY HELLO TO JULIO JOSE!
THAT'S MY BABY BOY!
YOU SHOULD BE PROUD, CHATO.
49

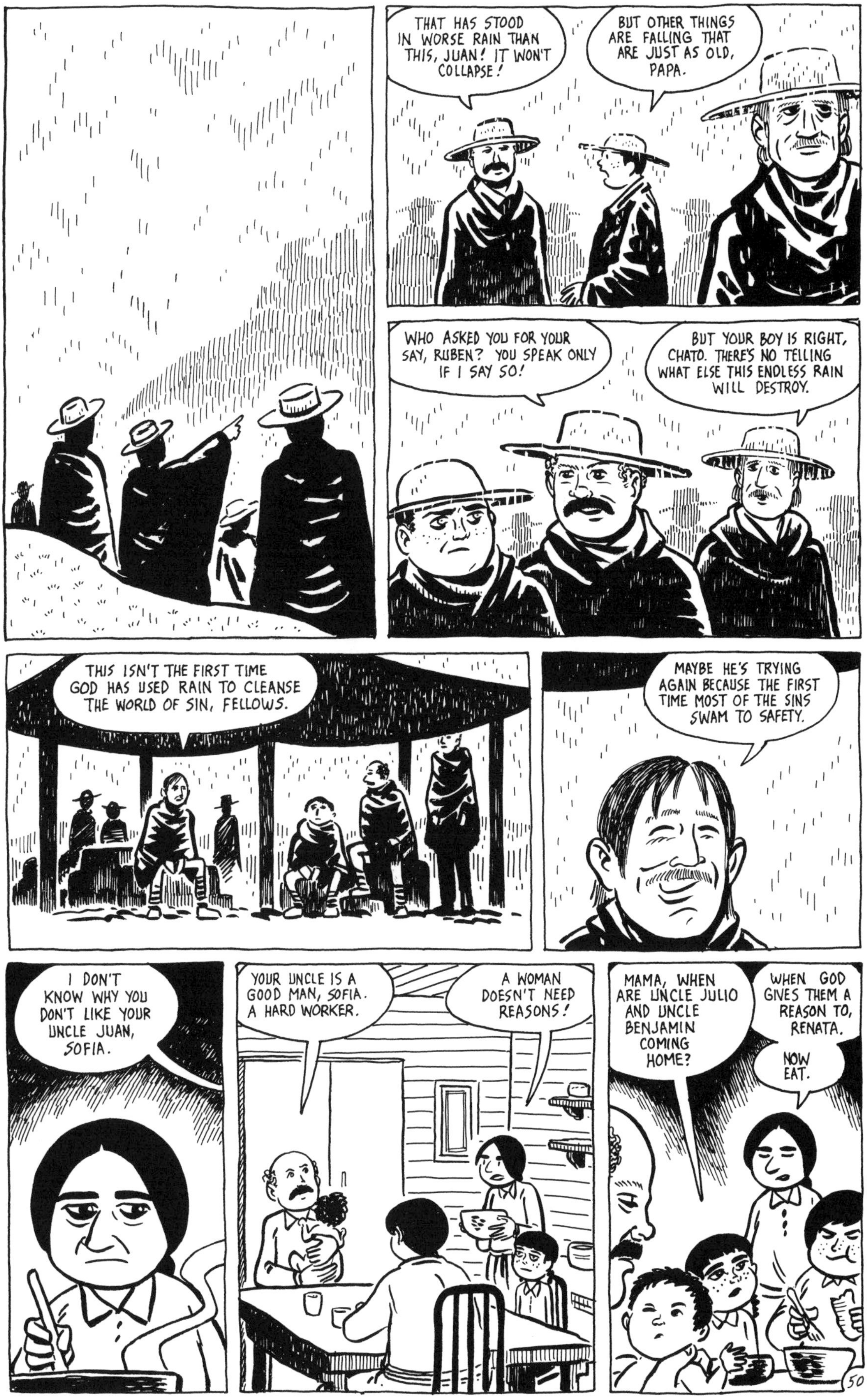
THAT HAS STOOD IN WORSE RAIN THAN THIS, JUAN! IT WON'T COLLAPSE!
BUT OTHER THINGS ARE FALLING THAT ARE JUST AS OLD, PAPA.
WHO ASKED YOU FOR YOUR SAY, RUBEN? YOU SPEAK ONLY IF I SAY SO!
BUT YOUR BOY IS RIGHT, CHATO. THERE'S NO TELLING WHAT ELSE THIS ENDLESS RAIN WILL DESTROY.
THIS ISN'T THE FIRST TIME GOD HAS USED RAIN TO CLEANSE THE WORLD OF SIN, FELLOWS.
MAYBE HE'S TRYING AGAIN BECAUSE THE FIRST TIME MOST OF THE SINS SWAM TO SAFETY.
I DON'T KNOW WHY YOU DON'T LIKE YOUR UNCLE JUAN, SOFIA.
YOUR UNCLE IS A GOOD MAN, SOFIA. A HARD WORKER.
A WOMAN DOESN'T NEED REASONS!
MAMA, WHEN ARE UNCLE JULIO AND UNCLE BENJAMIN COMING HOME?
WHEN GOD GIVES THEM A REASON TO, RENATA.
NOW EAT.

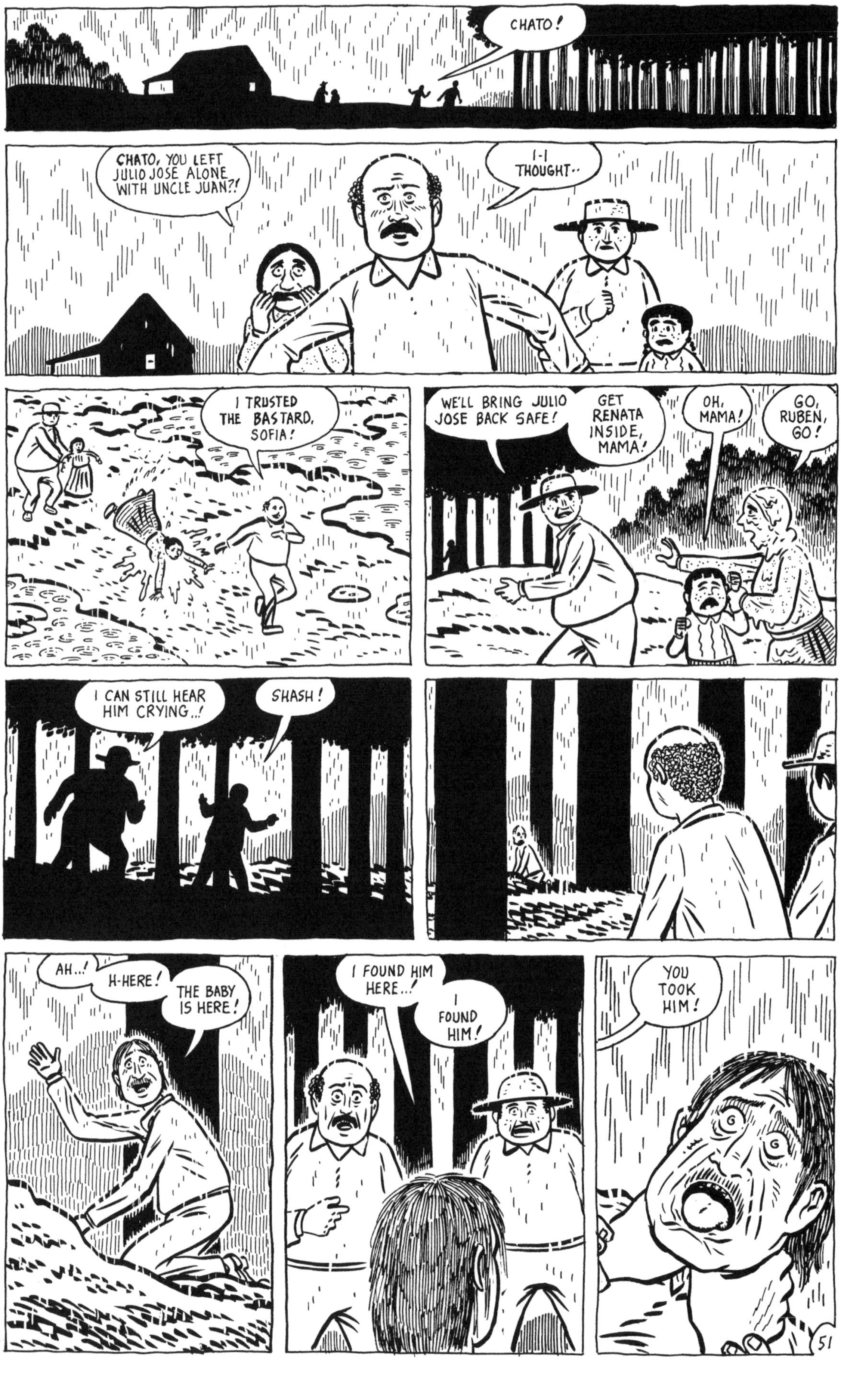
CHATO!
CHATO, YOU LEFT JULIO JOSE ALONE WITH UNCLE JUAN?!
I-I THOUGHT..
I TRUSTED THE BASTARD, SOFIA!
WE'LL BRING JULIO JOSE BACK SAFE!
GET RENATA INSIDE, MAMA!
OH, MAMA!
GO, RUBEN, GO!
I CAN STILL HEAR HIM CRYING..!
SHASH!
AH..!
H-HERE!
THE BABY IS HERE!
I FOUND HIM HERE..!
I FOUND HIM!
YOU TOOK HIM!

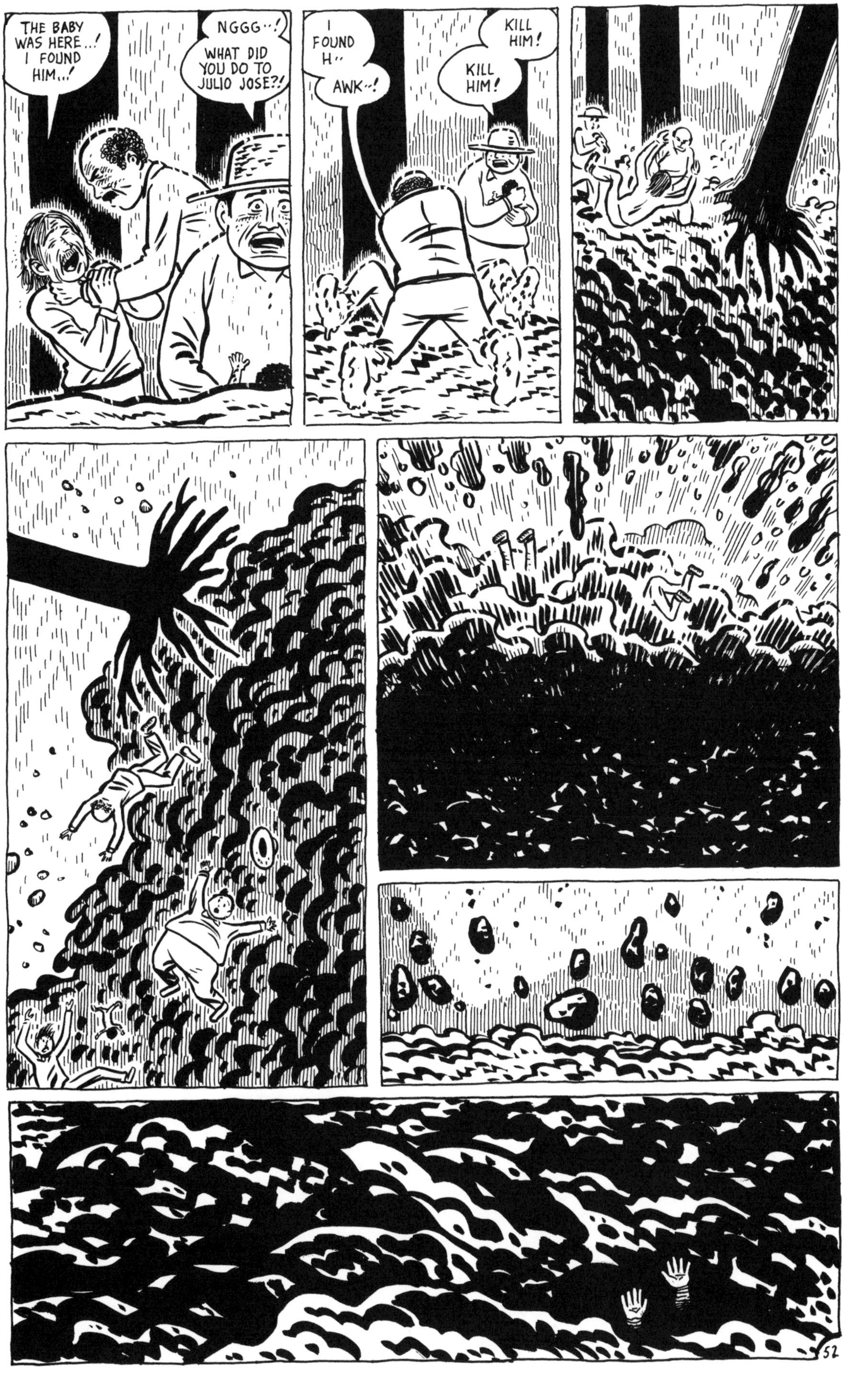
THE BABY WAS HERE...! I FOUND HIM...!
NGGG··!
WHAT DID YOU DO TO JULIO JOSE?!
I FOUND H··
AWK··!
KILL HIM!
KILL HIM!

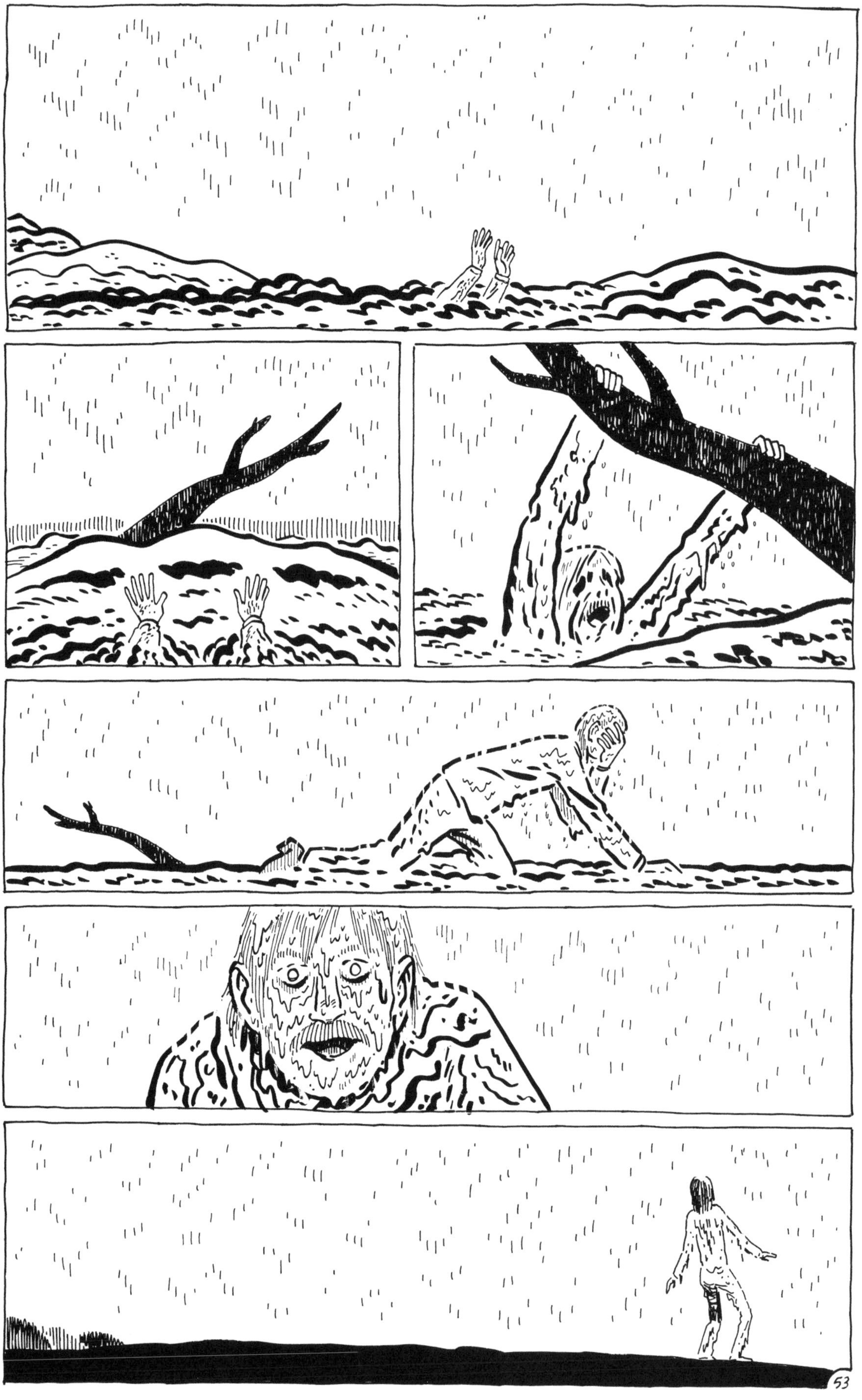

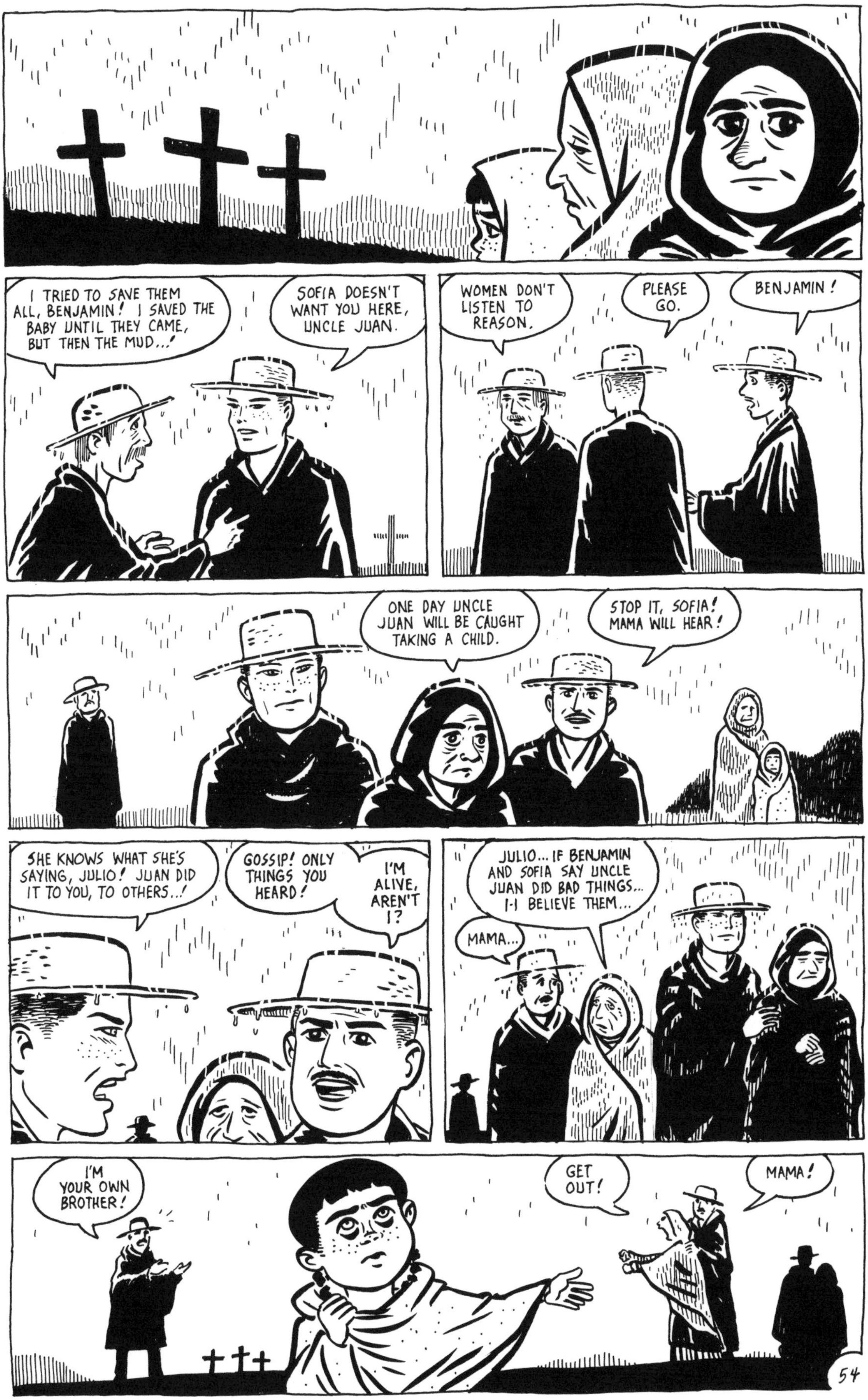

I TRIED TO SAVE THEM ALL, BENJAMIN! I SAVED THE BABY UNTIL THEY CAME, BUT THEN THE MUD...!
SOFIA DOESN'T WANT YOU HERE, UNCLE JUAN.
WOMEN DON'T LISTEN TO REASON.
PLEASE GO.
BENJAMIN!
ONE DAY UNCLE JUAN WILL BE CAUGHT TAKING A CHILD.
STOP IT, SOFIA! MAMA WILL HEAR!
SHE KNOWS WHAT SHE'S SAYING, JULIO! JUAN DID IT TO YOU, TO OTHERS...!
GOSSIP! ONLY THINGS YOU HEARD!
I'M ALIVE, AREN'T I?
JULIO... IF BENJAMIN AND SOFIA SAY UNCLE JUAN DID BAD THINGS... I-I BELIEVE THEM...
MAMA...
I'M YOUR OWN BROTHER!
GET OUT!
MAMA!

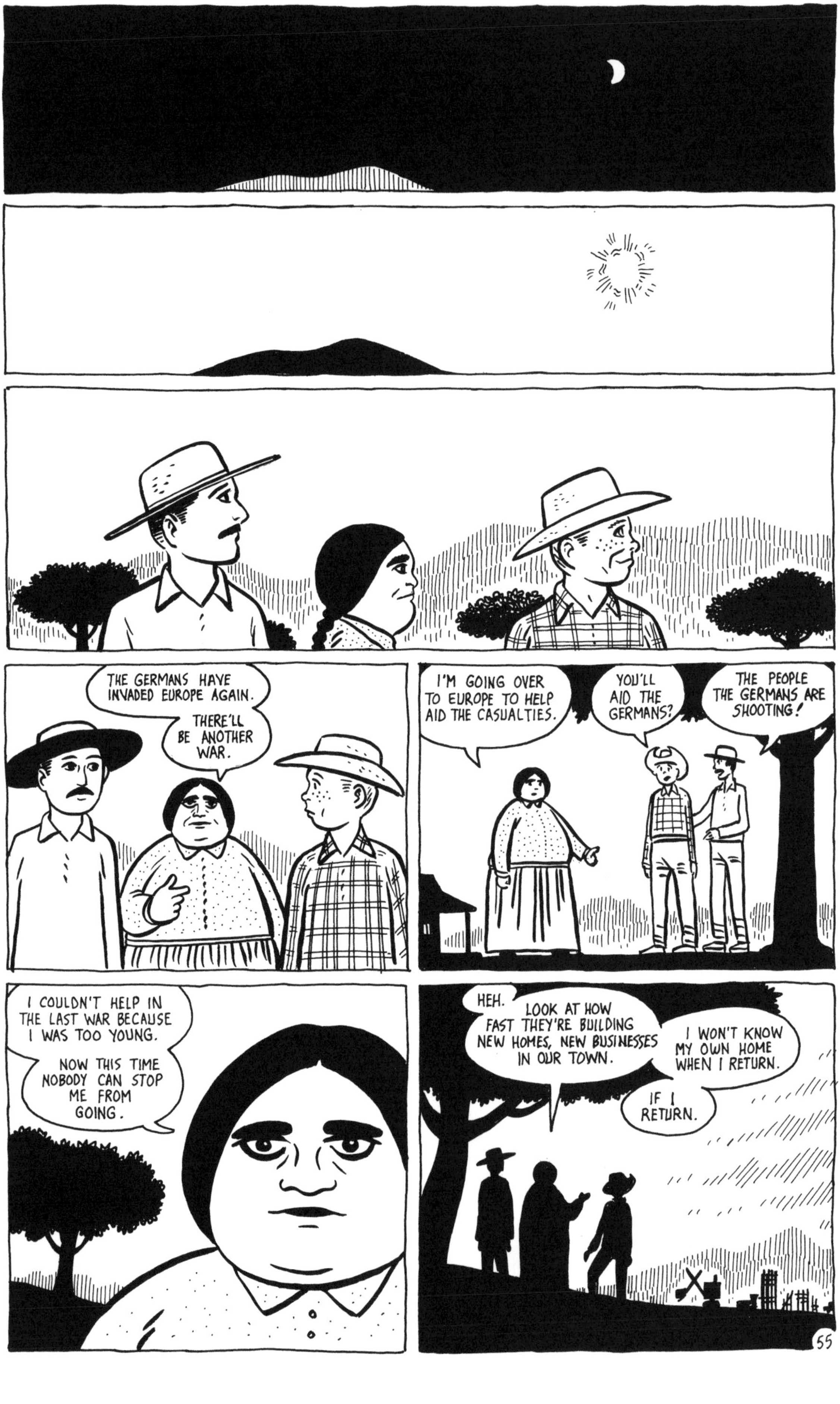
THE GERMANS HAVE INVADED EUROPE AGAIN.
THERE'LL BE ANOTHER WAR.
I'M GOING OVER TO EUROPE TO HELP AID THE CASUALTIES.
YOU'LL AID THE GERMANS?
THE PEOPLE THE GERMANS ARE SHOOTING!
I COULDN'T HELP IN THE LAST WAR BECAUSE I WAS TOO YOUNG.
NOW THIS TIME NOBODY CAN STOP ME FROM GOING.
HEH.
LOOK AT HOW FAST THEY'RE BUILDING NEW HOMES, NEW BUSINESSES IN OUR TOWN.
I WON'T KNOW MY OWN HOME WHEN I RETURN.
IF I RETURN.

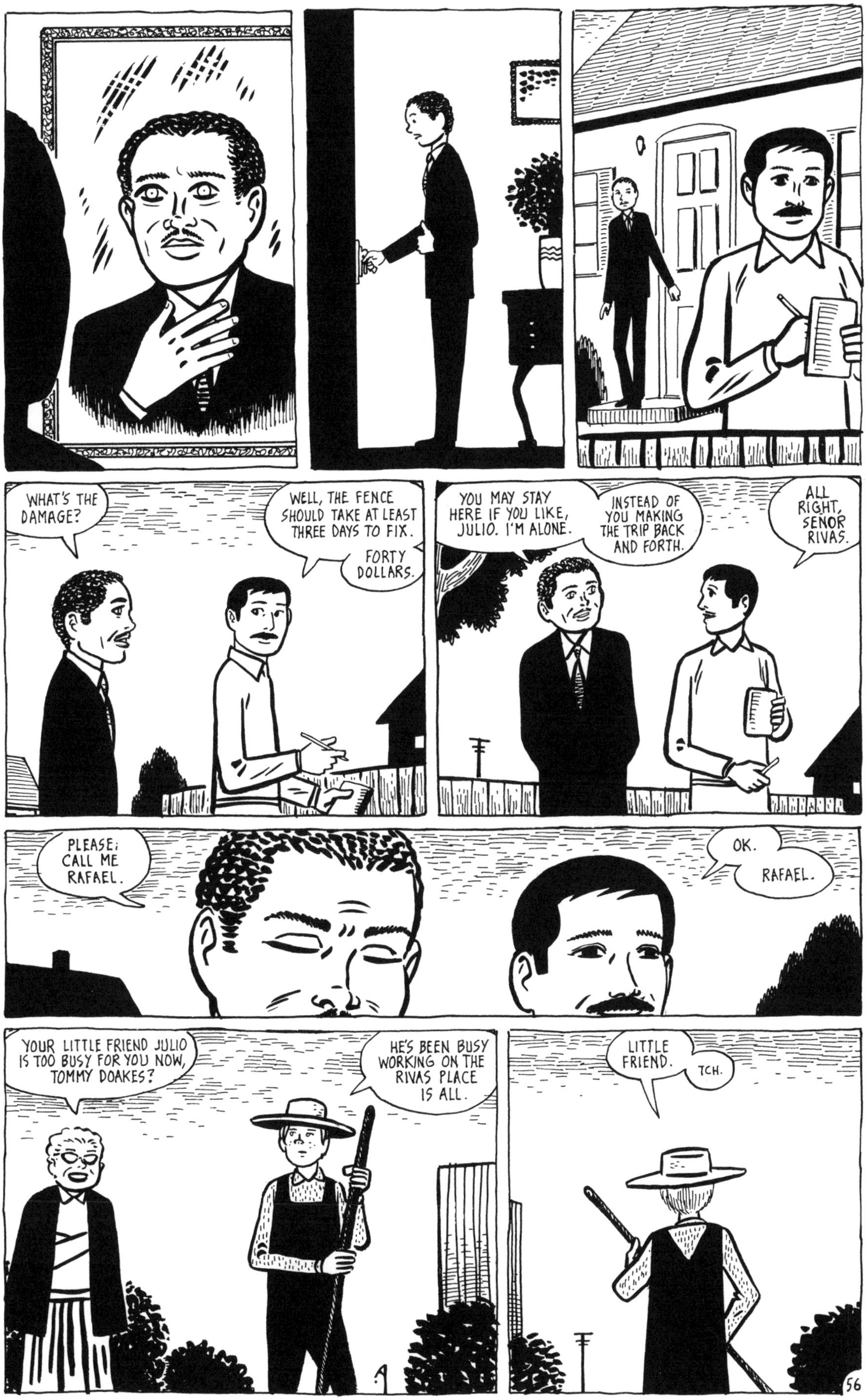
WHAT'S THE DAMAGE?
WELL, THE FENCE SHOULD TAKE AT LEAST THREE DAYS TO FIX.
FORTY DOLLARS.
YOU MAY STAY HERE IF YOU LIKE, JULIO. I'M ALONE.
INSTEAD OF YOU MAKING THE TRIP BACK AND FORTH.
ALL RIGHT, SENOR RIVAS.
PLEASE; CALL ME RAFAEL.
OK.
RAFAEL.
YOUR LITTLE FRIEND JULIO IS TOO BUSY FOR YOU NOW, TOMMY DOAKES?
HE'S BEEN BUSY WORKING ON THE RIVAS PLACE IS ALL.
LITTLE FRIEND.
TCH.

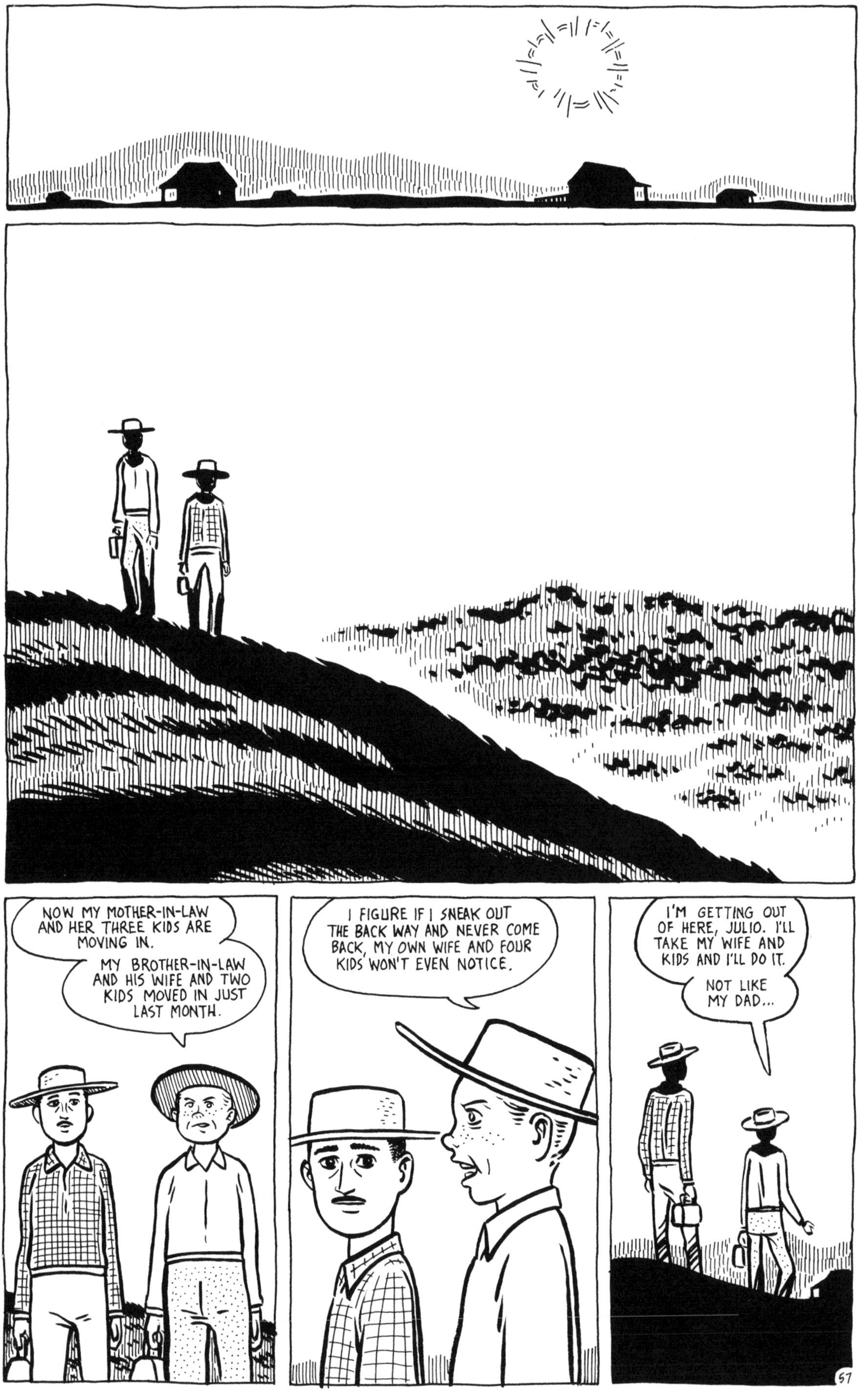
NOW MY MOTHER-IN-LAW AND HER THREE KIDS ARE MOVING IN.
MY BROTHER-IN-LAW AND HIS WIFE AND TWO KIDS MOVED IN JUST LAST MONTH.
I FIGURE IF I SNEAK OUT THE BACK WAY AND NEVER COME BACK, MY OWN WIFE AND FOUR KIDS WON'T EVEN NOTICE.
I'M GETTING OUT OF HERE, JULIO. I'LL TAKE MY WIFE AND KIDS AND I'LL DO IT.
NOT LIKE MY DAD...

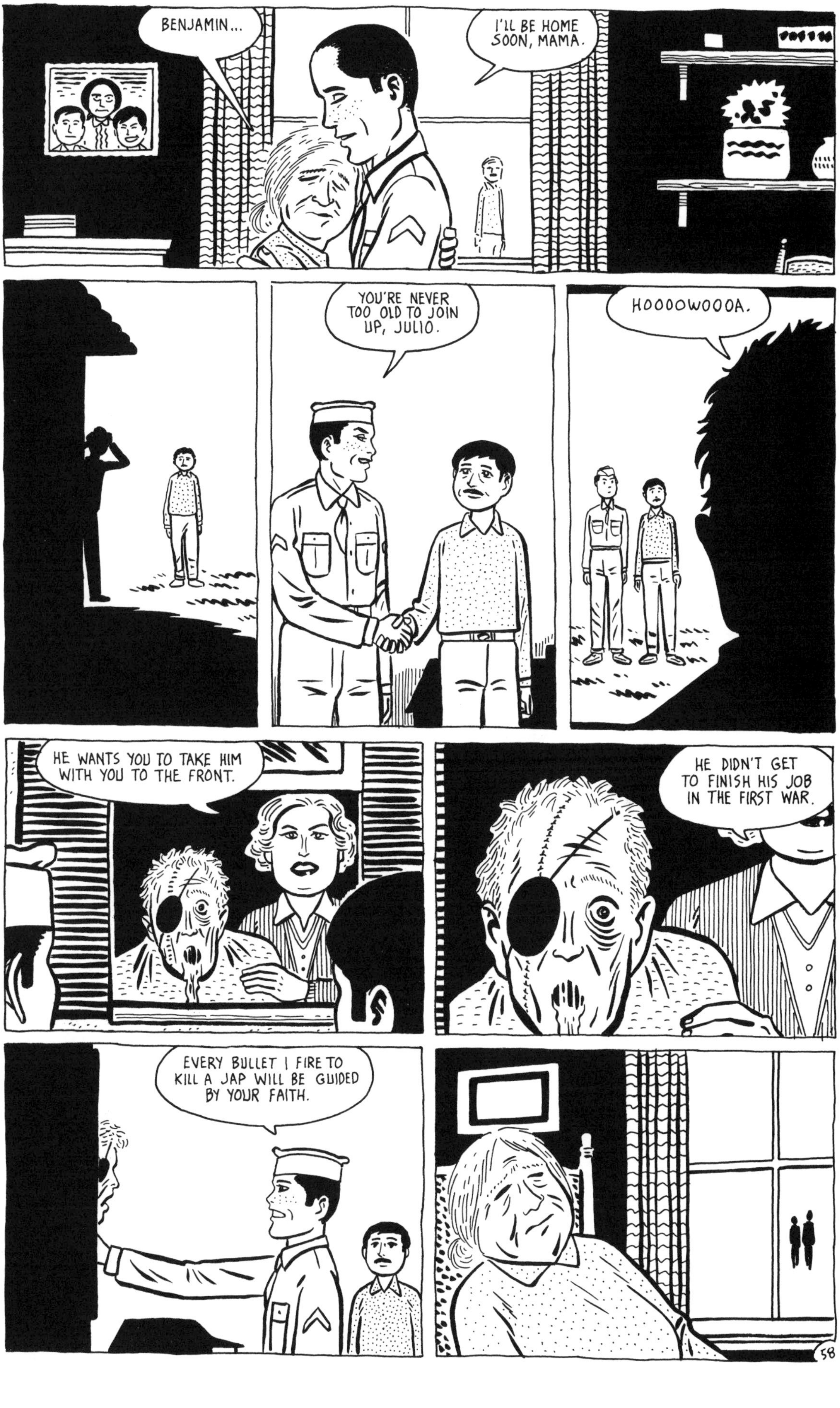
BENJAMIN...
I'LL BE HOME SOON, MAMA.
YOU'RE NEVER TOO OLD TO JOIN UP, JULIO.
HOOOOWOOOA.
HE WANTS YOU TO TAKE HIM WITH YOU TO THE FRONT.
HE DIDN'T GET TO FINISH HIS JOB IN THE FIRST WAR.
EVERY BULLET I FIRE TO KILL A JAP WILL BE GUIDED BY YOUR FAITH.

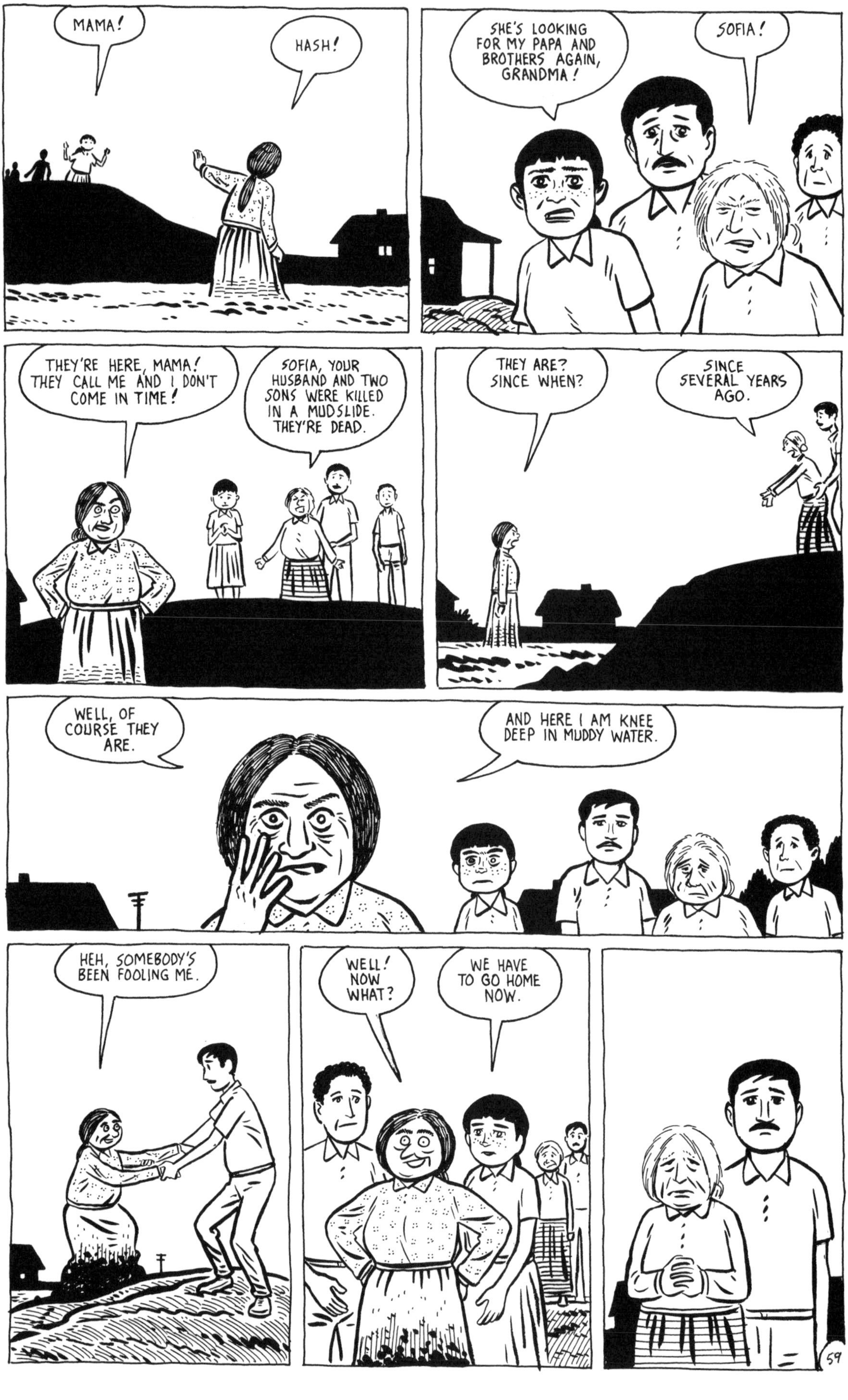
MAMA!
HASH!
SHE'S LOOKING FOR MY PAPA AND BROTHERS AGAIN, GRANDMA!
SOFIA!
THEY'RE HERE, MAMA! THEY CALL ME AND I DON'T COME IN TIME!
SOFIA, YOUR HUSBAND AND TWO SONS WERE KILLED IN A MUDSLIDE. THEY'RE DEAD.
THEY ARE? SINCE WHEN?
SINCE SEVERAL YEARS AGO.
WELL, OF COURSE THEY ARE.
AND HERE I AM KNEE DEEP IN MUDDY WATER.
HEH, SOMEBODY'S BEEN FOOLING ME.
WELL! NOW WHAT?
WE HAVE TO GO HOME NOW.

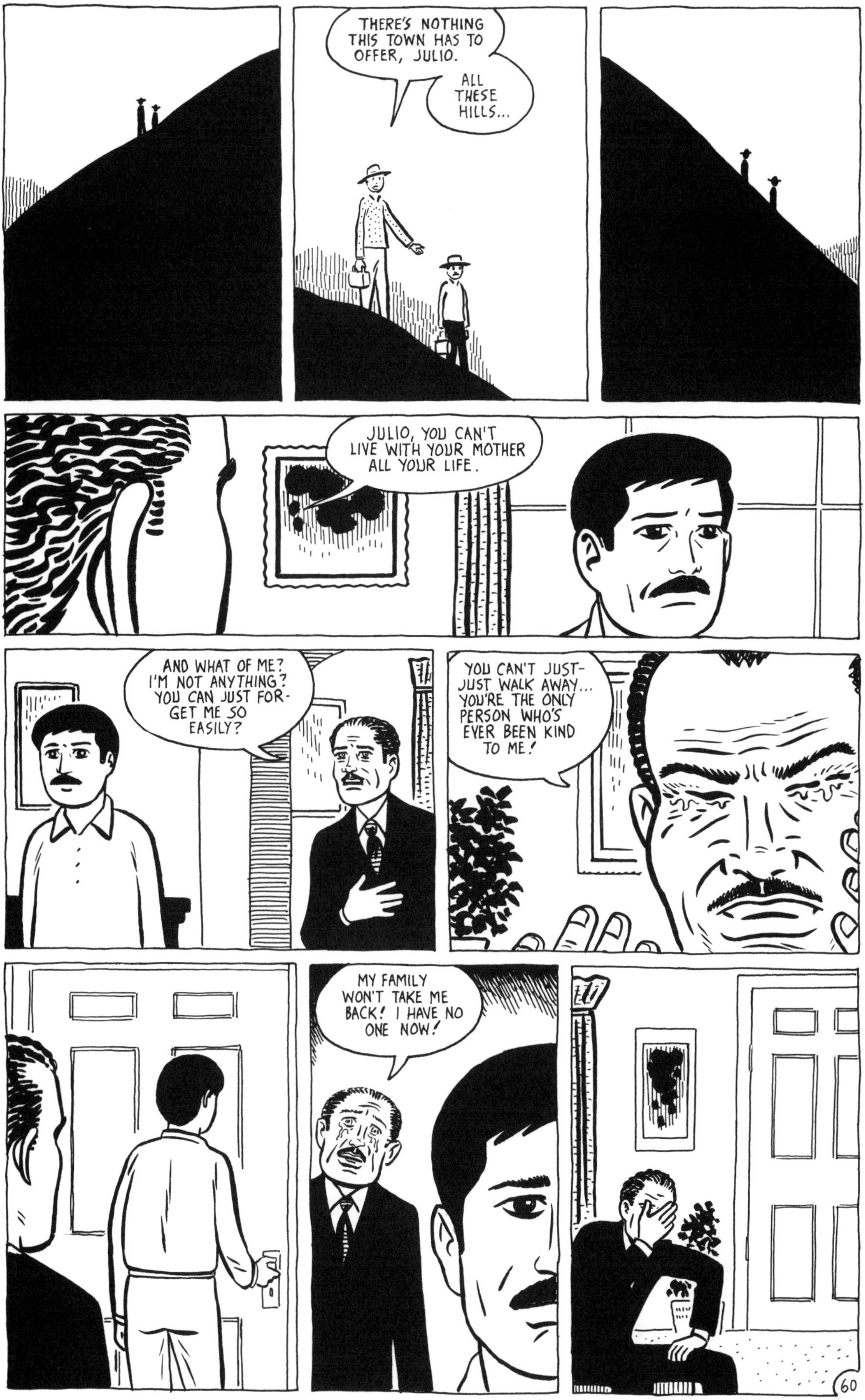
THERE'S NOTHING THIS TOWN HAS TO OFFER, JULIO.
ALL THESE HILLS...
JULIO, YOU CAN'T LIVE WITH YOUR MOTHER ALL YOUR LIFE.
AND WHAT OF ME? I'M NOT ANYTHING? YOU CAN JUST FORGET ME SO EASILY?
YOU CAN'T JUST-JUST WALK AWAY... YOU'RE THE ONLY PERSON WHO'S EVER BEEN KIND TO ME!
MY FAMILY WON'T TAKE ME BACK! I HAVE NO ONE NOW!

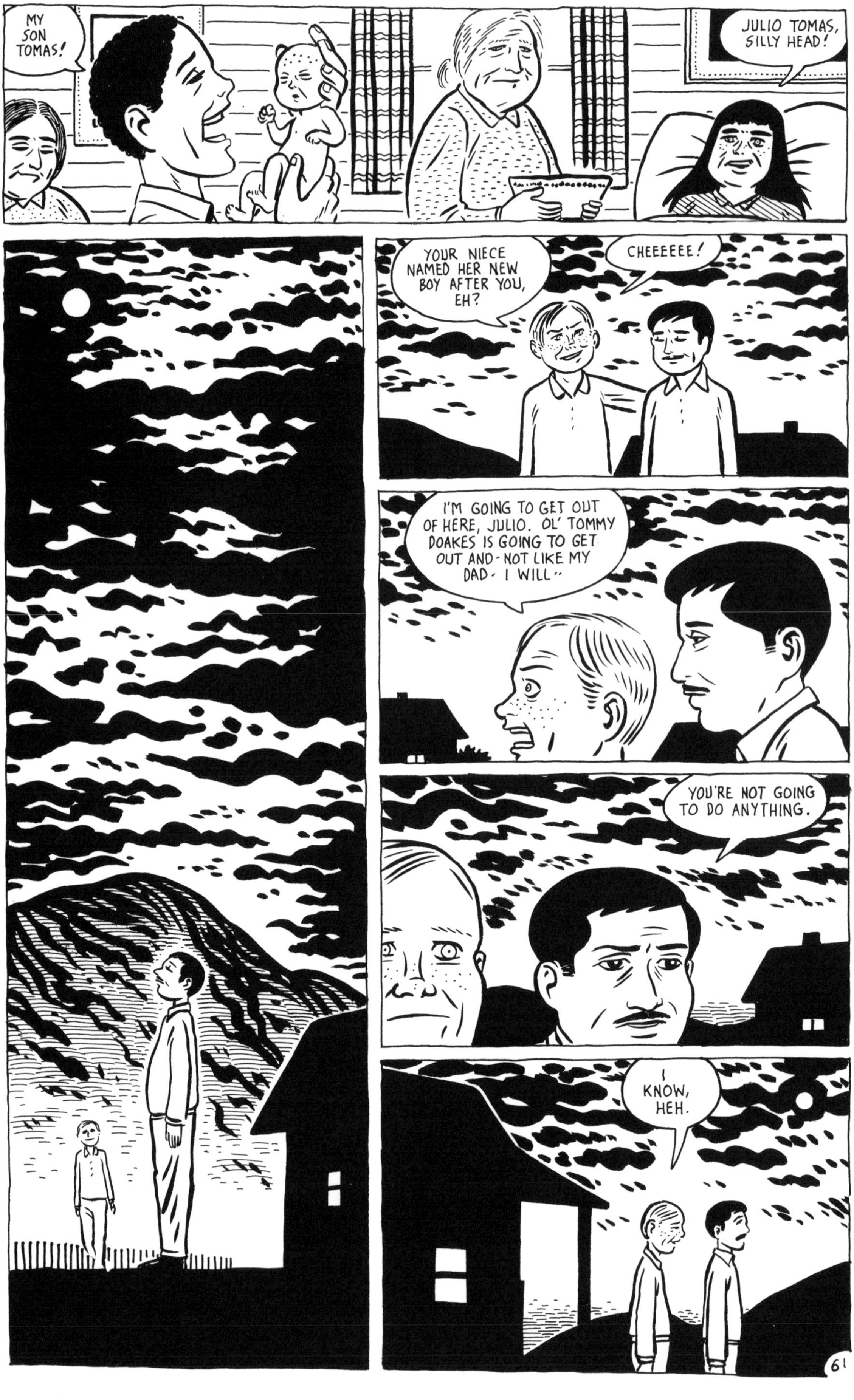
MY SON TOMAS!
JULIO TOMAS, SILLY HEAD!
YOUR NIECE NAMED HER NEW BOY AFTER YOU, EH?
CHEEEEEE!
I'M GOING TO GET OUT OF HERE, JULIO. OL' TOMMY DOAKES IS GOING TO GET OUT AND- NOT LIKE MY DAD- I WILL--
YOU'RE NOT GOING TO DO ANYTHING.
I KNOW, HEH.

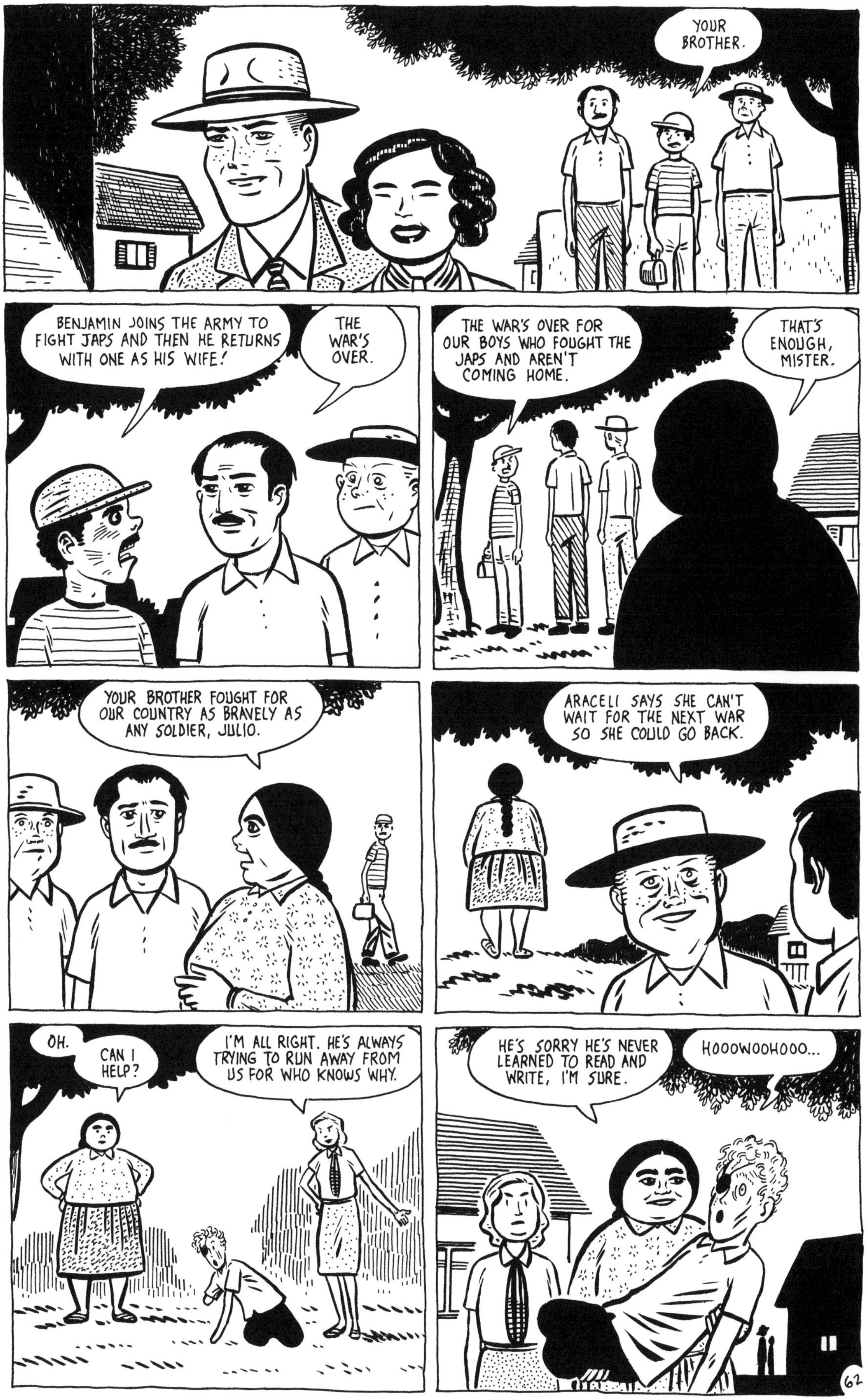
YOUR BROTHER.
BENJAMIN JOINS THE ARMY TO FIGHT JAPS AND THEN HE RETURNS WITH ONE AS HIS WIFE!
THE WAR'S OVER.
THE WAR'S OVER FOR OUR BOYS WHO FOUGHT THE JAPS AND AREN'T COMING HOME.
THAT'S ENOUGH, MISTER.
YOUR BROTHER FOUGHT FOR OUR COUNTRY AS BRAVELY AS ANY SOLDIER, JULIO.
ARACELI SAYS SHE CAN'T WAIT FOR THE NEXT WAR SO SHE COULD GO BACK.
OH.
CAN I HELP?
I'M ALL RIGHT. HE'S ALWAYS TRYING TO RUN AWAY FROM US FOR WHO KNOWS WHY.
HE'S SORRY HE'S NEVER LEARNED TO READ AND WRITE, I'M SURE.
HOOOWOOHOOO...

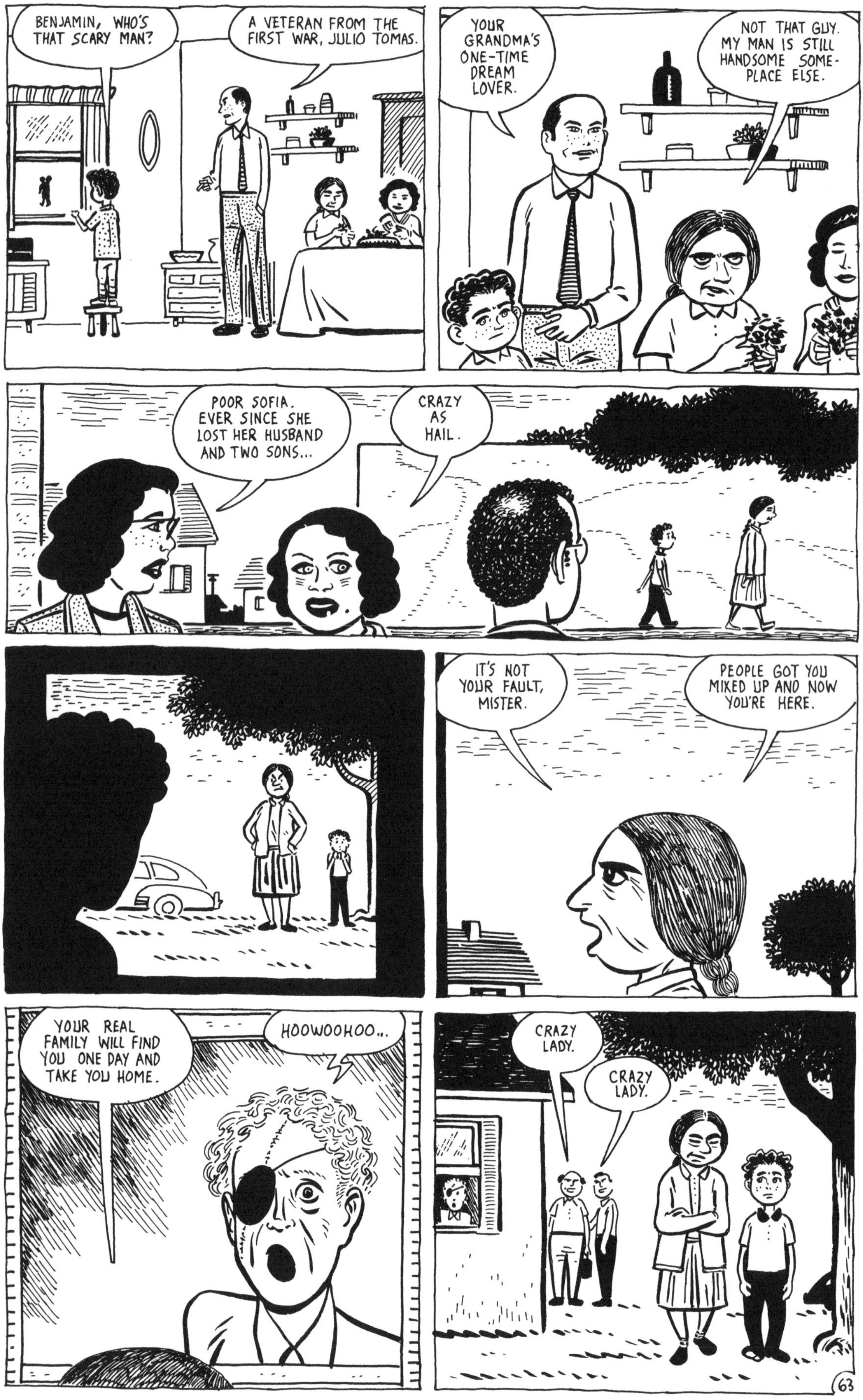
BENJAMIN, WHO'S THAT SCARY MAN?
A VETERAN FROM THE FIRST WAR, JULIO TOMAS.
YOUR GRANDMA'S ONE-TIME DREAM LOVER.
NOT THAT GUY. MY MAN IS STILL HANDSOME SOME-PLACE ELSE.
POOR SOFIA. EVER SINCE SHE LOST HER HUSBAND AND TWO SONS...
CRAZY AS HAIL.
IT'S NOT YOUR FAULT, MISTER.
PEOPLE GOT YOU MIXED UP AND NOW YOU'RE HERE.
YOUR REAL FAMILY WILL FIND YOU ONE DAY AND TAKE YOU HOME.
HOOWOOHOO...
CRAZY LADY.
CRAZY LADY.

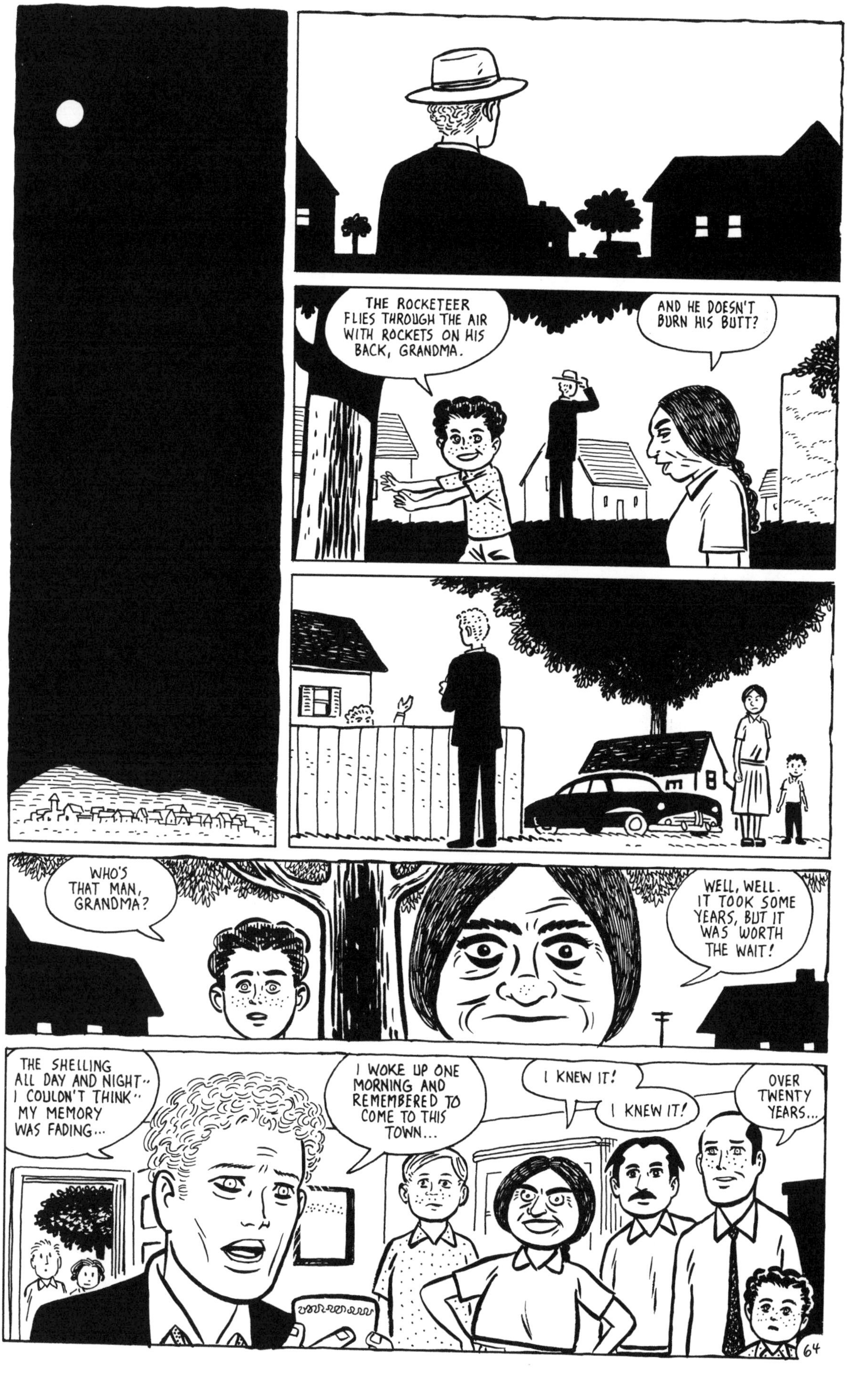

THE ROCKETEER FLIES THROUGH THE AIR WITH ROCKETS ON HIS BACK, GRANDMA.
AND HE DOESN'T BURN HIS BUTT?
WHO'S THAT MAN, GRANDMA?
WELL, WELL. IT TOOK SOME YEARS, BUT IT WAS WORTH THE WAIT!
THE SHELLING ALL DAY AND NIGHT.. I COULDN'T THINK.. MY MEMORY WAS FADING...
I WOKE UP ONE MORNING AND REMEMBERED TO COME TO THIS TOWN...
I KNEW IT!
I KNEW IT!
OVER TWENTY YEARS...

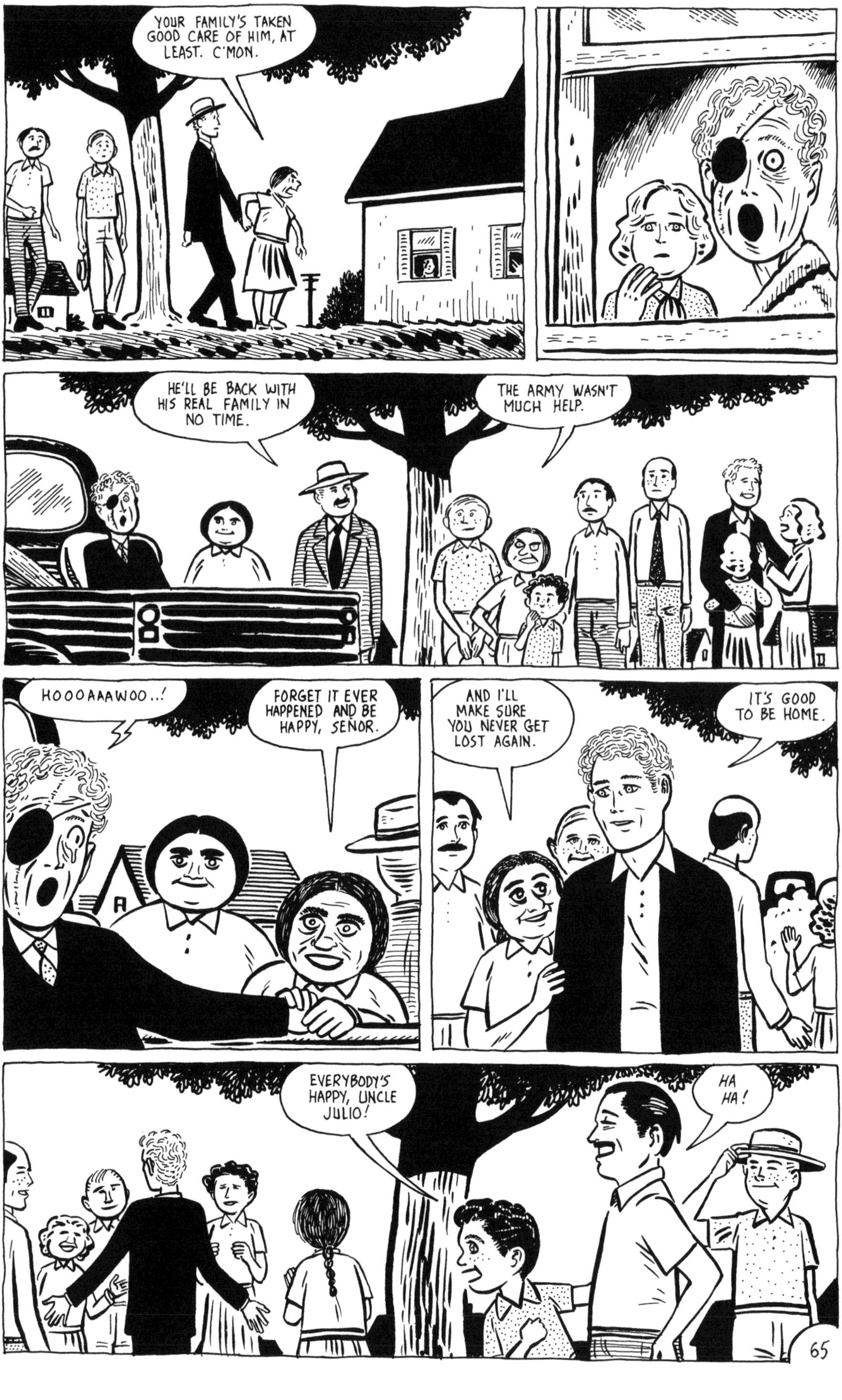
YOUR FAMILY'S TAKEN GOOD CARE OF HIM, AT LEAST. C'MON.
HE'LL BE BACK WITH HIS REAL FAMILY IN NO TIME.
THE ARMY WASN'T MUCH HELP.
HOOOAAAWOO..!
FORGET IT EVER HAPPENED AND BE HAPPY, SEÑOR.
AND I'LL MAKE SURE YOU NEVER GET LOST AGAIN.
IT'S GOOD TO BE HOME.
EVERYBODY'S HAPPY, UNCLE JULIO!
HA HA!

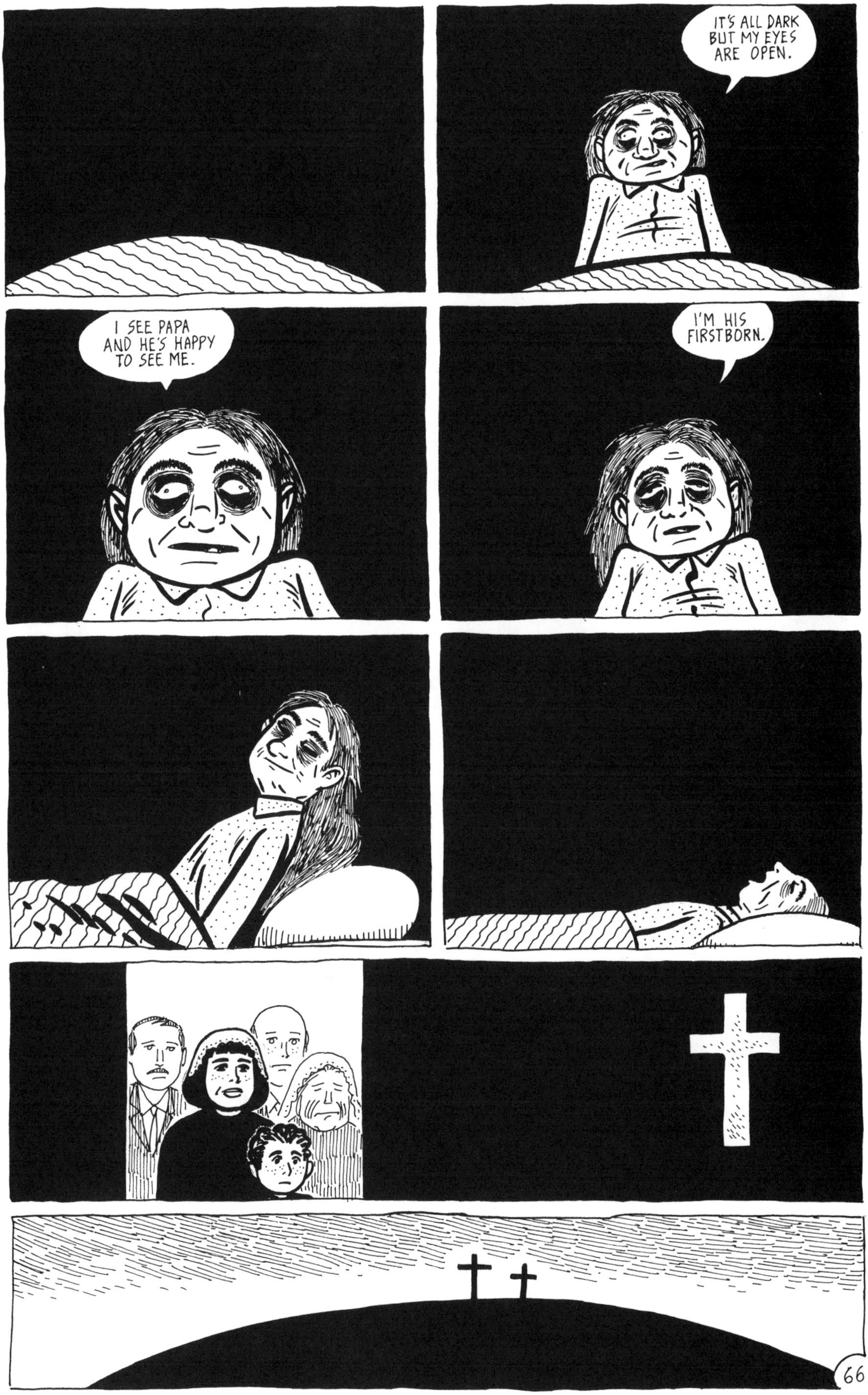
IT'S ALL DARK BUT MY EYES ARE OPEN.
I SEE PAPA AND HE'S HAPPY TO SEE ME.
I'M HIS FIRSTBORN.

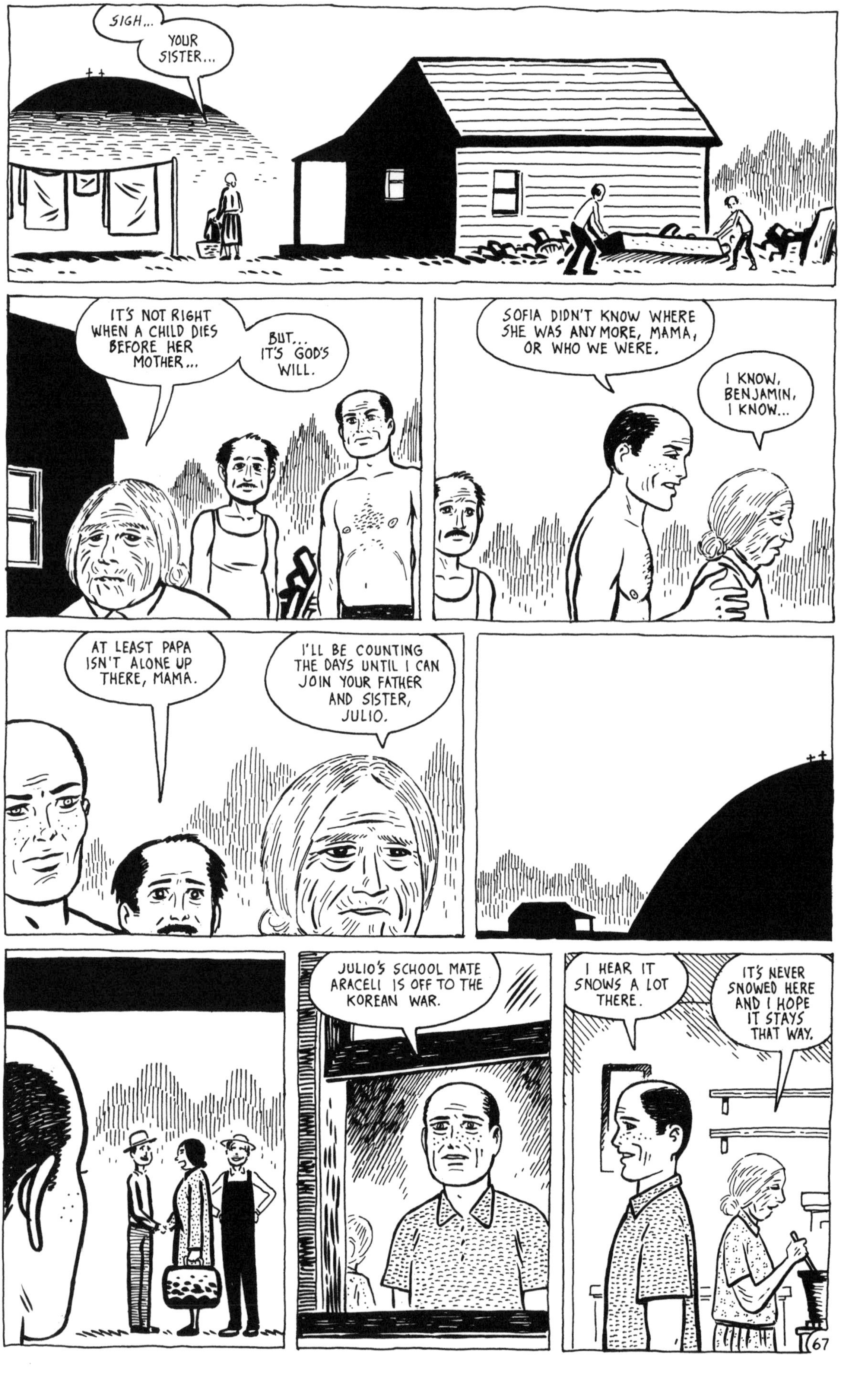
SIGH...
YOUR SISTER...
IT'S NOT RIGHT WHEN A CHILD DIES BEFORE HER MOTHER...
BUT... IT'S GOD'S WILL.
SOFIA DIDN'T KNOW WHERE SHE WAS ANYMORE, MAMA, OR WHO WE WERE.
I KNOW, BENJAMIN, I KNOW...
AT LEAST PAPA ISN'T ALONE UP THERE, MAMA.
I'LL BE COUNTING THE DAYS UNTIL I CAN JOIN YOUR FATHER AND SISTER, JULIO.
JULIO'S SCHOOL MATE ARACELI IS OFF TO THE KOREAN WAR.
I HEAR IT SNOWS A LOT THERE.
IT'S NEVER SNOWED HERE AND I HOPE IT STAYS THAT WAY.

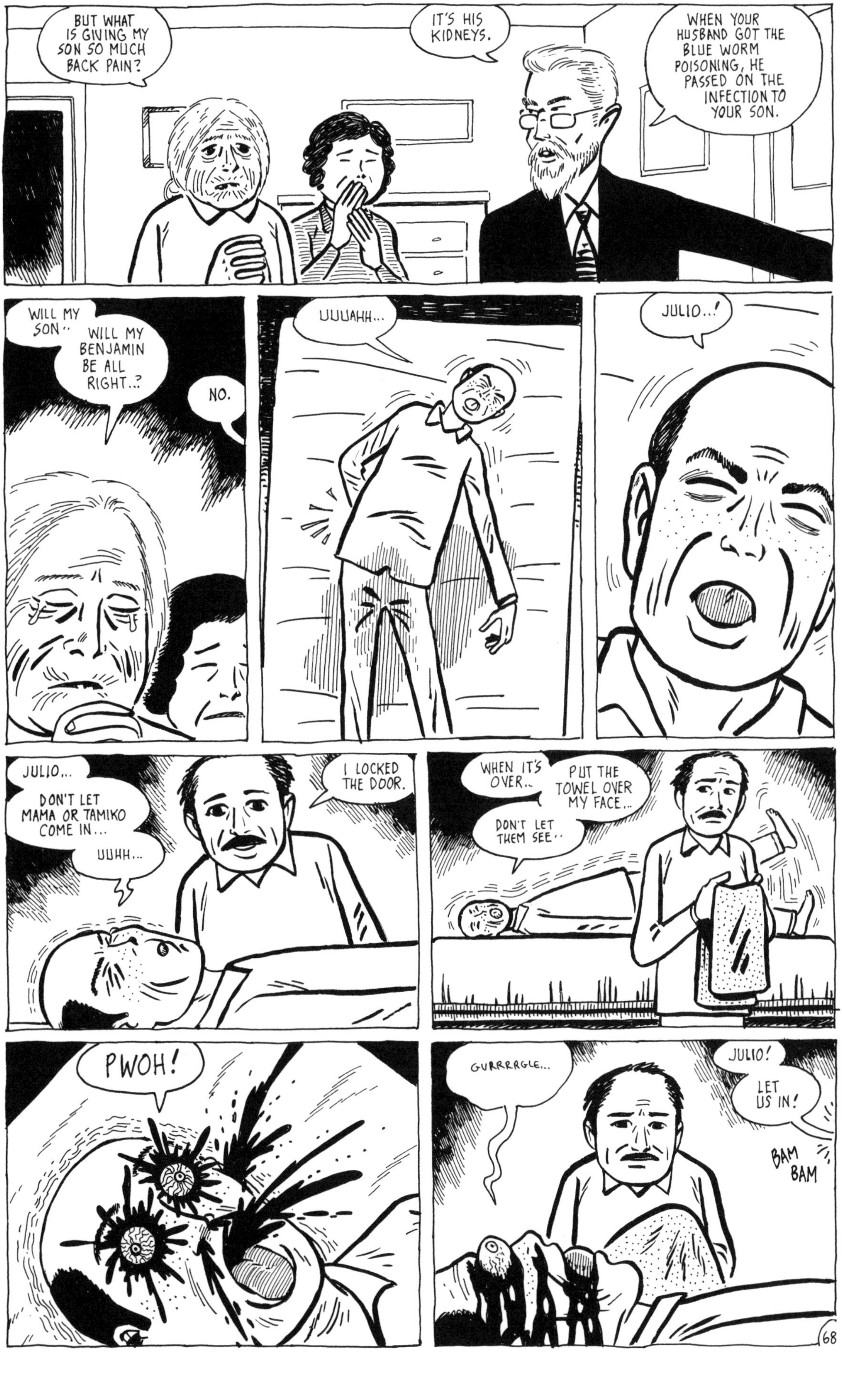
BUT WHAT IS GIVING MY SON SO MUCH BACK PAIN?
IT'S HIS KIDNEYS.
WHEN YOUR HUSBAND GOT THE BLUE WORM POISONING, HE PASSED ON THE INFECTION TO YOUR SON.
WILL MY SON.. WILL MY BENJAMIN BE ALL RIGHT..?
NO.
UUUAHH...
JULIO...!
JULIO...
DON'T LET MAMA OR TAMIKO COME IN...
UUHH...
I LOCKED THE DOOR.
WHEN IT'S OVER..
PUT THE TOWEL OVER MY FACE...
DON'T LET THEM SEE..
PWOH!
GURRRRGLE...
JULIO!
LET US IN!
BAM BAM

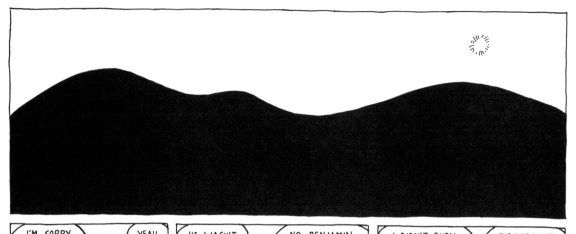

I'M SORRY ABOUT YOUR BROTHER, JULIO.

YEAH.

HE WASN'T SO OLD.

NO, BENJAMIN WAS BORN WITH BAD KIDNEYS.

I DIDN'T EVEN KNOW ABOUT YOUR SISTER.

SHE DIED THREE YEARS AGO. YOU WERE IN KOREA.

IT'S JUST YOU AND YOUR MAMA NOW.

YEAH.

DID IT SNOW IN KOREA?

MOST OF THE TIME.

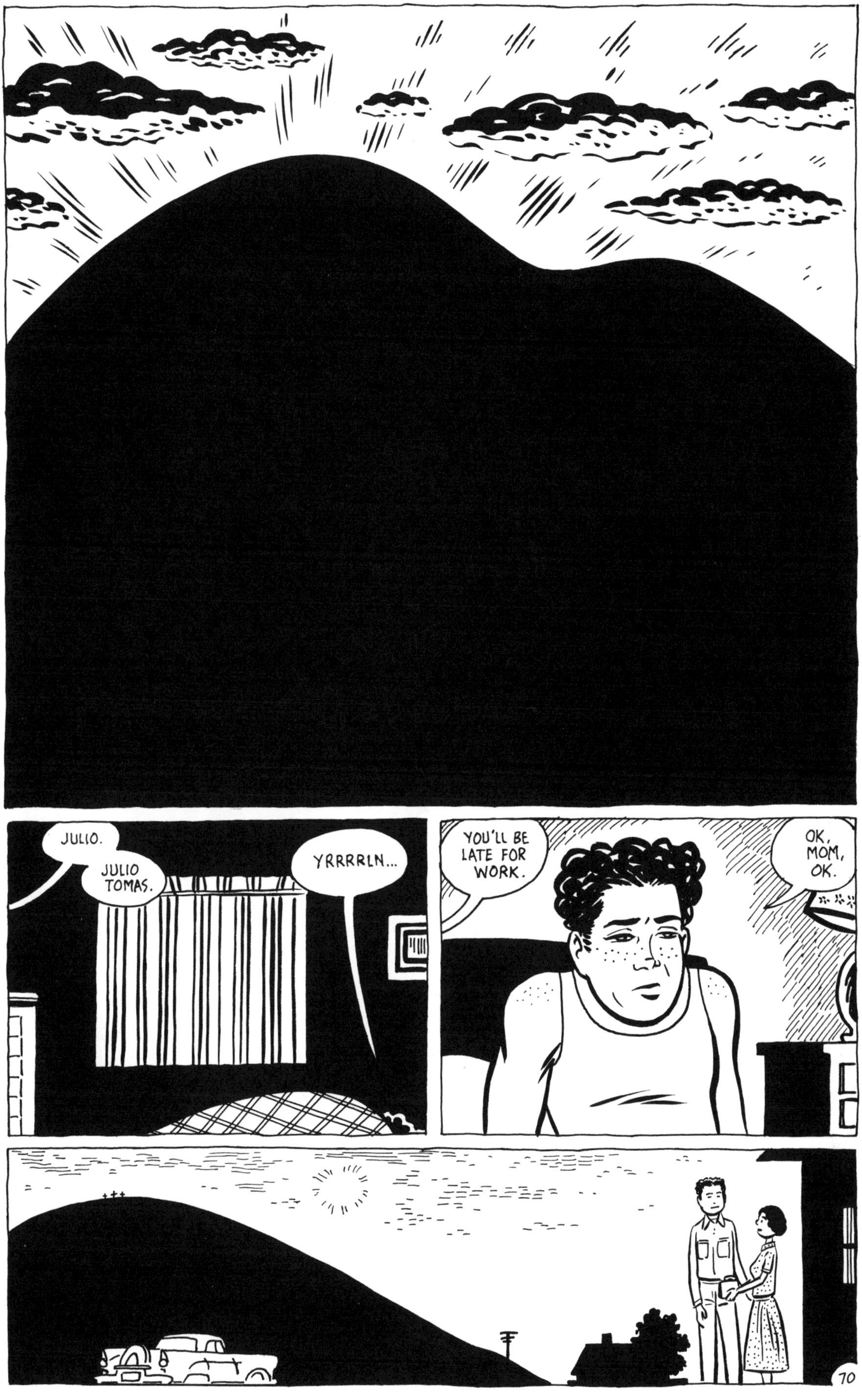
JULIO.
JULIO TOMAS.
YRRRRLN...
YOU'LL BE LATE FOR WORK.
OK, MOM, OK.

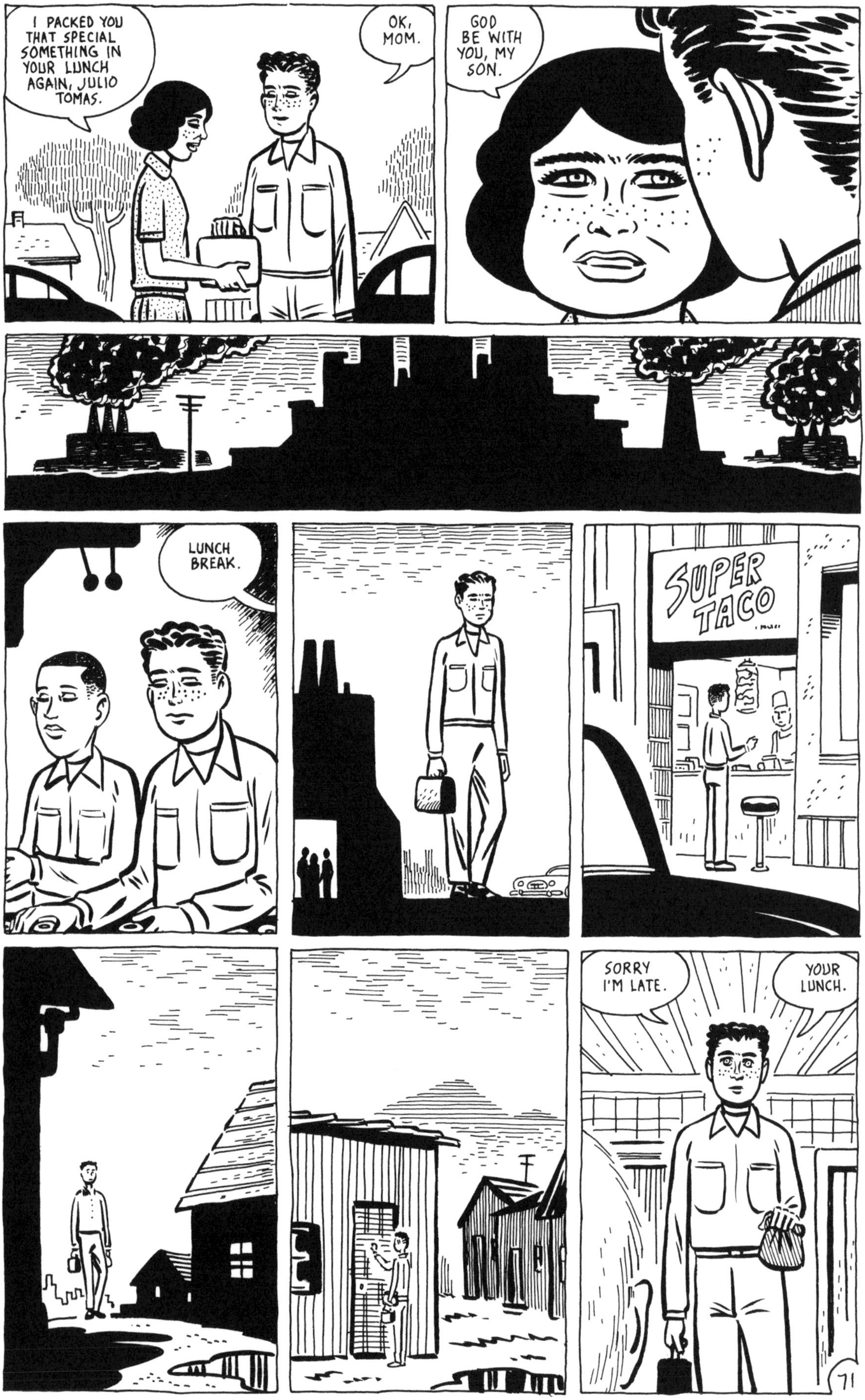
I PACKED YOU THAT SPECIAL SOMETHING IN YOUR LUNCH AGAIN, JULIO TOMAS.
OK, MOM.
GOD BE WITH YOU, MY SON.
LUNCH BREAK.
SUPER TACO
SORRY I'M LATE.
YOUR LUNCH.

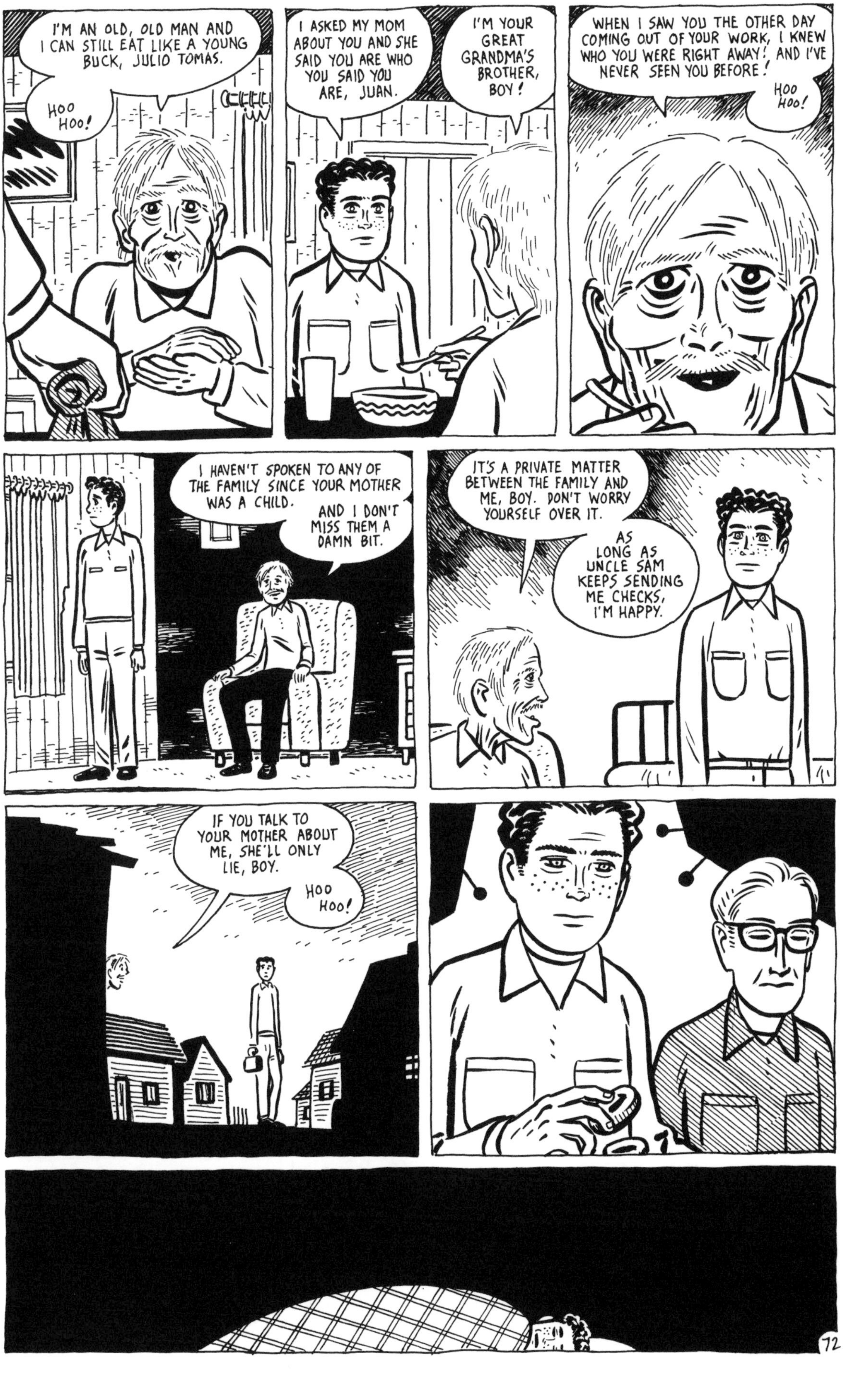
I'M AN OLD, OLD MAN AND I CAN STILL EAT LIKE A YOUNG BUCK, JULIO TOMAS.
HOO HOO!
I ASKED MY MOM ABOUT YOU AND SHE SAID YOU ARE WHO YOU SAID YOU ARE, JUAN.
I'M YOUR GREAT GRANDMA'S BROTHER, BOY!
WHEN I SAW YOU THE OTHER DAY COMING OUT OF YOUR WORK, I KNEW WHO YOU WERE RIGHT AWAY! AND I'VE NEVER SEEN YOU BEFORE!
HOO HOO!
I HAVEN'T SPOKEN TO ANY OF THE FAMILY SINCE YOUR MOTHER WAS A CHILD.
AND I DON'T MISS THEM A DAMN BIT.
IT'S A PRIVATE MATTER BETWEEN THE FAMILY AND ME, BOY. DON'T WORRY YOURSELF OVER IT.
AS LONG AS UNCLE SAM KEEPS SENDING ME CHECKS, I'M HAPPY.
IF YOU TALK TO YOUR MOTHER ABOUT ME, SHE'LL ONLY LIE, BOY.
HOO HOO!

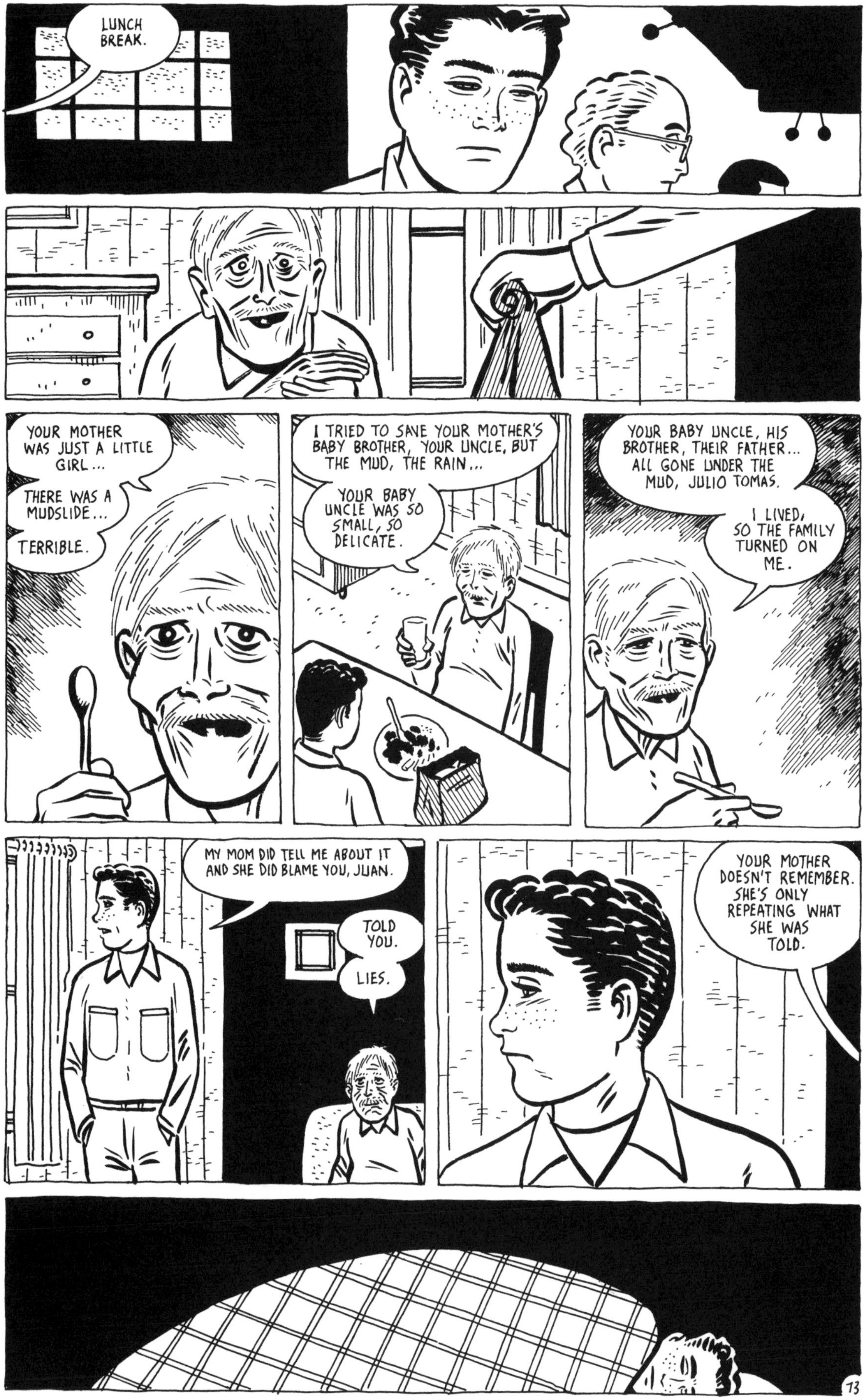
LUNCH BREAK.
YOUR MOTHER WAS JUST A LITTLE GIRL...
THERE WAS A MUDSLIDE...
TERRIBLE.
I TRIED TO SAVE YOUR MOTHER'S BABY BROTHER, YOUR UNCLE, BUT THE MUD, THE RAIN...
YOUR BABY UNCLE WAS SO SMALL, SO DELICATE.
YOUR BABY UNCLE, HIS BROTHER, THEIR FATHER... ALL GONE UNDER THE MUD, JULIO TOMAS.
I LIVED, SO THE FAMILY TURNED ON ME.
MY MOM DID TELL ME ABOUT IT AND SHE DID BLAME YOU, JUAN.
TOLD YOU.
LIES.
YOUR MOTHER DOESN'T REMEMBER. SHE'S ONLY REPEATING WHAT SHE WAS TOLD.

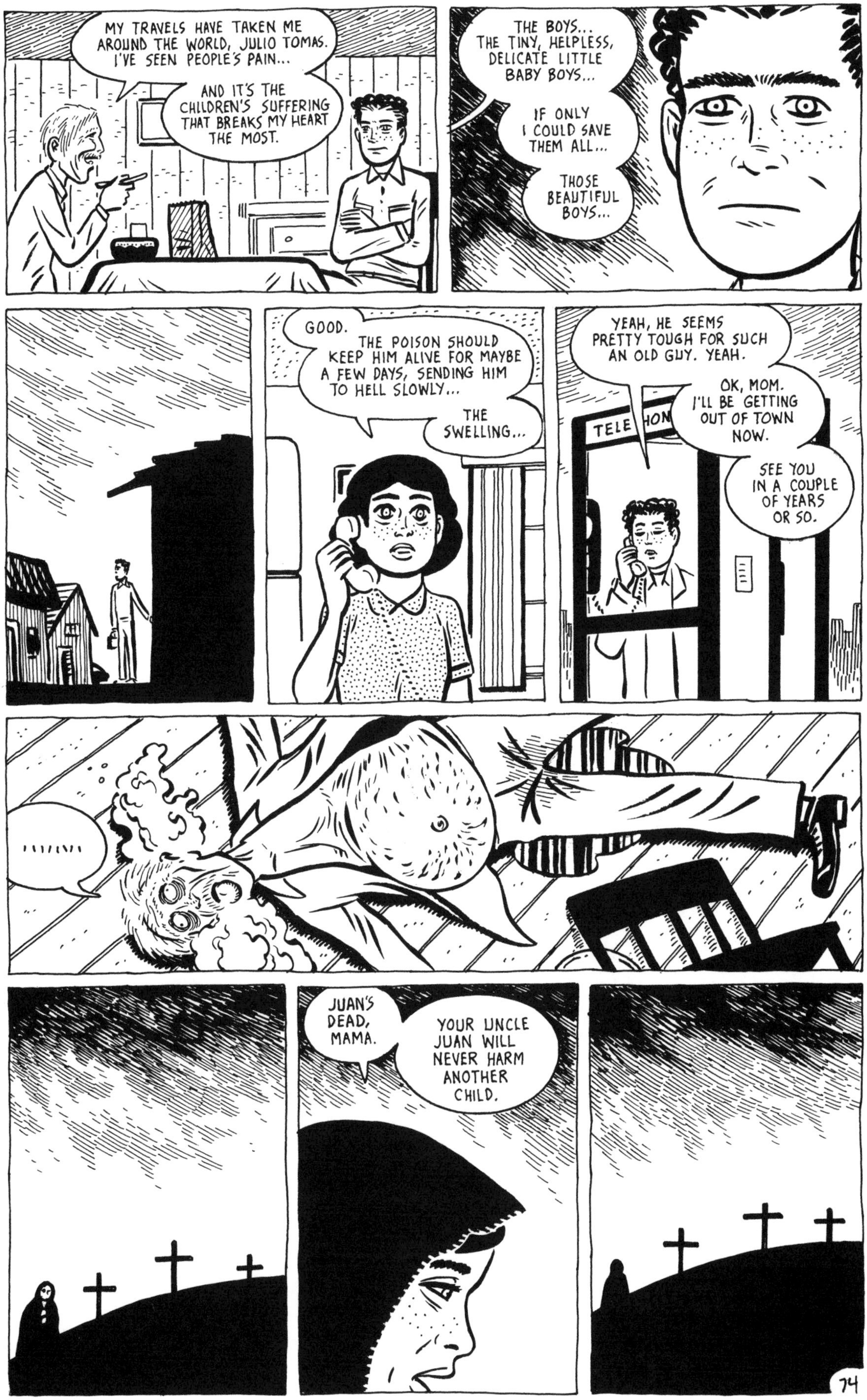
MY TRAVELS HAVE TAKEN ME AROUND THE WORLD, JULIO TOMAS. I'VE SEEN PEOPLE'S PAIN...
AND IT'S THE CHILDREN'S SUFFERING THAT BREAKS MY HEART THE MOST.
THE BOYS... THE TINY, HELPLESS, DELICATE LITTLE BABY BOYS...
IF ONLY I COULD SAVE THEM ALL...
THOSE BEAUTIFUL BOYS...
GOOD.
THE POISON SHOULD KEEP HIM ALIVE FOR MAYBE A FEW DAYS, SENDING HIM TO HELL SLOWLY...
THE SWELLING...
YEAH, HE SEEMS PRETTY TOUGH FOR SUCH AN OLD GUY. YEAH.
TELE HON
OK, MOM. I'LL BE GETTING OUT OF TOWN NOW.
SEE YOU IN A COUPLE OF YEARS OR SO.
JUAN'S DEAD, MAMA.
YOUR UNCLE JUAN WILL NEVER HARM ANOTHER CHILD.

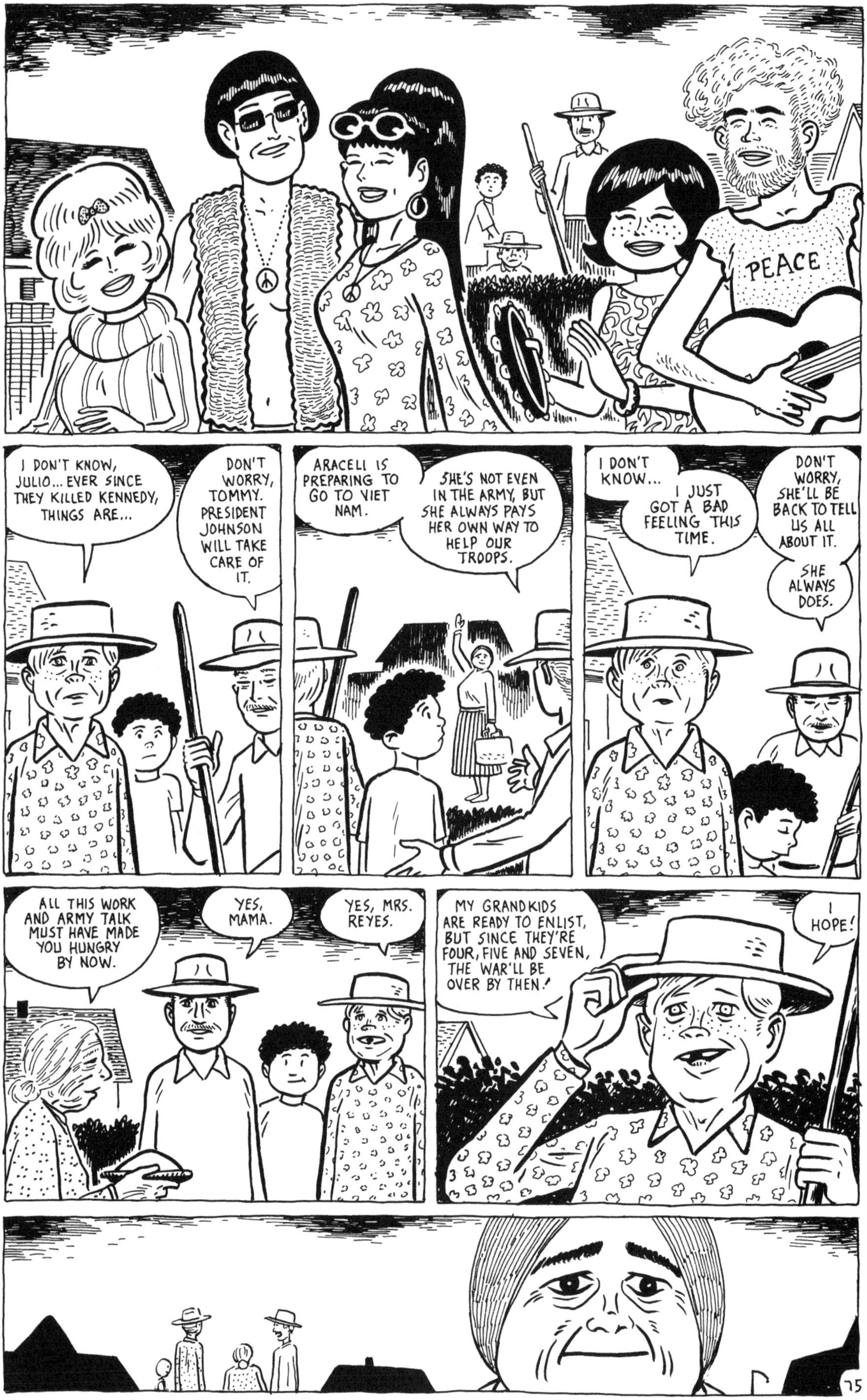

PEACE
I DON'T KNOW, JULIO... EVER SINCE THEY KILLED KENNEDY, THINGS ARE...
DON'T WORRY, TOMMY. PRESIDENT JOHNSON WILL TAKE CARE OF IT.
ARACELI IS PREPARING TO GO TO VIET NAM.
SHE'S NOT EVEN IN THE ARMY, BUT SHE ALWAYS PAYS HER OWN WAY TO HELP OUR TROOPS.
I DON'T KNOW...
I JUST GOT A BAD FEELING THIS TIME.
DON'T WORRY, SHE'LL BE BACK TO TELL US ALL ABOUT IT.
SHE ALWAYS DOES.
ALL THIS WORK AND ARMY TALK MUST HAVE MADE YOU HUNGRY BY NOW.
YES, MAMA.
YES, MRS. REYES.
MY GRANDKIDS ARE READY TO ENLIST, BUT SINCE THEY'RE FOUR, FIVE AND SEVEN, THE WAR'LL BE OVER BY THEN!
I HOPE!

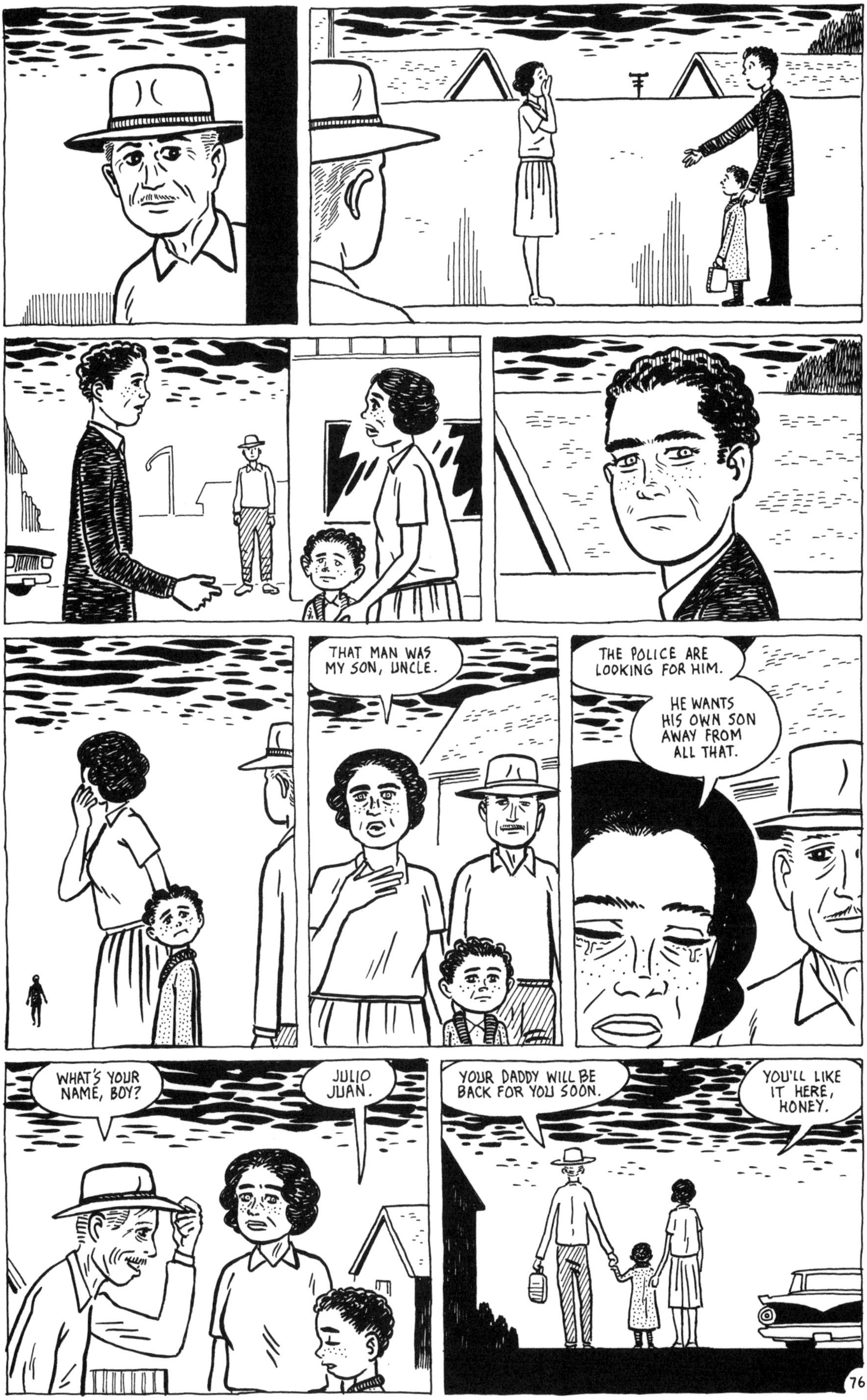
THAT MAN WAS MY SON, UNCLE.
THE POLICE ARE LOOKING FOR HIM.
HE WANTS HIS OWN SON AWAY FROM ALL THAT.
WHAT'S YOUR NAME, BOY?
JULIO JUAN.
YOUR DADDY WILL BE BACK FOR YOU SOON.
YOU'LL LIKE IT HERE, HONEY.

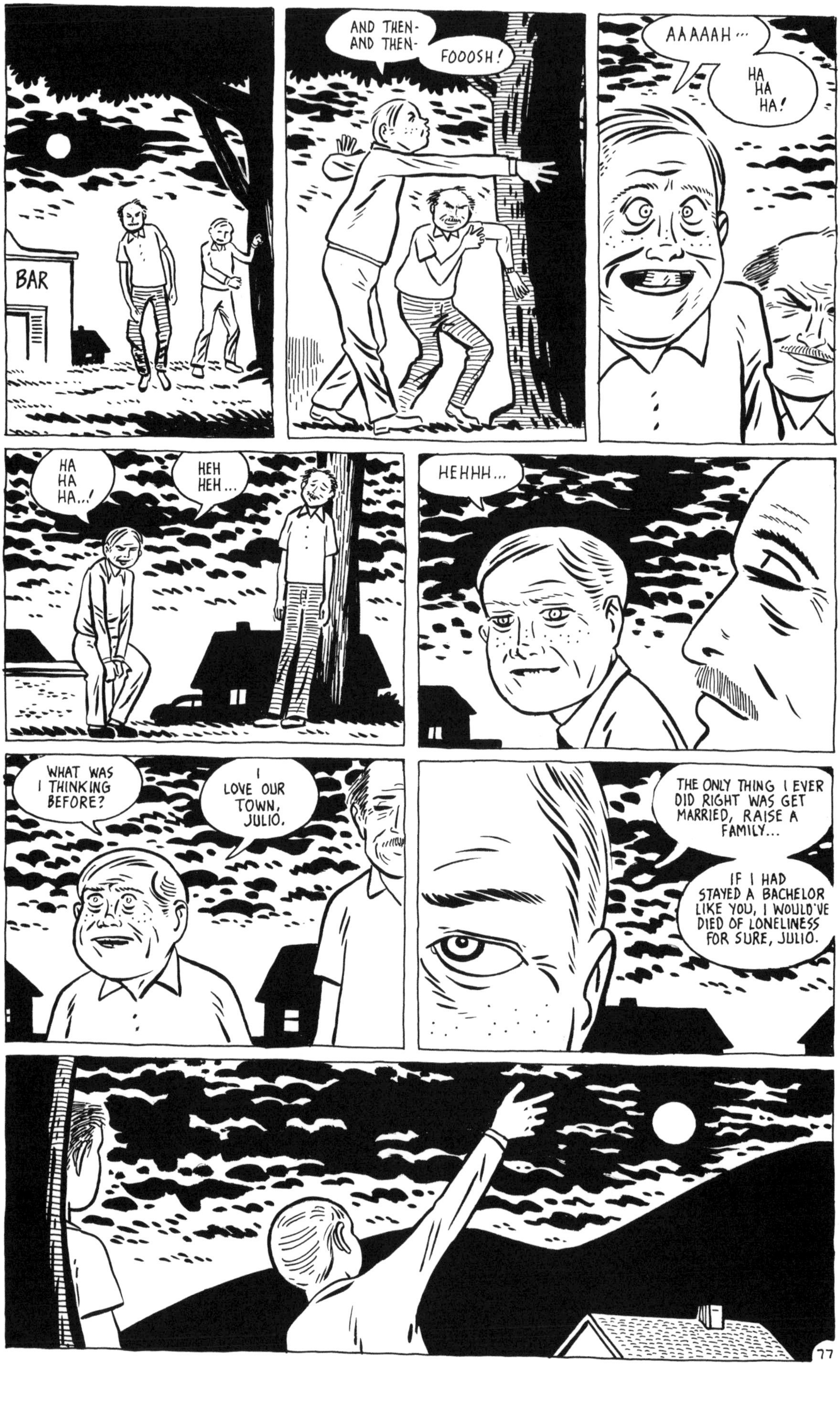
BAR
AND THEN-
AND THEN-
FOOOSH!
AAAAAH...
HA
HA
HA!
HA
HA
HA...!
HEH
HEH...
HEHHH...
WHAT WAS
I THINKING
BEFORE?
I
LOVE OUR
TOWN,
JULIO.
THE ONLY THING I EVER
DID RIGHT WAS GET
MARRIED, RAISE A
FAMILY...
IF I HAD
STAYED A BACHELOR
LIKE YOU, I WOULD'VE
DIED OF LONELINESS
FOR SURE, JULIO.

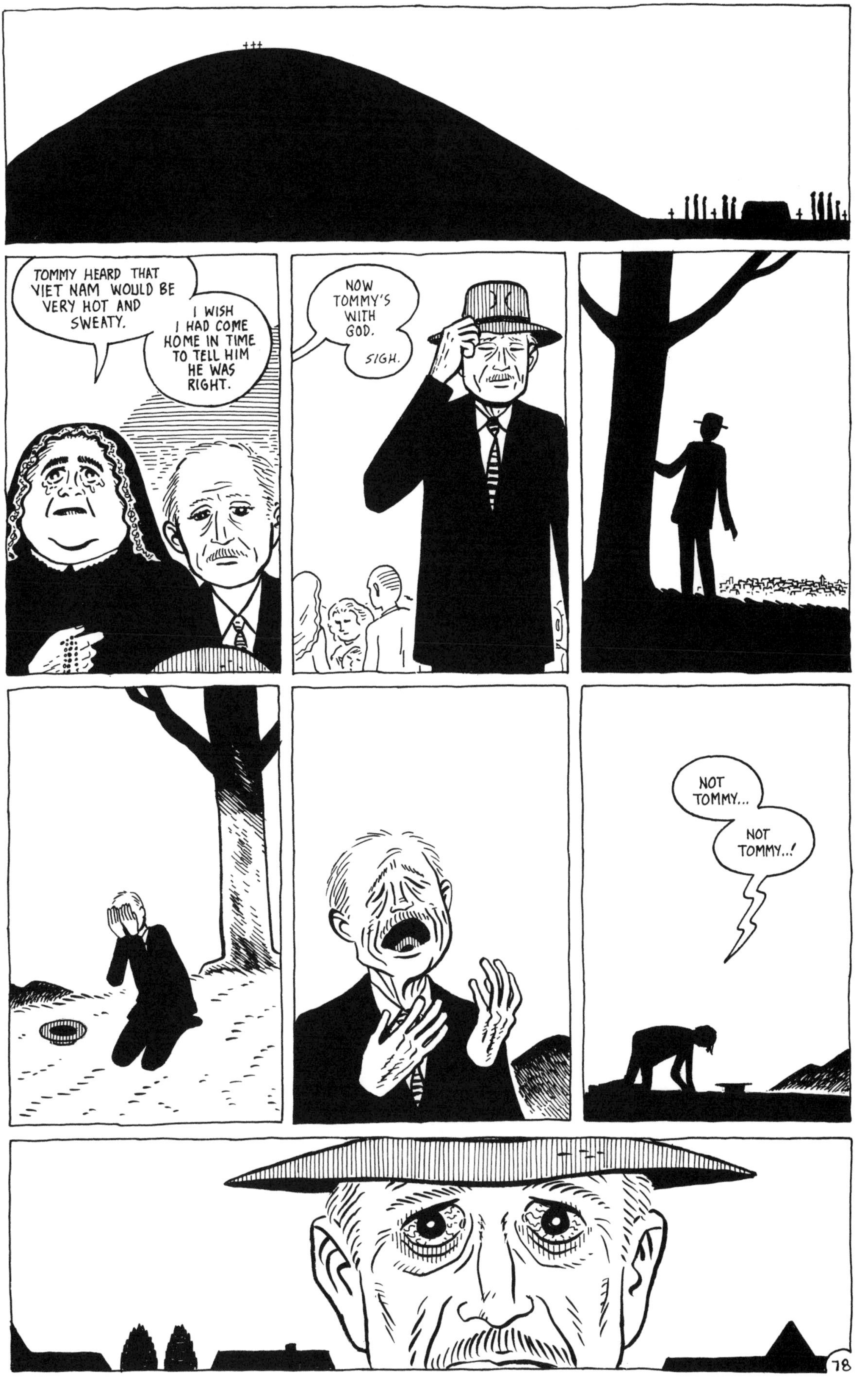
TOMMY HEARD THAT VIET NAM WOULD BE VERY HOT AND SWEATY.
I WISH I HAD COME HOME IN TIME TO TELL HIM HE WAS RIGHT.
NOW TOMMY'S WITH GOD.
SIGH.
NOT TOMMY...
NOT TOMMY..!

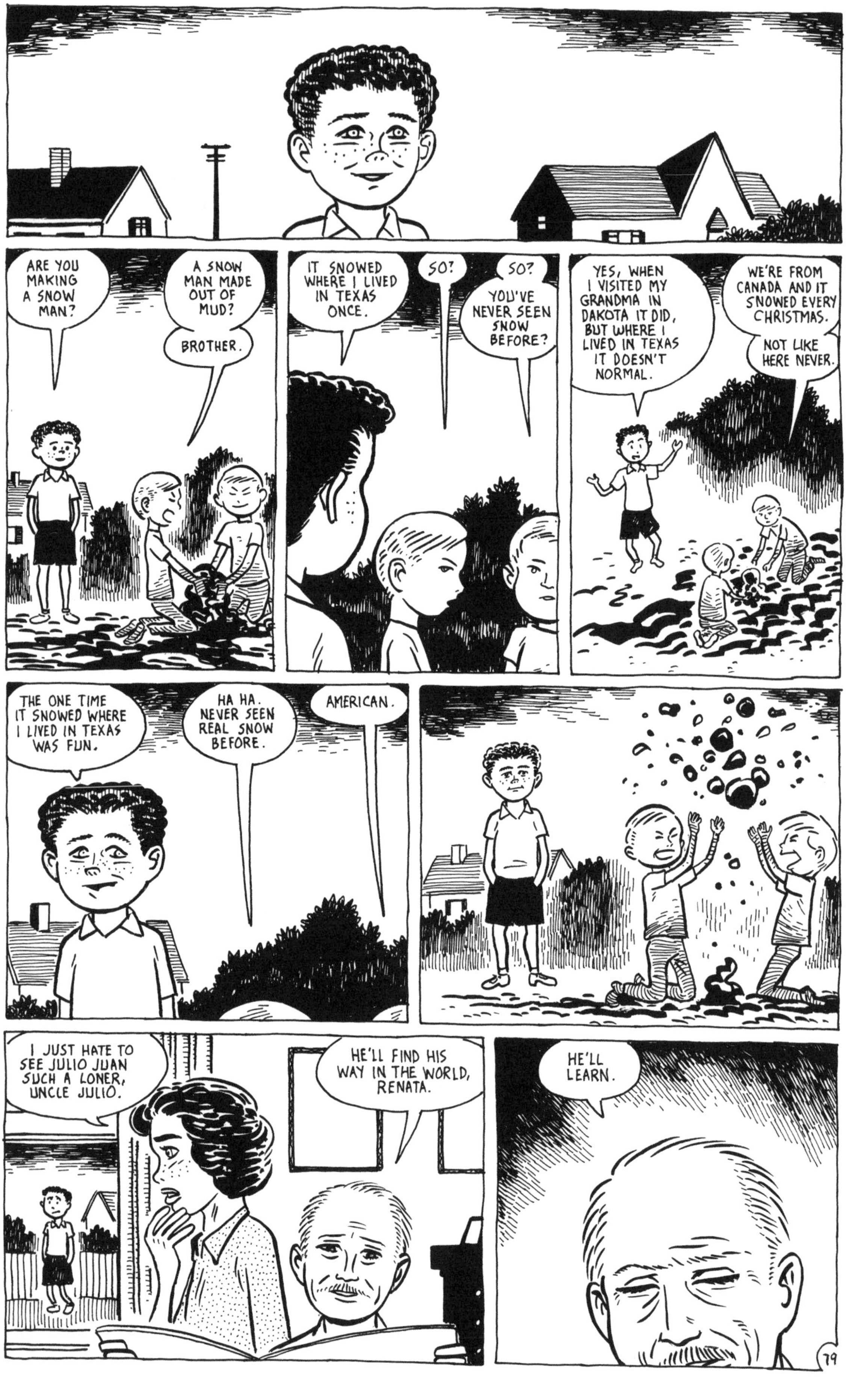
ARE YOU MAKING A SNOW MAN?
A SNOW MAN MADE OUT OF MUD?
BROTHER.
IT SNOWED WHERE I LIVED IN TEXAS ONCE.
SO?
SO?
YOU'VE NEVER SEEN SNOW BEFORE?
YES, WHEN I VISITED MY GRANDMA IN DAKOTA IT DID, BUT WHERE I LIVED IN TEXAS IT DOESN'T NORMAL.
WE'RE FROM CANADA AND IT SNOWED EVERY CHRISTMAS.
NOT LIKE HERE NEVER.
THE ONE TIME IT SNOWED WHERE I LIVED IN TEXAS WAS FUN.
HA HA. NEVER SEEN REAL SNOW BEFORE.
AMERICAN.
I JUST HATE TO SEE JULIO JUAN SUCH A LONER, UNCLE JULIO.
HE'LL FIND HIS WAY IN THE WORLD, RENATA.
HE'LL LEARN.

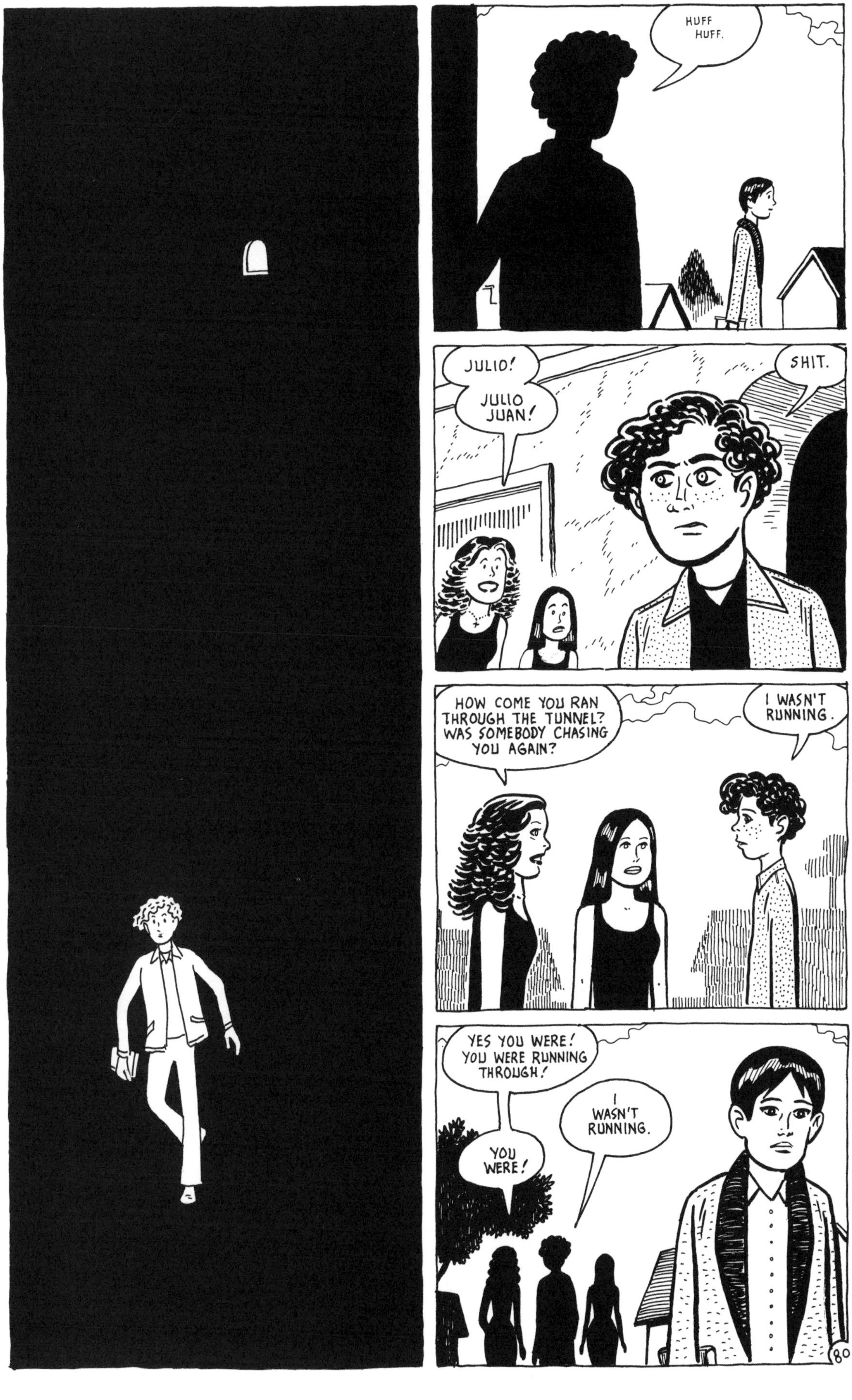
HUFF
HUFF.
JULIO!
JULIO JUAN!
SHIT.
HOW COME YOU RAN THROUGH THE TUNNEL? WAS SOMEBODY CHASING YOU AGAIN?
I WASN'T RUNNING.
YES YOU WERE! YOU WERE RUNNING THROUGH!
YOU WERE!
I WASN'T RUNNING.

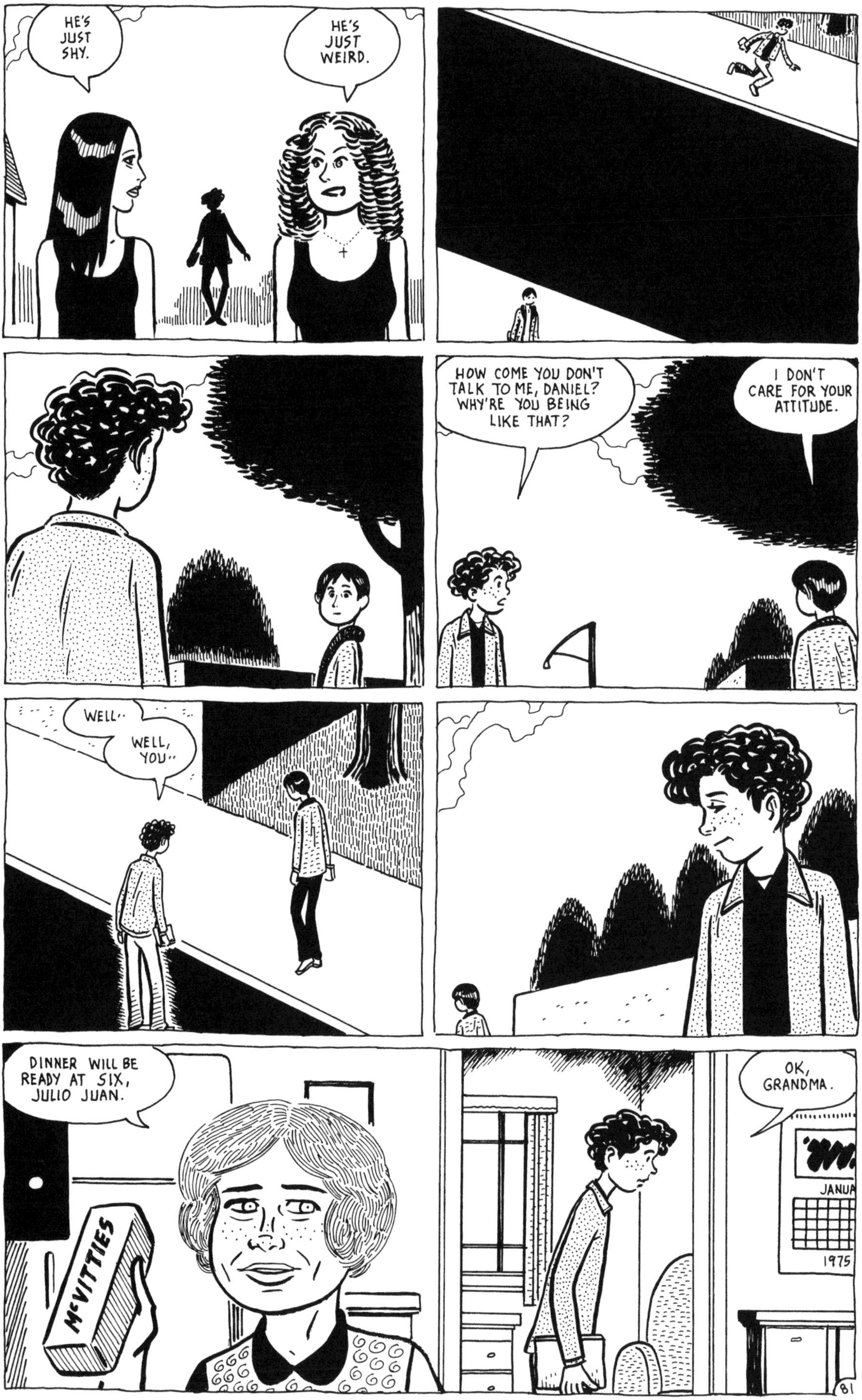
HE'S JUST SHY.
HE'S JUST WEIRD.
HOW COME YOU DON'T TALK TO ME, DANIEL? WHY'RE YOU BEING LIKE THAT?
I DON'T CARE FOR YOUR ATTITUDE.
WELL..
WELL, YOU..
DINNER WILL BE READY AT SIX, JULIO JUAN.
McVITTIES
OK, GRANDMA.
JANUA
1975

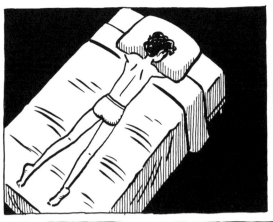

SNIFF.

I KNOW YOU RAN THROUGH THE TUNNEL AS A SHORT CUT TO CATCH UP WITH ME, JULIO.

82

I'M GLAD YOU'RE TALKING TO ME STILL.

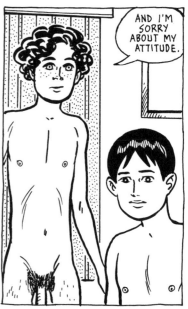

AND I'M SORRY ABOUT MY ATTITUDE.

I JUST GOT SCARED, JULIO.

DANIEL, I WON'T LET ANYTHING BAD HAPPEN TO YOU.

I MEANT I GOT SCARED FOR YOU, JULIO.

NOTHING BAD WILL HAPPEN TO ME.

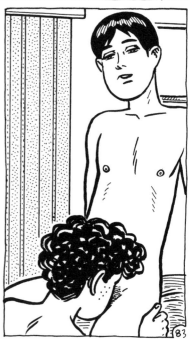

183

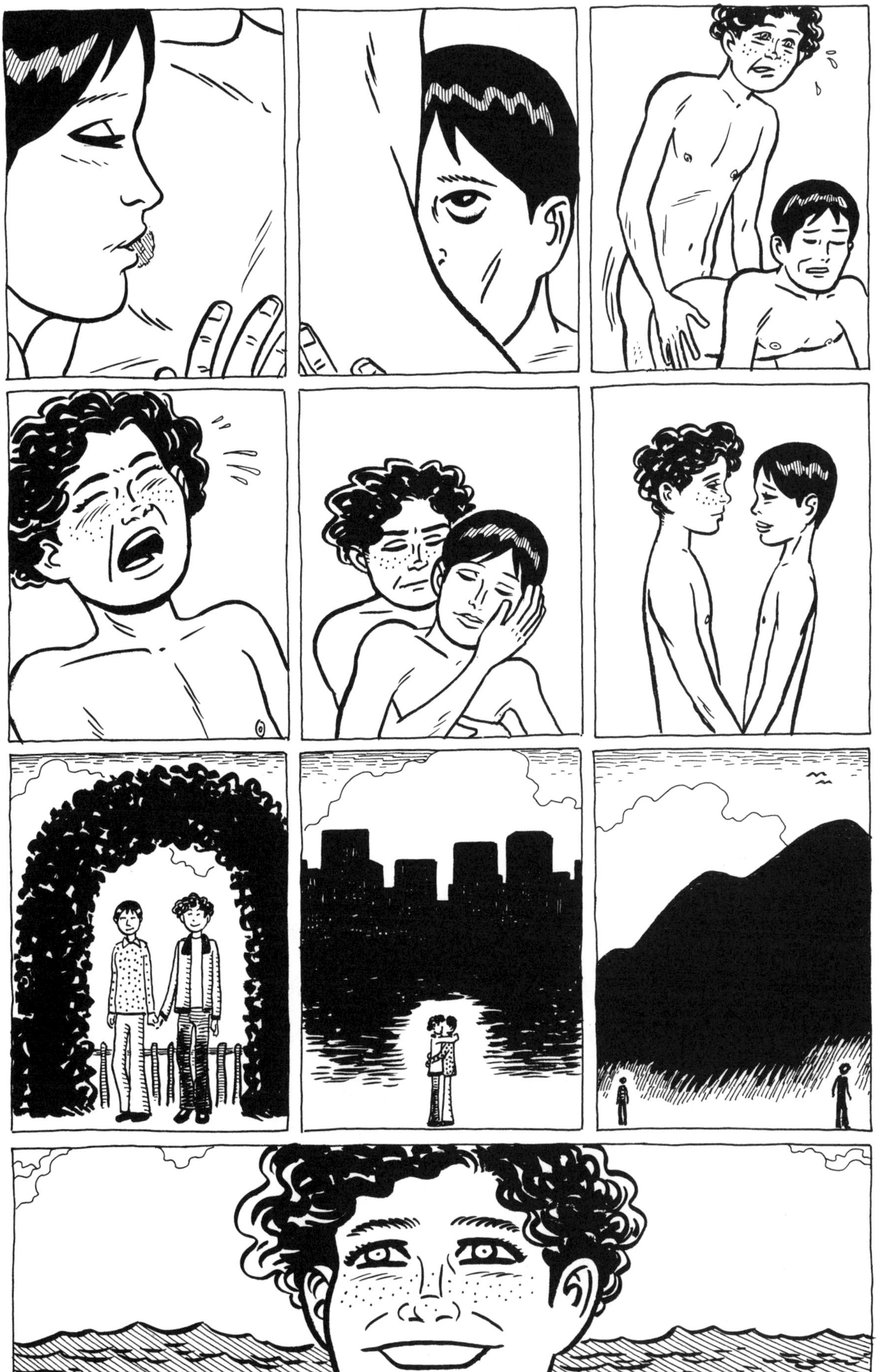

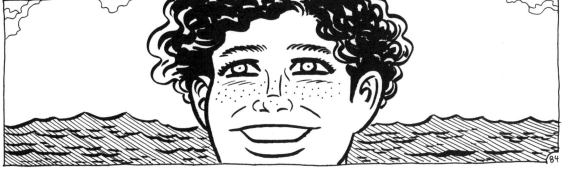

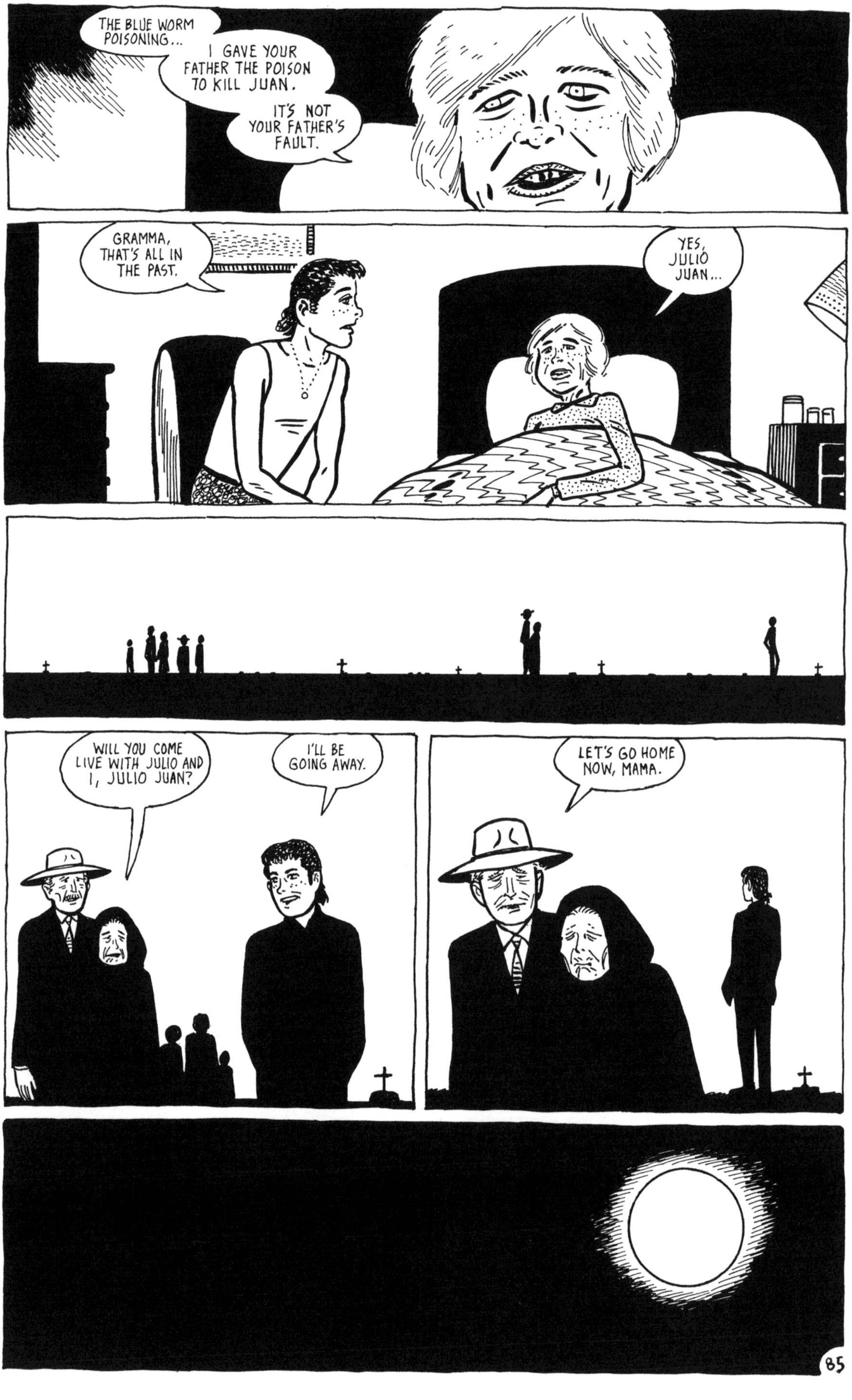
THE BLUE WORM POISONING...
I GAVE YOUR FATHER THE POISON TO KILL JUAN.
IT'S NOT YOUR FATHER'S FAULT.
GRAMMA, THAT'S ALL IN THE PAST.
YES, JULIO JUAN...
WILL YOU COME LIVE WITH JULIO AND I, JULIO JUAN?
I'LL BE GOING AWAY.
LET'S GO HOME NOW, MAMA.

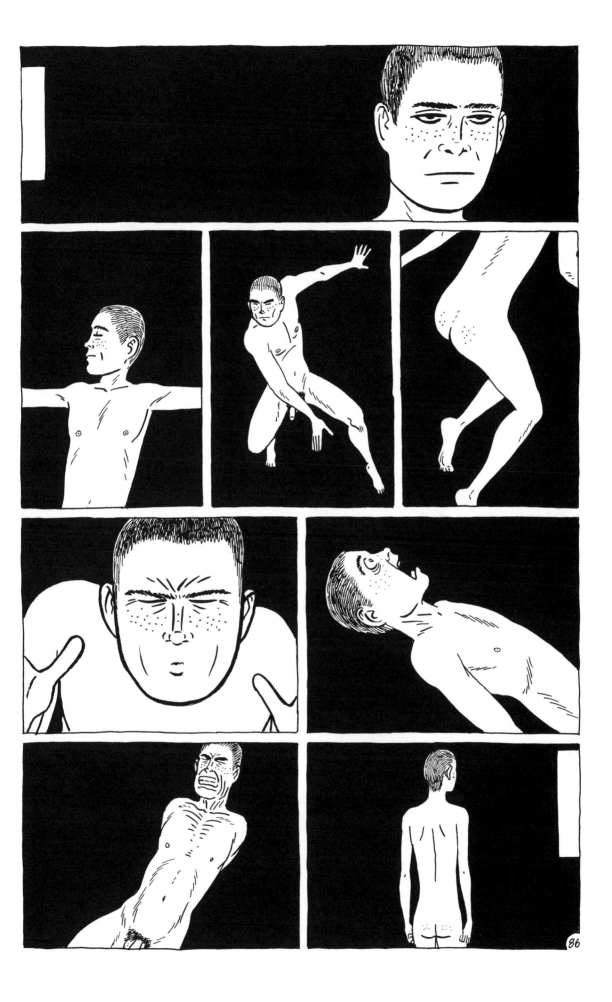

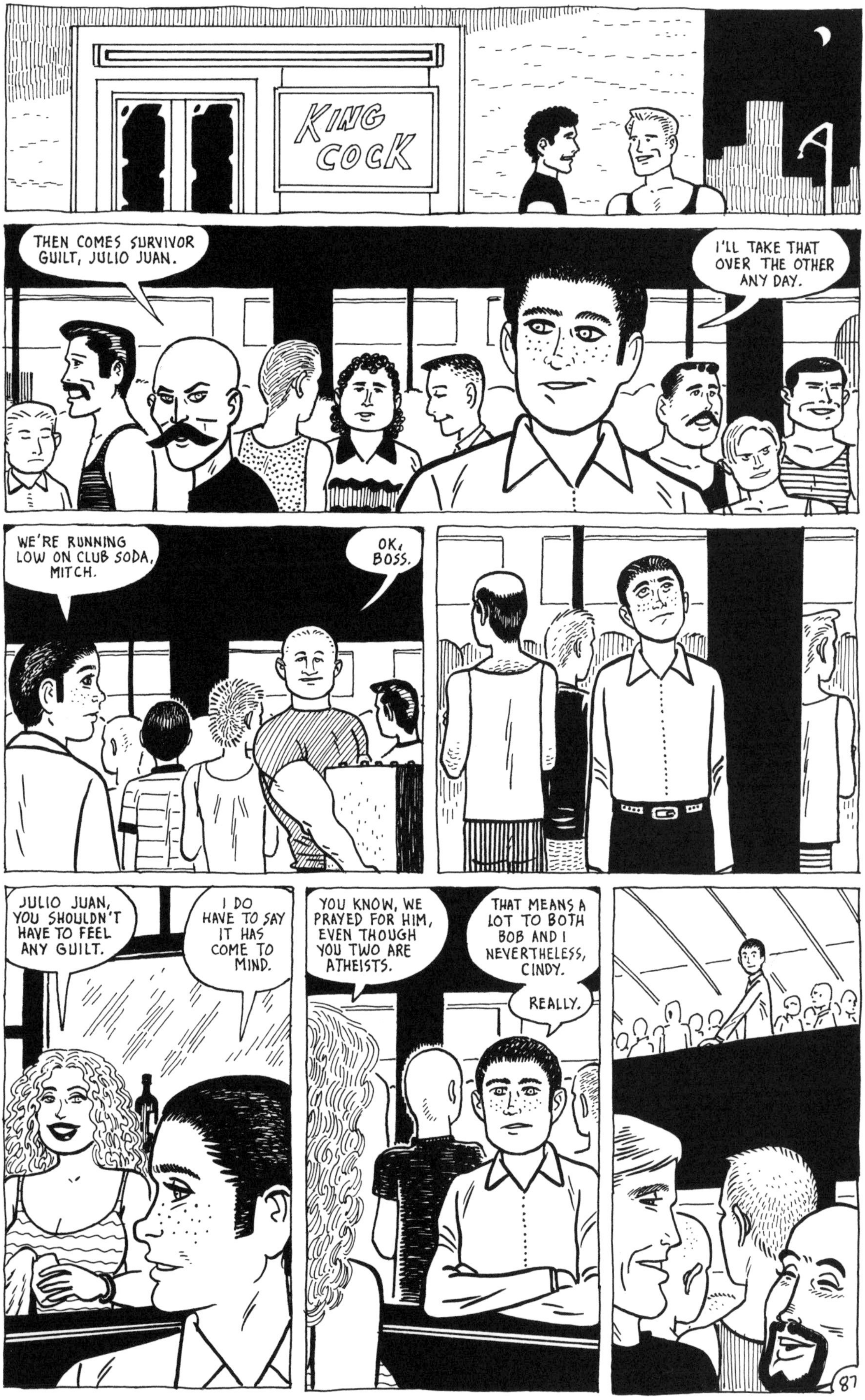

KING COCK
THEN COMES SURVIVOR GUILT, JULIO JUAN.
I'LL TAKE THAT OVER THE OTHER ANY DAY.
WE'RE RUNNING LOW ON CLUB SODA, MITCH.
OK, BOSS.
JULIO JUAN, YOU SHOULDN'T HAVE TO FEEL ANY GUILT.
I DO HAVE TO SAY IT HAS COME TO MIND.
YOU KNOW, WE PRAYED FOR HIM, EVEN THOUGH YOU TWO ARE ATHEISTS.
THAT MEANS A LOT TO BOTH BOB AND I NEVERTHELESS, CINDY.
REALLY.

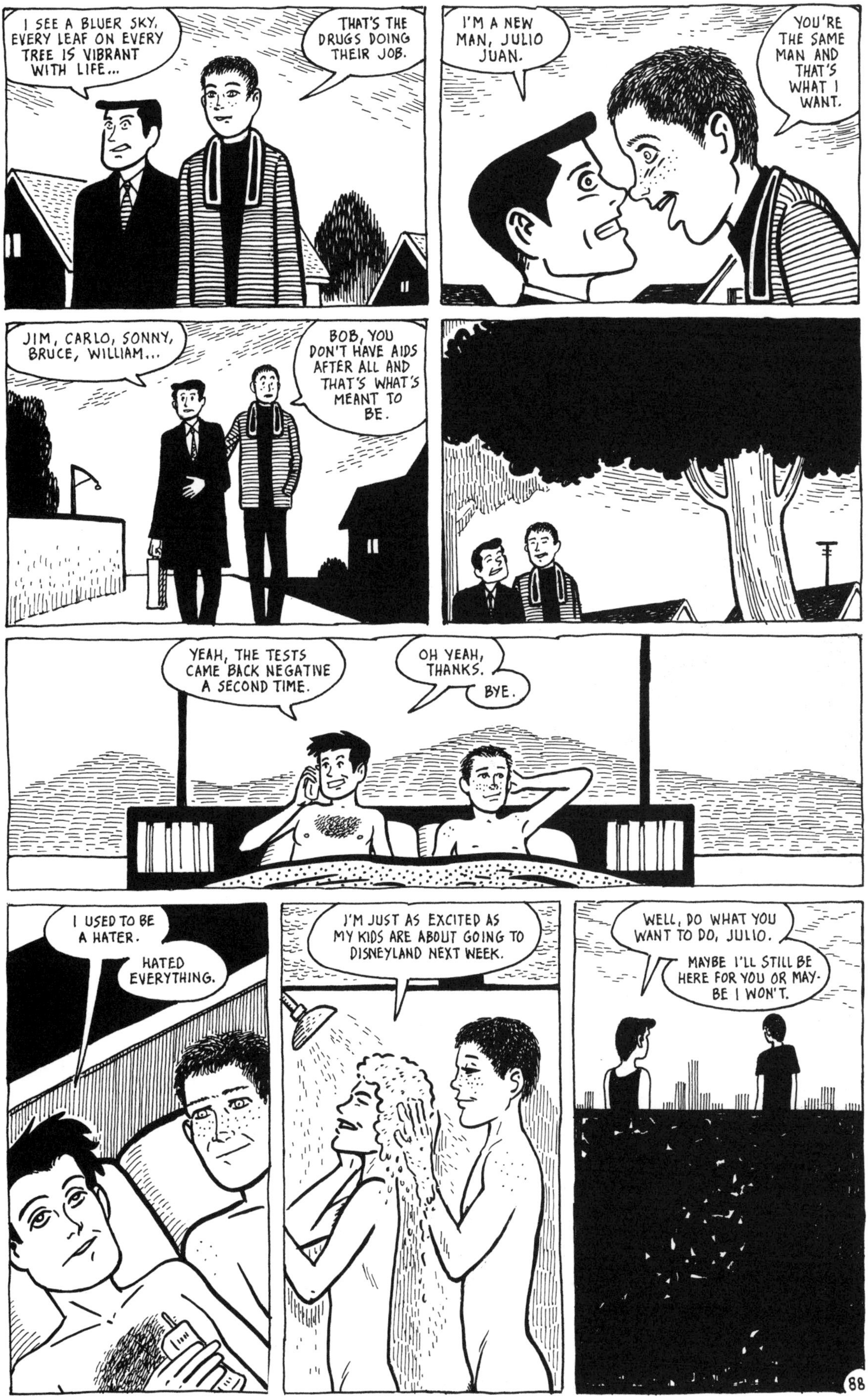
I SEE A BLUER SKY, EVERY LEAF ON EVERY TREE IS VIBRANT WITH LIFE...
THAT'S THE DRUGS DOING THEIR JOB.
I'M A NEW MAN, JULIO JUAN.
YOU'RE THE SAME MAN AND THAT'S WHAT I WANT.
JIM, CARLO, SONNY, BRUCE, WILLIAM...
BOB, YOU DON'T HAVE AIDS AFTER ALL AND THAT'S WHAT'S MEANT TO BE.
YEAH, THE TESTS CAME BACK NEGATIVE A SECOND TIME.
OH YEAH, THANKS.
BYE.
I USED TO BE A HATER.
HATED EVERYTHING.
I'M JUST AS EXCITED AS MY KIDS ARE ABOUT GOING TO DISNEYLAND NEXT WEEK.
WELL, DO WHAT YOU WANT TO DO, JULIO.
MAYBE I'LL STILL BE HERE FOR YOU OR MAY-BE I WON'T.

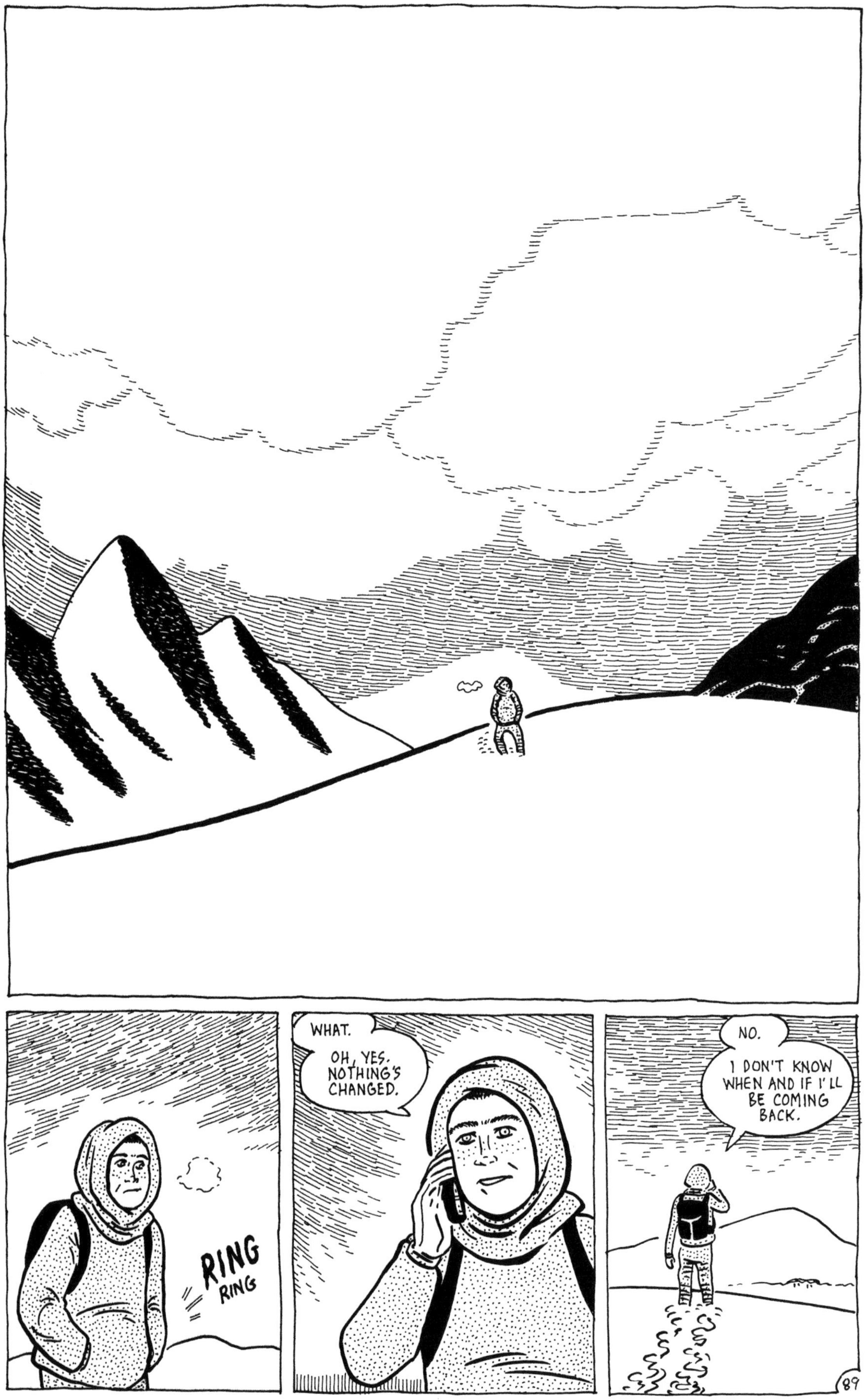
RING
RING
WHAT.
OH, YES. NOTHING'S CHANGED.
NO.
I DON'T KNOW WHEN AND IF I'LL BE COMING BACK.

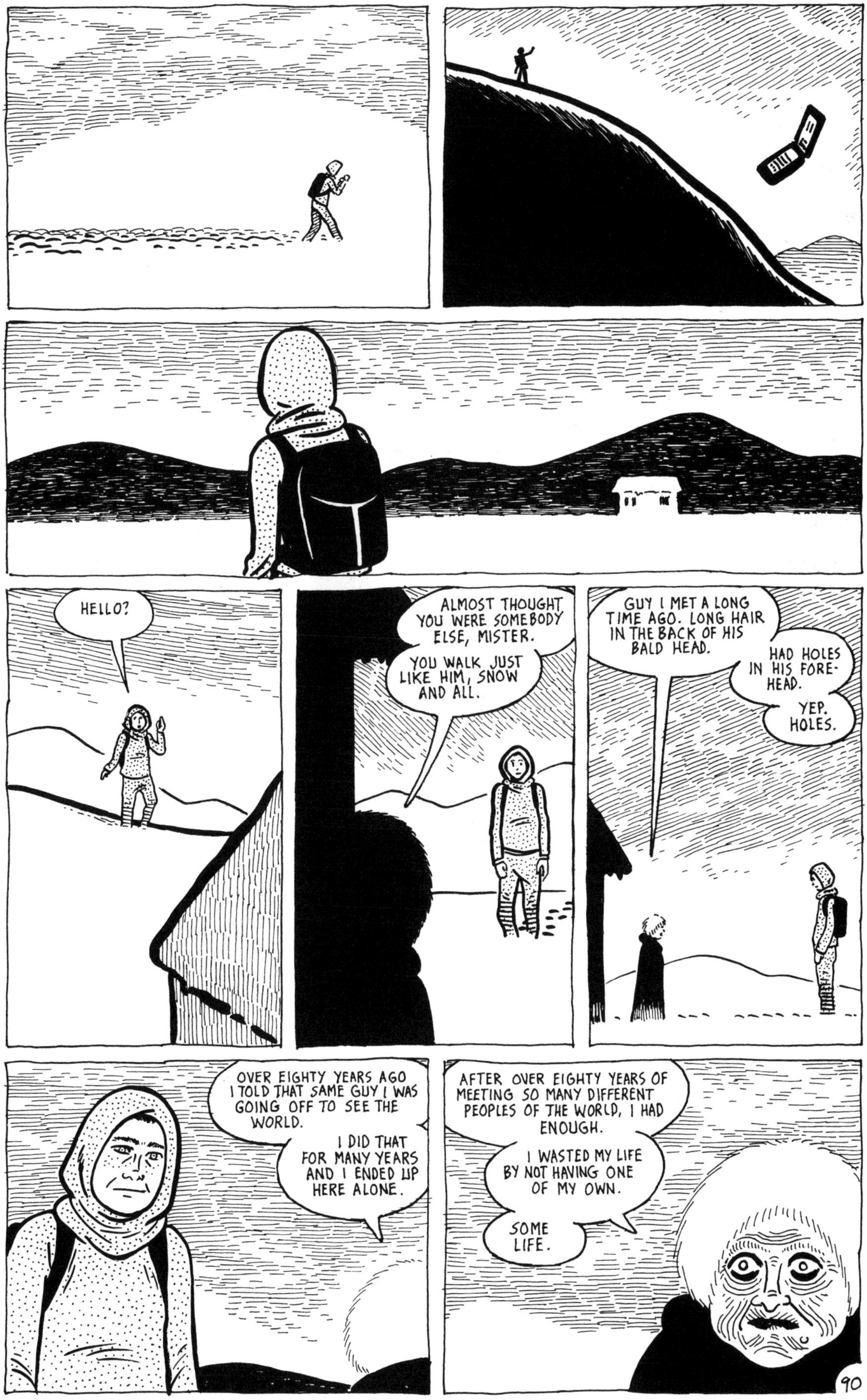
HELLO?
ALMOST THOUGHT YOU WERE SOMEBODY ELSE, MISTER.
YOU WALK JUST LIKE HIM, SNOW AND ALL.
GUY I MET A LONG TIME AGO. LONG HAIR IN THE BACK OF HIS BALD HEAD.
HAD HOLES IN HIS FORE-HEAD.
YEP. HOLES.
OVER EIGHTY YEARS AGO I TOLD THAT SAME GUY I WAS GOING OFF TO SEE THE WORLD.
I DID THAT FOR MANY YEARS AND I ENDED UP HERE ALONE.
AFTER OVER EIGHTY YEARS OF MEETING SO MANY DIFFERENT PEOPLES OF THE WORLD, I HAD ENOUGH.
I WASTED MY LIFE BY NOT HAVING ONE OF MY OWN.
SOME LIFE.

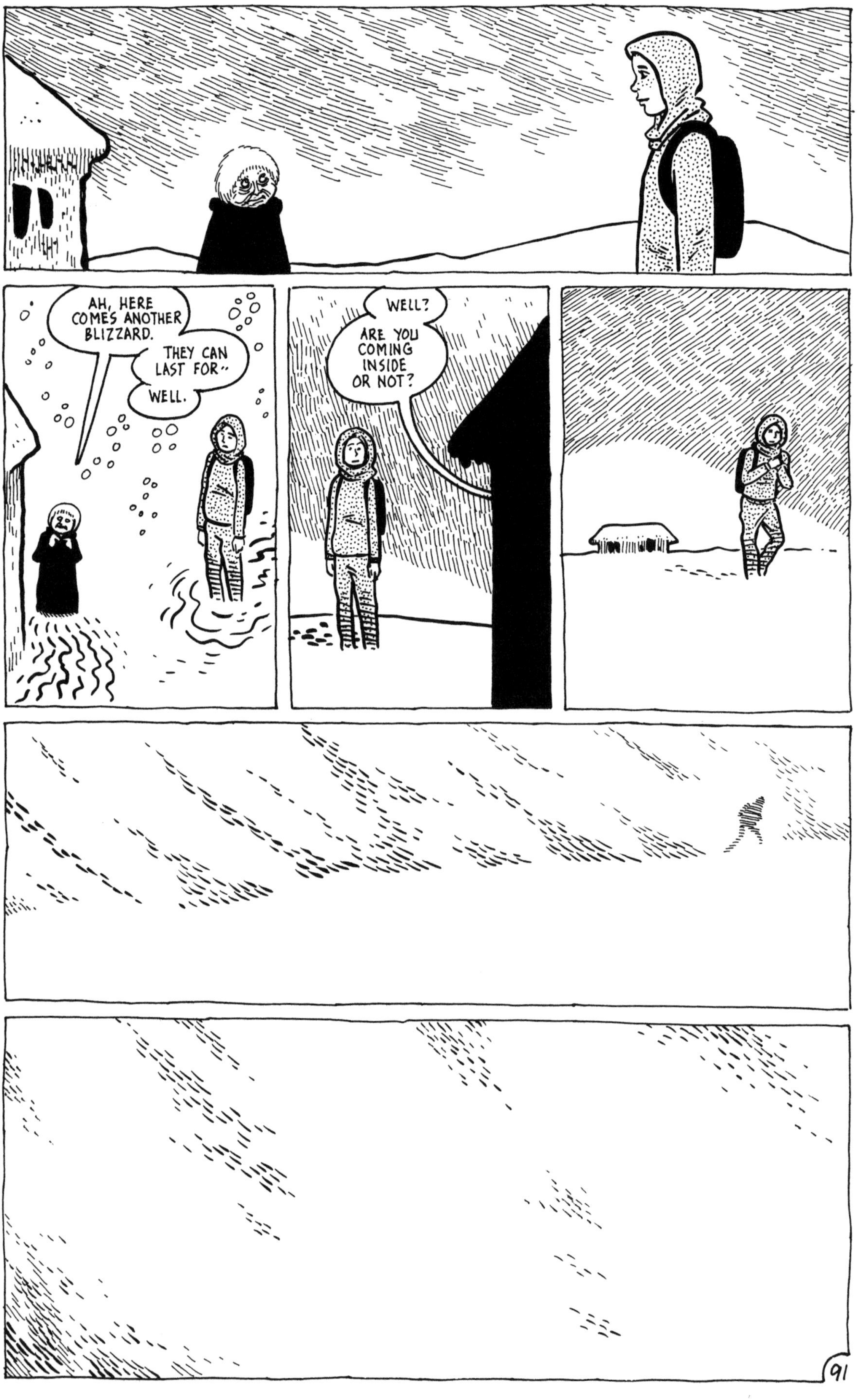
AH, HERE COMES ANOTHER BLIZZARD.
THEY CAN LAST FOR--
WELL.
WELL?
ARE YOU COMING INSIDE OR NOT?

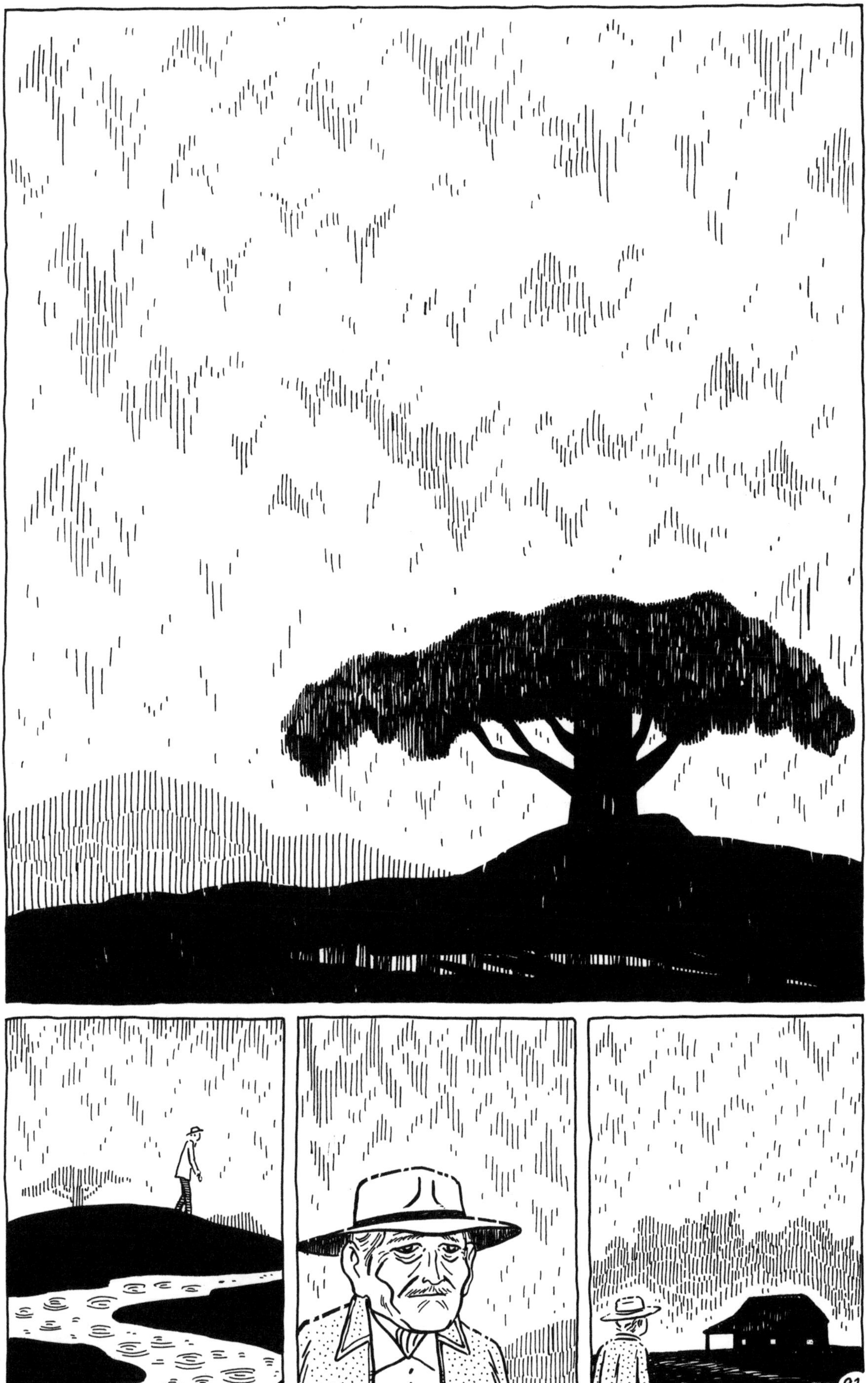

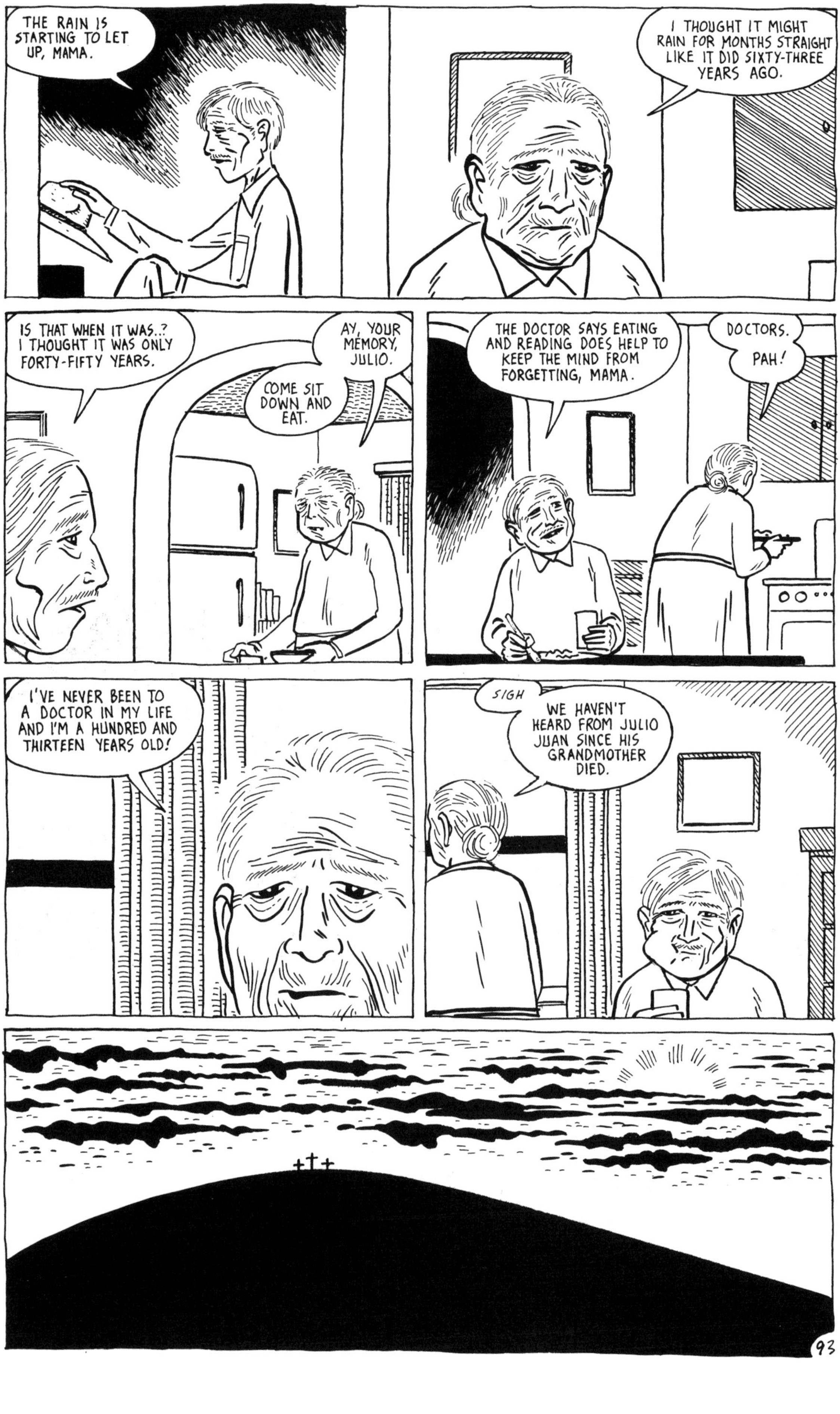
THE RAIN IS STARTING TO LET UP, MAMA.
I THOUGHT IT MIGHT RAIN FOR MONTHS STRAIGHT LIKE IT DID SIXTY-THREE YEARS AGO.
IS THAT WHEN IT WAS..? I THOUGHT IT WAS ONLY FORTY-FIFTY YEARS.
AY, YOUR MEMORY, JULIO.
COME SIT DOWN AND EAT.
THE DOCTOR SAYS EATING AND READING DOES HELP TO KEEP THE MIND FROM FORGETTING, MAMA.
DOCTORS.
PAH!
I'VE NEVER BEEN TO A DOCTOR IN MY LIFE AND I'M A HUNDRED AND THIRTEEN YEARS OLD!
SIGH
WE HAVEN'T HEARD FROM JULIO JUAN SINCE HIS GRANDMOTHER DIED.

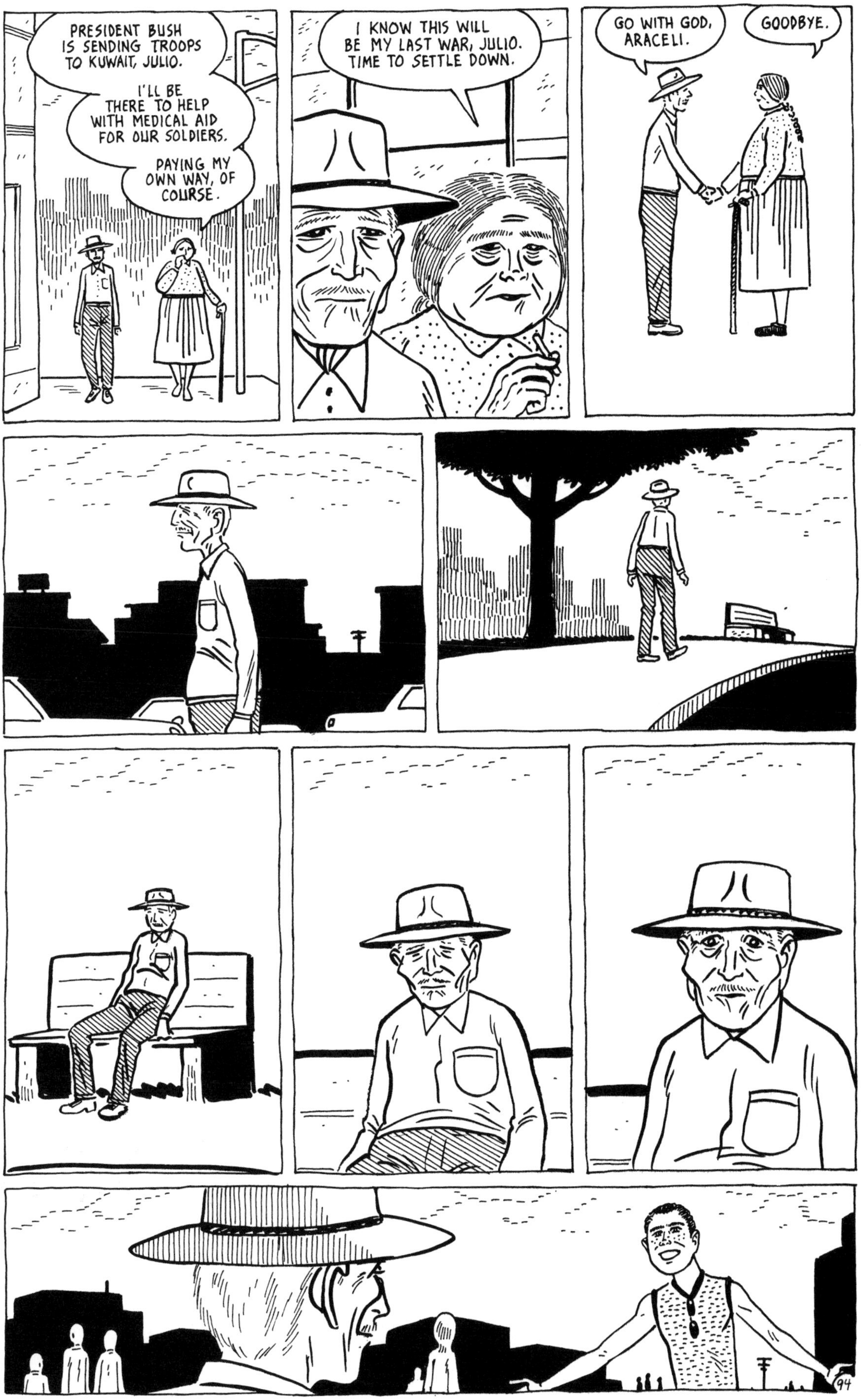
PRESIDENT BUSH IS SENDING TROOPS TO KUWAIT, JULIO.
I'LL BE THERE TO HELP WITH MEDICAL AID FOR OUR SOLDIERS.
PAYING MY OWN WAY, OF COURSE.
I KNOW THIS WILL BE MY LAST WAR, JULIO. TIME TO SETTLE DOWN.
GO WITH GOD, ARACELI.
GOODBYE.

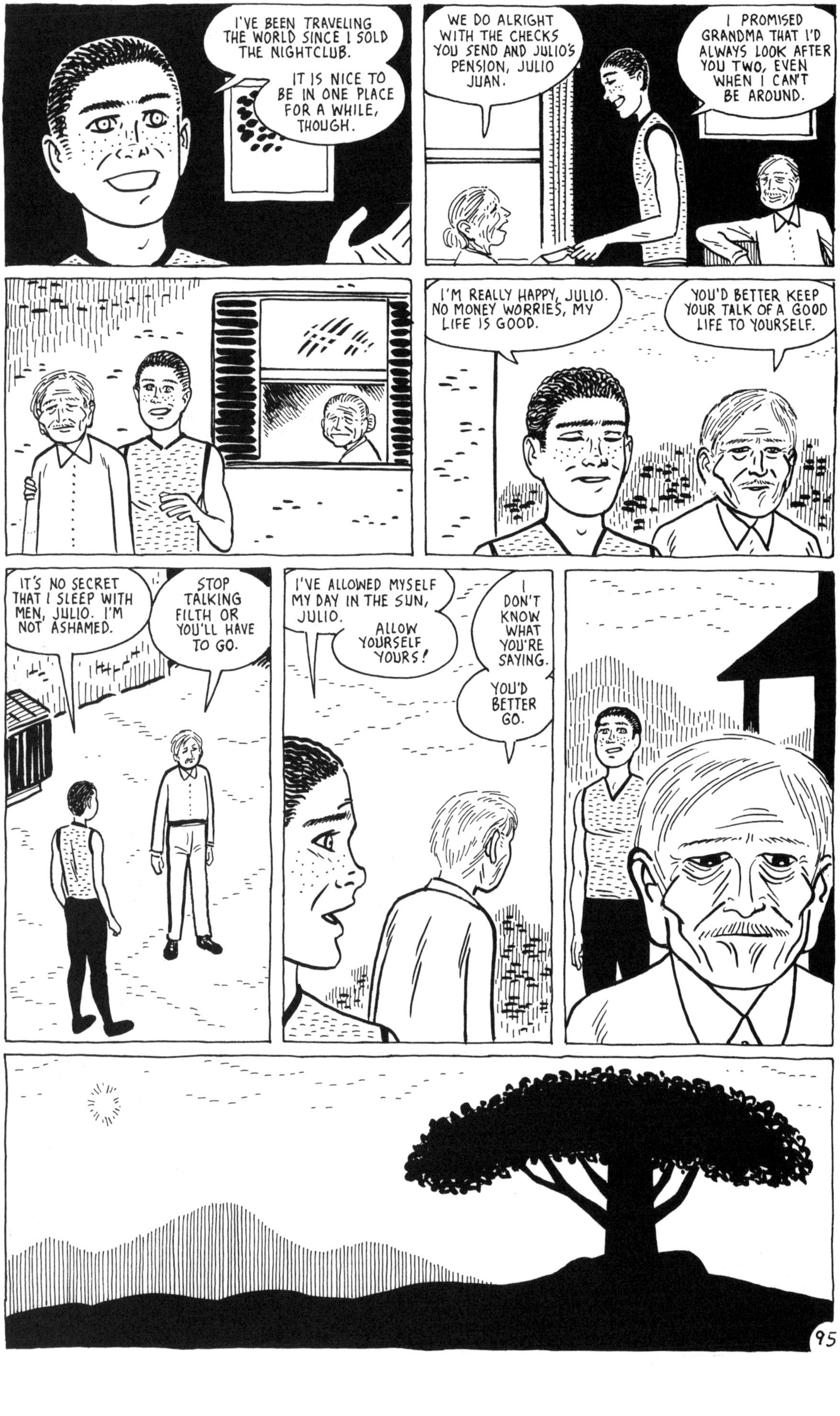
I'VE BEEN TRAVELING THE WORLD SINCE I SOLD THE NIGHTCLUB.
IT IS NICE TO BE IN ONE PLACE FOR A WHILE, THOUGH.
WE DO ALRIGHT WITH THE CHECKS YOU SEND AND JULIO'S PENSION, JULIO JUAN.
I PROMISED GRANDMA THAT I'D ALWAYS LOOK AFTER YOU TWO, EVEN WHEN I CAN'T BE AROUND.
I'M REALLY HAPPY, JULIO. NO MONEY WORRIES, MY LIFE IS GOOD.
YOU'D BETTER KEEP YOUR TALK OF A GOOD LIFE TO YOURSELF.
IT'S NO SECRET THAT I SLEEP WITH MEN, JULIO. I'M NOT ASHAMED.
STOP TALKING FILTH OR YOU'LL HAVE TO GO.
I'VE ALLOWED MYSELF MY DAY IN THE SUN, JULIO.
ALLOW YOURSELF YOURS!
I DON'T KNOW WHAT YOU'RE SAYING.
YOU'D BETTER GO.

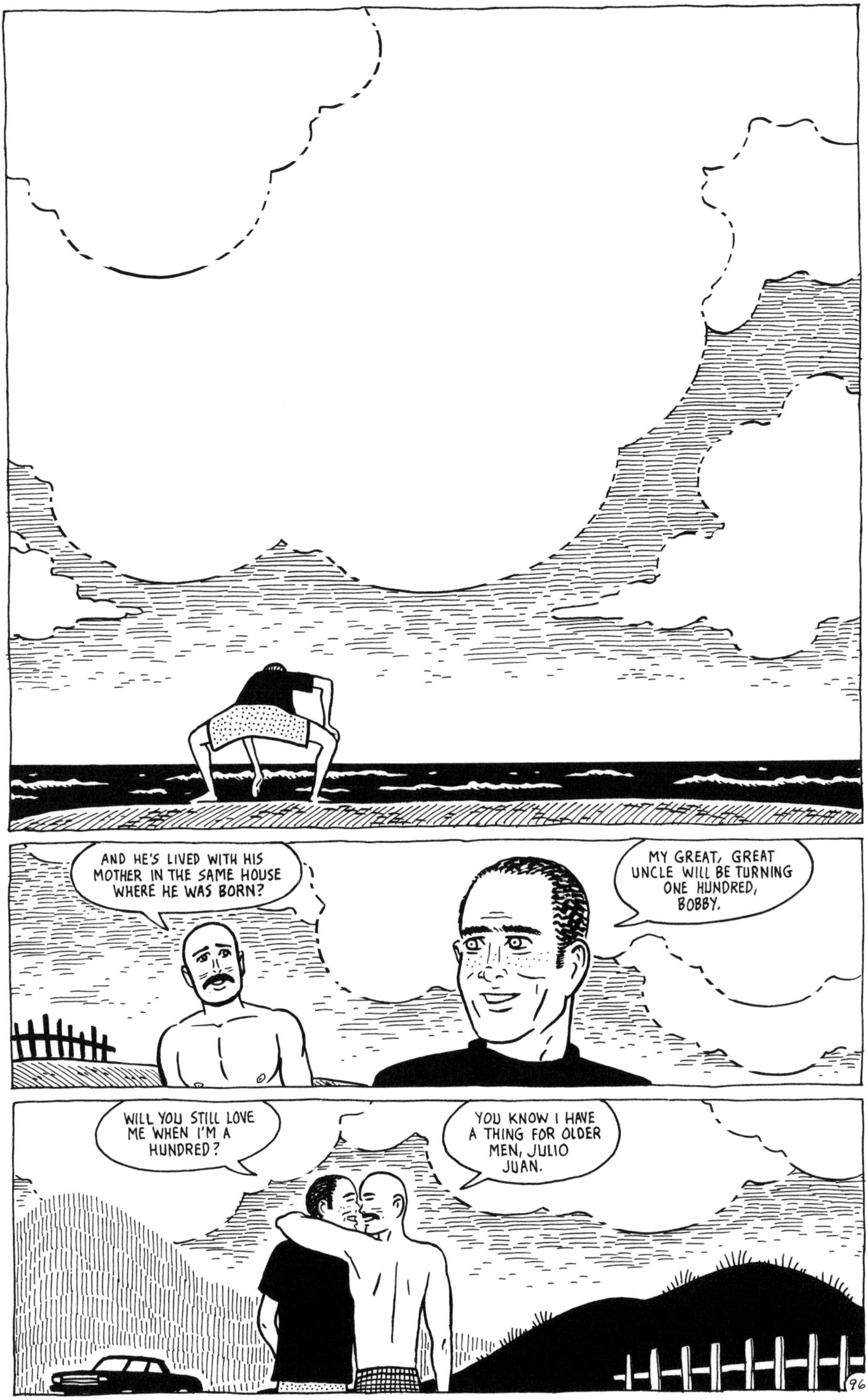
AND HE'S LIVED WITH HIS MOTHER IN THE SAME HOUSE WHERE HE WAS BORN?
MY GREAT, GREAT UNCLE WILL BE TURNING ONE HUNDRED, BOBBY.
WILL YOU STILL LOVE ME WHEN I'M A HUNDRED?
YOU KNOW I HAVE A THING FOR OLDER MEN, JULIO JUAN.
96

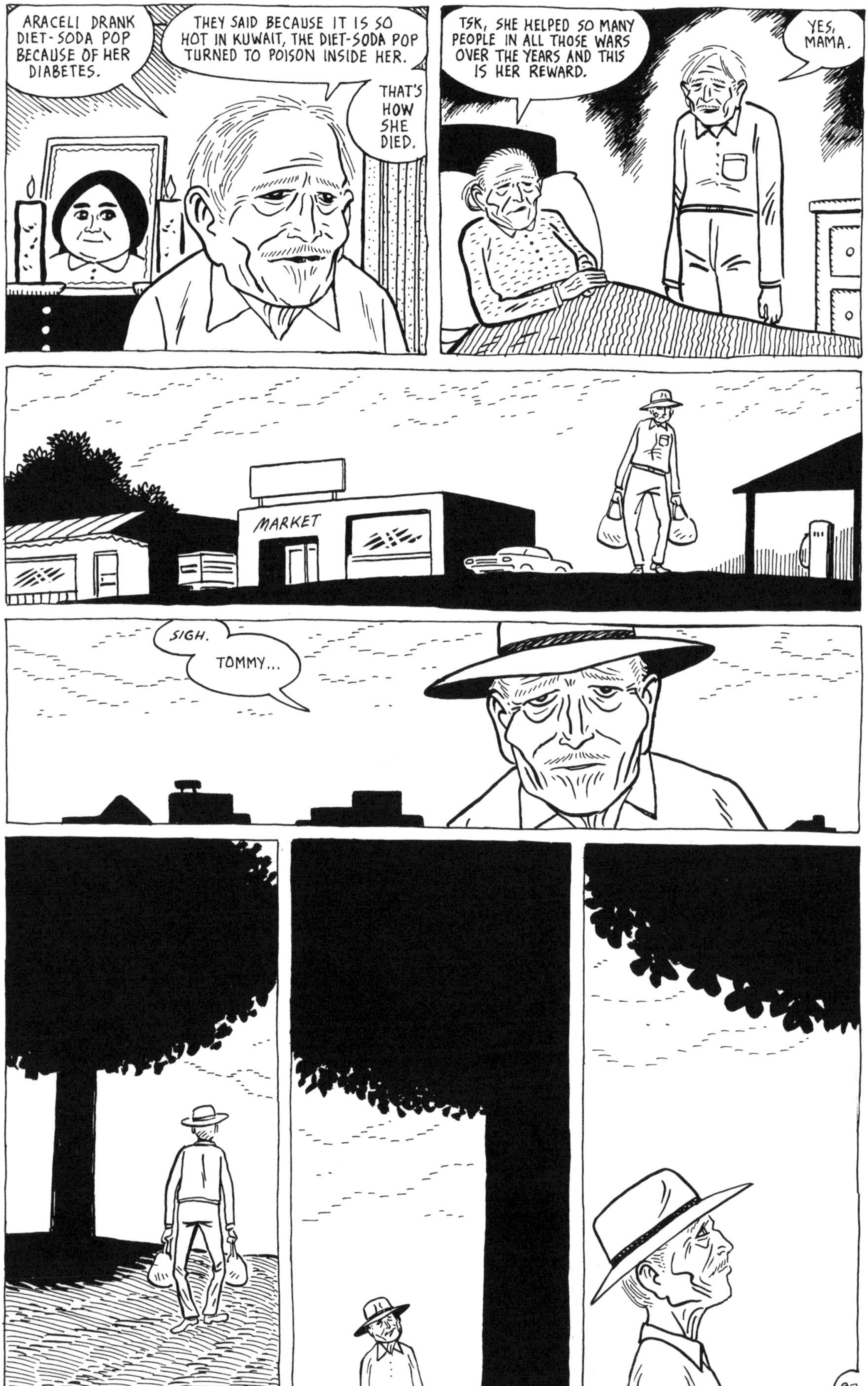
ARACELI DRANK DIET-SODA POP BECAUSE OF HER DIABETES.
THEY SAID BECAUSE IT IS SO HOT IN KUWAIT, THE DIET-SODA POP TURNED TO POISON INSIDE HER.
THAT'S HOW SHE DIED.
TSK, SHE HELPED SO MANY PEOPLE IN ALL THOSE WARS OVER THE YEARS AND THIS IS HER REWARD.
YES, MAMA.
MARKET
SIGH.
TOMMY...

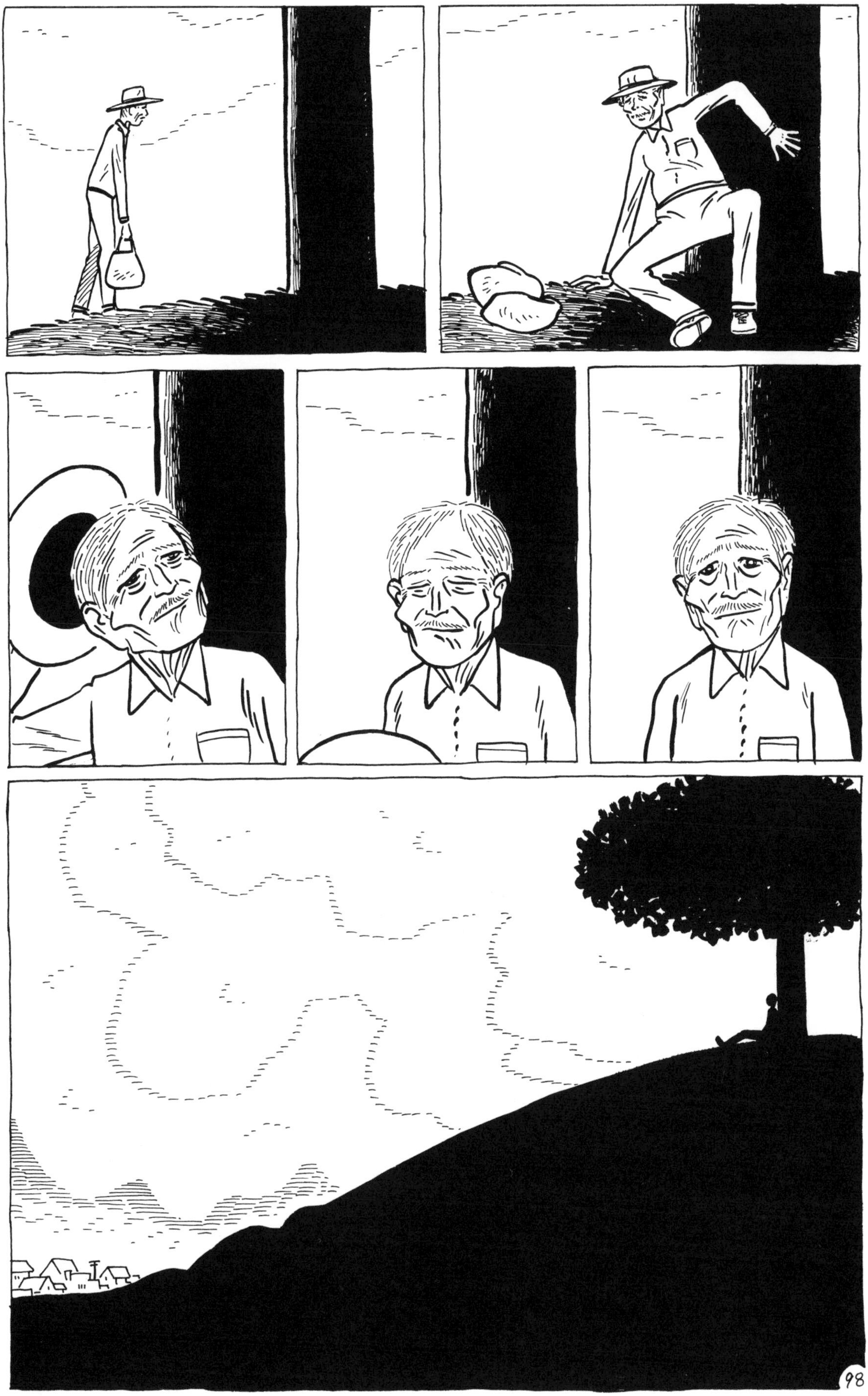

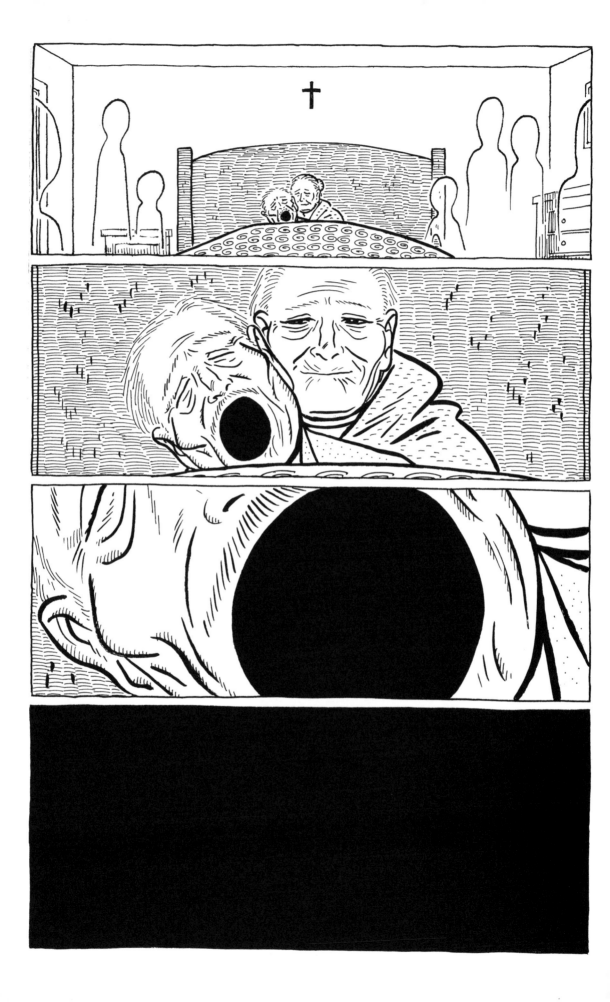

GILBERT HERNANDEZ

Gilbert Hernandez, born in 1957, enjoyed a pleasant childhood in Oxnard, California with four brothers and one sister. In Gilbert's words, they were "born into a world with comic books in the house." His childhood enthusiasm for the medium was equaled only by his appetite for punk rock. Both he and his brother Jaime created eye-catching poster art for local bands like the Angry Samoans, Agent Orange, Black Flag and others through the early '80s.

Initiated by older brother Mario and bankrolled by younger brother Ismael, Gilbert created *Love and Rockets* #1 with his brother Jaime in 1981. Over 30 years later, the series is regarded as a modern classic and the Hernandez brothers continue to create some of the most startling, original, and intelligent comic art ever seen.

COMICS HERNANDEZ

Hernandez, Gilbert.

Julio's day